Leadership for a Global Economy:
A Pathway to Sustainable Freedom

Leadership for a Global Economy:
A Pathway to Sustainable Freedom

Editors

Robert J. Manley, Ph.D
John F. Manley, Ph.D
Deepa Sharma, Ph.D
Carlos Trejo-Pech, Ph.D
Richard Bernato, Ed.D

NA

NorthAmerican
Business Press

Atlanta – Seattle – South Florida – Toronto

North American Business Press, Inc
Atlanta, Georgia
Seattle, Washington
South Florida
Toronto, Canada

Leadership for a Global Economy: A Pathway to Sustainable Freedom

ISBN: 9780985394974
© 2013 All Rights Reserved.

Along with trade books for various business disciplines, the North American Business Press also publishes a variety of academic-peer reviewed journals.

Library of Congress Control Number: 2012955282

Library of Congress
Cataloging in Publication Division
101 Independence Ave., SE
Washington, DC 20540-4320
Printed in theUnited States of America

First Edition

Vision

Through diversity and collaboration, we will raise productivity, innovation, and the pacific development of human potential among all of our students.

Mission

We will expand the capacity of students across the globe to learn how to lead social agencies as stewards of venerable human aspirations.

Purpose

We will develop profound understandings of ethical leadership in a global economy for students with international interests. We will expand democratic practices that benefit all citizens of the world. We will enable our graduates to lead social agencies with the courage to confront weaknesses and the prudence to expand human capacity. We will help our students achieve cherished goals that their institutions and their communities share.

Preface from India

When the manuscript came to my hands, I started going through the articles and found I could not lay aside these loose pages. I read them thoroughly with great interest. As I read, I thought of Francis Bacon who wrote, "Some books are to be tasted, some to be swallowed and some to be chewed and digested."

We, in the industrial world, have been discussing growth in Gross Domestic Production. We choose to analyze nationwide production statistics, currency values, and a great deal more about economics in general, but little attention do we pay to the basis and foundations on which a civilized society can stand and flourish. When the city of Sparta was in the design stage, the architects who were in charge brought the designs, estimates for bricks, mortar and stones that would be required to King Agasthanese. He threw the designs away and told the architects, "Nay, Nay, cities are not built of bricks and stones and mortar. They are built of men. Show me the men who are to live in them."

Chanakya put it very aptly some 2300 years ago when he stated that society stands upon four pillars: Education, Culture, Research and Health. Lord Krishna identified the responsibilities and accountability leaders must accept in Shrimad Bhagwat Gita: "Whatsoever a great person does, the same is done by other common man, whatever standards he sets, the other people follow them."

In Chapter I, Robert J. Manley discloses what to look for in this book. He explains what leadership is according to great thinkers. Quoting various philosophers and great men, present and past, he explains the parameters under which leadership functions. Leaders must have vision, be ethical and to succeed in their mission, they must lift up society.

This book contains words of wisdom and advice from educationalists like Deepa Sharma and Gita Patil who examine the changes that higher education will face. Diogenes Laertius observes, "The other meaning of life is change." Change is the only constant in life. Beneficial change comes from a solid conceptual base and an evolutionary nature. As we travel through the pages of this book, new ideas on leadership continuously emerge.

Edward F. Lyons, an international business executive explains global leadership. He says that one person's leader may be another person's tyrant. He presents a descriptive analysis of leaders who succeed in business.

The discussions of leadership throughout this book remind me of the words of Booker T. Washington: "Success is to be measured not by the station one achieves in life, but by the difficulties and obstacles one has to overcome." How a leader reacts to crisis; how decisively one acts and how effectively one communicates determine the success of a leader. Measures of how much wealth increases, or the institution grows in size, or quality of staff grows or client numbers increase are not evidence of leadership. The real test of leadership measures how much better the lives of employees and customers have become because of what the leader has done.

When addressing the qualities of a leader, I recall Bhartuhari's view,
> A leader ought to be of great moral stature,
> Great experts of law and social behavior or moral practices
> May praise or criticize,
> Wealth may come and go as it pleases,
> Death may come now or after ages,
> But the path of truth and justice that a leader has taken,
> He will not deviate from it.

The authors of these chapters whose origins are in India, Mexico, Peru, and the United States present such diverse insights and attitudes that I feel obliged to recall for the reader a simple story of a Soldier and his Captain:
> Soldier: "Sir, we are surrounded by enemies from all sides."
> Captain: "Excellent, that means we can attack in any direction."

Our authors show how leadership and attitude matter. They demonstrate how a good leader is the one who sees positive opportunities in all surroundings, and is not disheartened by negative situations.

Authors, Ranjana Mishra and Ceena Paul, write about women as an emerging economic force. It seems true that women have begun to take their rightful place in the affairs of the world, be it education, industry, politics, and any other subject. They seem to be forging ahead and very happily acquiring positions of importance. However, we have a long way to go to establish a real sense of equality among men and women. The women and men who are authors of chapters in this book address our common need for freedom and equality. They offer a sustainable pathway to freedom.

Ultimately, I would say this book is a great work, a document that has been produced very diligently by people who are learned and who know well the subject of "Leadership for a Global Economy: A Pathway to Freedom and Sustainability."

Chairperson for Board of Trustees

Bombay College of Pharmacy
Shri Vile Parle Mahila Sangh College
Mumbai, India (11-7-2012)

Table of Contents

Foreward

As the title implies, this book is about leadership and globalization. Ed Lyons, in the chapter "Leadership in Business," states that leadership is a complex topic by itself: *"Leadership may not be easily defined, but you know it when either you see or do not see it."* That complexity and richness of multicultural leadership becomes more profound when leadership is addressed from a global perspective, as in this book.

Furthermore, it could be said that the very conception of this book is global. The plan for the book was devised by scholars from different nationalities and cultures for students equally diverse. Researchers and business leaders from the USA, Mexico, and India devised the plan for this book during an international research conference in Udaipur, India. They visualized the implementation of a university level course taught by volunteer scholars that would enable students from these three countries to learn from their readings and discussions with one another using the Internet.

The book is the product of the efforts of twenty professors that embraced the idea of an international learning community. The chapters in the book are similar to the main reading material of the course that students attended on line. Fifty students from different majors at Iona College (New York, EU), Dowling College (New York, EU), Universidad Panamericana (Guadalajara, México), and Shri M. D. Shah Mahila College of Arts and Commerce (Mumbai, India) participated in the course during spring 2010.

The last chapter, by Thomas Franza, technology leader of this course, describes the technology requirements to implement such a course. As this group of students benefited from the exchange of multiple cultural and professional perspectives by reading these articles, the publication of this book would allow this benefit to be extended to others in different contexts.

Even though the book is comprised of chapters that were conceived independently of each other, the reader will note a natural interconnection of themes and multiple viewpoints. It seems that a collective inaudible conversation exists within the minds of people that have leadership responsibilities in different disciplines. This internal conversation is captured in unique and surprising ways within this book. The first chapter, by Robert Manley, establishes the basis or background on leadership, which is then extended in other chapters to different contexts, sectors, or functional areas of the firm. Manley introduces the topic to the reader by discussing from the perspectives of traditional (e.g. Sun-tzu and Machiavelli) and modern thinkers (e.g. Drucker), the values that make leaders succeed or fail.

The authors of this book are from different disciplines. Some are scholars with leadership positions in colleges, others are entrepreneurs of successful business in the international arena, and others have been top level executives in transnational firms while some serve as government representatives. All of them share a common interest in leadership and education. They care about education. They volunteered to participate in this international lecture series as full or invited professors, members of research associates, or speakers in academic forums to provide diverse students with few opportunities to engage in an international learning community an opportunity to expand their own leadership capacity.

Some chapters of the book cover the generalities of leadership (Manley, chapter 1; McGuire, chapter 13; Walter, chapter 9). Other chapters focus on leadership in education (Bernato, chapter 15; Higuera and Manley, chapter 10: Sharma and Patil, chapter 4). Additional authors discuss leadership for a democratic society, covering aspects of gender and non-for-profit organizations (Hawkins, chapter 16; Mishra and Paul, chapter 11; Sussman, chapter 6). There are interesting and diverse examinations on technology (Morote, chapter 2; Chheda, chapter 12; Franza, chapter 17) and on finance (Trejo-Pech, chapter 3; Manley, John, chapter 7; Shetty, chapter 16) or business sustainability (Lyons, chapter 5; Cusack, chapter 8).

I think this book could be useful for business students and for people starting their careers in a leadership position, a career which probably will be vast and full of challenges. As Kevin McGuire [chapter 14: *Intentional Leadership*] suggests: "*One of the amazing dimensions of leadership is its complexity, as it is replete with paradoxes that present challenges to all who chose to assume a leadership mantle. That's because from a career perspective, leadership is dangerous and difficult work.*"

To survive and serve others effectively in a leadership position requires one to face paradoxes one after another, to act and to self reflect continuously on the motivations related to one's purpose and the moral beliefs common to all peoples and the actual results one achieves.

Dr. José Antonio Esquivias-Romero
Vice President
Universidad Panamericana, Campus Guadalajara, Mexico

Introduction

The origin of this book dates back to 1994, when Dr. Ravikala Kamath, a Fulbright Scholar and Professor of Human Development at S.N.D.T. Women's University, Juhu Campus, Santa Cruz, Mumbai, India saw a news show on CNN. She saw quality educational processes were being instituted in public schools of West Babylon, New York. Dr. Kamath suggested to her graduate student, Deepa Sharma, that she write to the superintendent of the schools that were featured in the show for more information on the implementation of the W. Edwards Deming system theory in USA public schools.

Mrs. Deepa Sharma, soon to be Dr. Deepa Sharma, wrote an airmail letter to Superintendent of Schools, Dr. Robert Manley, that began their international exchange of ideas and aspirations for the human development of students. In 2006, Drs. Sharma and Kamath celebrated the publication of their book, Quality in Education, by Kalpaz Publications, Delhi, India.

For several years, Dr. Deepa Sharma and Dr. Robert Manley continued to consult about student and leader developmental issues on the Internet. In July 2008, Dr. Manley wrote to Dr. Sharma about the International Business and Economy Conference (IBEC) that was to be held in Udaipur, India in the month of January, 2009. He asked if she and a colleague or family member might attend.

She invited her "virtual colleague" and his associates to visit and participate in a Symposium on Quality in Higher Education at Shri Shah M. D. Mahila College of Commerce and Arts in Mumbai, India. A few days before they attended the IBEC meeting in Udaipur, India, they served on a panel of international scholars at Mahila College. One Mexican, four Americans, and three Indian colleagues interacted with students at the Mahila College Quality Symposium for Higher Education. Additional conversations about the needs of students for deeper international understandings continued at the Udaipur IBEC Conference.

Finance Professor John Manley, Adjunct Professor John Cusack from Iona College, and Finance Professor Carlos Trejo-Pech from Universidad Panamericana; Dr. Deepa Sharma, Mahila College Principal, Dr. Edward Lyons, Vice Chairman of Filtration Group, USA, and Dr. Robert Manley, Professor of Education at Dowling College devised a plan to solicit colleagues who would volunteer to conduct an International Discussion of Moral Leadership for a Global Economy.

They wanted to offer a diverse and engaging opportunity for students with an interest in leadership to discuss social, educational and business enterprises that were connected to a global economy. They hoped that their students would grasp more profoundly the essence of human development through the exchanges of multiple cultural and experiential perspectives. Finally, they wanted their students to feel the sacred trust that those who accept the mantle of leadership must sustain.

In the spring of 2010, with the help of Dr. Thomas Franza, Director of Instructional Technology at Dowling College, 20 volunteer professors agreed to dedicate one week of their time to present a digital lecture on Blackboard and conduct an electronic and asynchronous discussion of leadership in a global economy for students in Mumbai, India; Guadalajara, Mexico and New York, United States.

In this book, we offer a synthesis of those efforts. Our purpose is to expand global understandings of moral leadership and to describe how moral leaders prepare pathways to freedom and sustainability for all citizens of the world.

Chapter One
Leadership for the Twenty-first Century
-Robert J. Manley

Leaders of social agencies in a global economy face many choices in their daily duties that require a high level of personal discipline and foresight in government, not for profit or for profit enterprises. Can men and women learn to be better leaders or are they born with the dispositions and cognitive skills to lead?

The question about natural talent to lead is irrelevant in our environment where we require that leaders for every social setting and every human enterprise operate prudently across the globe. Leaders have to be developed to meet human needs for guidance, development, prediction and aspirations. A few people have natural gifts for oratory, pattern recognition, planning and execution that enable them to lead with greater ease than many other people. Most people can learn these skills and they can adopt the virtues and disciplines necessary for successful leadership. The moral self-knowledge that imbues leadership with significant meaning and positive outcomes for many people is more difficult to acquire than technical skills.

Sun-tzu (500 B.C.), a Chinese General, noted in the *Art of War* that the Moral Law causes people to be in accord with their leader. Successful leaders stand for the virtues of wisdom, sincerity, benevolence, courage and strictness (in Giles, L., translation, p. 21).

Sun-tzu recorded five dangerous faults in a leader: recklessness, cowardice, a hasty temper easily provoked by insults, a delicacy of honor that is sensitive to shame, and over solicitude for one's followers that exposes the leader to excessive worry (in Giles, L., translation, p. 42).

In Italy, two thousand years later, Niccolo Machiavelli, wrote a political treatise on the behavior of rulers. In his tome, *The Prince,* he wrote: "You must know that there are two ways of contesting, the one by law, the other by force; the first method is proper to men, the second to beasts; but because the first is frequently not sufficient; it is necessary to recourse to the second" (Machiavelli, The Prince (1501), translated by Marriott, W. K., p. 97).

Machiavelli wrote about the dispositions and skills that a leader must possess. Machiavelli noted that a leader "ought to be slow to believe and to act, nor should he show fear, but proceed in a temperate manner with prudence and humanity, so that too much confidence may not make him incautious and too much distrust render him intolerable" (in Marriott's translation, p. 92).

Richard Bushkirk in his book, Modern Management and Machiavelli, proposed that Machiavelli "held no brief for such contemptible behavior <of the Prince>, but in the

1

name of accurate reporting he was compelled to present and evaluate it" (p. 18). Many can argue about Machiavelli's dispositions and miss the analysis of leader behavior that he offered. From the perspective of a political historian who witnessed effective and ineffective leaders and, at times, was a victim of their decisions, Machiavelli presents a dramatic analysis of behavior that leaders exhibited in his age.

Students of leadership study Sun-tzu and Machiavelli because they present an historical analysis of leadership across cultures and time. They examine in profound ways the emotions, beliefs, aspirations, fears and benefits that leaders and followers exchange in their daily interactions.

In the Sixteenth Century, Machiavelli wrote that "everyone sees what you appear to be; few really know what you are" (p. 100). He observed that a leader "had to be a fox to discover the snares and a lion to terrify wolves" (p. 98). He suggested a wise leader "cannot, nor ought he to, keep faith when such observance may be turned against him and when the reasons that caused him to pledge it exist no longer" (p. 98).

In the Twenty-first Century, because of Google, Facebook, Twitter, 24-hour news shows, and digital records of leader behavior within a multiplicity of devices, the promises and private communications of every leader are open for scrutiny. How does a fallible, ever developing man or woman lead in the digital, global community where nations share one economy and followers separate themselves by distinctive icons of faith, religion, ethnic identity, national pride and history?

Peter Drucker, writing in the Harvard Business Review of March-April 1999, observed that "Success in the knowledge economy comes to those who know themselves-their strengths, their values, and how they best perform" (p. 185). In his article, Managing Oneself, Drucker observed that great achievers always managed themselves. He offered this insight:

> Most people think they know what they are good at. They are usually wrong. More often, people know what they are not good at- and even then more people are wrong than right. And yet, a person can perform only from strength. One cannot build performance on weaknesses, let alone on something one cannot do at all. (p. 66)

Drucker believed that the only way to discover one's strengths was through feedback. He offered a simple self-regulating process:

> Whenever you make a key decision or take a key action, write down what you expect will happen. Nine or 12 months later, compare the actual results with your expectations. (p. 66)

He believed that new actions should follow from feedback analysis that enabled the user to concentrate on and improve strengths, to acquire new and needed skills, to discover one's intellectual arrogance, and to remedy one's bad habits.

Drucker often focused on execution as a key leadership skill. He noted how often leaders fail to follow through on their plans:

> It is equally essential to remedy your bad habits- the things you do or fail to do that inhibit your effectiveness and performance. Such habits will quickly show up in the feedback. For example, a planner may find that his beautiful plans fail because he does not follow through on them. Like so

many brilliant people, he believes ideas move mountains. But bulldozers move mountains; ideas show where the bulldozers should go to work. This planner will have to learn that the work does not stop when the plan is completed. He must find people to carry-out the plan and explain it to them. He must adapt and change it as he puts it into action. And finally, he must decide when to stop pushing the plan. (p. 66)

Also, Drucker felt the feedback revealed, that when the pushback came from subordinates, it came from a lack of manners. Manners, for him, were "the lubricating oil of an organization" (p. 67). He taught that manners, saying 'please and thank you', knowing people's names, asking about their families and concerns, enabled people to work together.

He recognized that each of us have preferred learning styles. Some learn best by reading, or listening, or writing or speaking. Few learn equally well using multiple learning styles. He presents Beethoven as an example of a person who wrote things in a sketchbook so that he would not forget.

Drucker wants all leaders to ask: How do I perform? How do I learn? Do I work well with people? Am I a loner? Do I work best as a subordinate, as an advisor, or as a decision maker? Drucker offers us the insight that strong decision makers need strong advisors in the second spot on the hierarchy to force them to think. He reports that leaders must know if they perform well under stress, or if they are better suited for highly structured and predictable environments.

In my own experience as a CEO of a large school system with a highly unionized workforce, I found that my environment and role had structures that were similar to world soccer games where referees knew all of their powers and authorities and all of the rules of the game. World Cup officials are highly trained and they officiate within the confines of field boundaries with a book of rules that operate as policy guidelines.

Still, the stress of competition and the emotion of players, coaches and fans may prevent them from executing a fair and well-adjudicated game. If the referees fail to act as a team or if individual referees succumb to personal biases or let their ego needs drive their decisions, they lose control of the game and risk the ire of the fans. They have to manage their own fears and aspirations, observe carefully and position themselves to see events clearly. They have to lead the players by exercising their competence in their chosen field and not impose on the players unnecessary restrictions that would inhibit their performance as athletes.

At all times, referees must adhere to the highest professional values. If they are to be effective, they must manage their own emotions. Frequently, the Chief Executive Officer must referee talented, highly committed and goal oriented personnel who challenge every call and every directive.

Drucker points out that to manage others, one must manage oneself; one must know with great clarity what one values. He distinguishes values from ethics. Ethics, he notes, are the rules that are the same for everybody. He says they are tested in the mirror every morning. When we look in the mirror each morning, we know if we lived by the rules of ethics the previous 24 hours. We know the truth when we answer a simple question: Did I act rightly or wrongly, selfishly or fairly?

Drucker places ethics within a value system. He suggests that each of us ascribes to the fundamental principles of ethics and that ethical behavior in one organization would be the same in all organizations. He notes that organizations may value personnel differently and cause us to be uncomfortable with values that favor outsiders for high executive office and expect junior officers to leave the company to find advancement.

Such expectations or values are not unethical, nor illegal, although they may be counterproductive if used exclusively within an enterprise. Organizations that are committed to short-term goals instead of long-term goals reflect values. What one values and what one believes must be compatible with one's strengths, goals and work, if one is to be in harmony with oneself.

Sometimes, one's beliefs focus on material or spiritual rewards and those beliefs reflect values that we have internalized and accepted as the driving force within our existence. Such values can motivate Mother Teresa to serve the poor or drive Hitler to exterminate a minority of his people as part of a warped drive for power. All leaders must reflect on the values that drive their behavior, their thoughts and aspirations.

Drucker says that leaders in knowledge industries must answer a basic question if they want a good future and hope to avoid contributing to the evil in the world: "What should my contribution be?" By asking a question that causes a leader to create a vision of him or herself for the immediate future, Drucker believes that he has found a way to guide managers and leaders to create more positive and satisfying enterprises.

He suggests that no one can look ahead very far and most plans should not try to go beyond 18 months. Leaders can learn to ask what do I want to contribute to my enterprise in the next 18 months or "Where and how can I achieve results that will make a difference within the next year and a half" (Drucker, p. 71)?

Drucker notes that to be effective, leaders must work with others and "know the strengths, performance modes, and the values of coworkers" (p. 71). Also, they must know their bosses and "find out how they work, and adapt themselves to what makes their bosses most effective" (p. 72).

Organizations, Drucker observes, sustain themselves with trust and not force. He states: "The existence of trust between two people does not necessarily mean that they like one another. It means that they understand one another" (p.72). In Drucker's view, leaders take responsibility for relationships.

Daniel Goleman (1995), in his book, Emotional Intelligence, reports that the most successful leaders know how to manage their own emotions and those of others.

> And that is the problem: academic intelligence offers virtually no preparation for the turmoil – or opportunity- life's vicissitudes bring. Yet, even though a high IQ (intelligence quotient) is no guarantee of prosperity, prestige or happiness in life, our schools and our culture fixate on academic abilities, ignoring emotional intelligence, a set of traits- some might call it character- that also matters for our personal destiny. Emotional life is a domain that, as surely as math or reading, can be handled with greater or lesser skill and requires its unique set of competencies. And how adept a person is at those is crucial to understanding why one person thrives in life while another, of equal intellect, dead-ends… (p. 37)

Goleman reminds us "leadership is not domination, but the art of persuading people to work toward a common goal" (p. 149). He notes how system theory emphasizes feedback as an essential data exchange about every element or unit in a process that helps all participants know if they are doing the job well. "Feedback is the life blood of the organization" (Goleman, p. 151).

4

Leaders have a responsibility to take and give feedback that is positive and negative and to behave in ways that promote greater effort, change and innovation. Goleman observes that one of the more common forms of destructive feedback at work is criticism voiced as personal attacks, sarcasm and contempt. He reports, "inept criticism was ahead of mistrust, personality struggles, and disputes over power and pay as a reason for conflict on the job" (p. 152).

He advises that effective criticism focuses on what was done and how it could be improved: it is specific, face-to-face, solution oriented, empathetic and clear. He cautions recipients of a critique not to become defensive and to take responsibility for their part in the outcome. He encourages all of us to see criticism as information and look for opportunities where valuable feedback can guide our actions and help us to improve working relationships with peers and those to whom we report as well as those we serve.

Goleman suggests that all leaders must develop self-awareness by learning to identify, express and manage their feelings. They need to practice self-reflection, impulse control, and the self-discipline to delay gratification, manage stress and anxiety and actively listen to others for important feedback (p. 256).

In his book, Social Intelligence (2006), Goleman offers the observation that Machiavelli in the sixteenth century described a leader, The Prince, who had only his own interests at heart, who cared little for those he ruled and worried not about those he crushed. Goleman notes how such leaders justify their own behavior and their drives for power by cloaking their desires with the larger purpose of creating great organizations. They fool many followers at the beginning of a relationship and as time passes, they reveal themselves to be uncaring manipulators of other human beings that no one can trust (p. 125-126).

In the book, The Future of Leadership, Thomas Stewart offers in Chapter Six a broad analysis of trust:

> Real trust is hard even between people who have chosen to be together and have years to work on it, like spouses. It's harder still where they have little or no say in selecting their colleagues and where time is short. Impossible where an organization is large. The goal of real interpersonal trust might be misguided as well as unattainable: certainly there are limits to the trust between colleagues or between boss and subordinate, since everyone retains the option to end the relationship. Trust at work therefore needs support- forces that create incentives for trustworthy behavior and reassurance for people who rely on others. (p. 70)

Stewart identifies five forces at work that promote trust: the competence that people believe coworkers and super-ordinates have, communities of informal groups with a common discipline, set of values and mission, commitment which is best expressed with a sense of loyalty to the organization, open communication about successes and failures, and fair, democratic and published rewards (pp. 71-75). He believes that leaders are responsible for the forces at work that promote trust.

Stewart cautions leaders to remember that in the digital age there are no secrets. Networks exist within and outside the enterprise. Members of those networks constantly communicate about happenings within the company and the industry. Leaders must lead with truth and be guided by values that almost all employees, clients and customers cherish. Leaders who make a difference in their community exhibit a profound concern for the well being of all, create jobs and safe places to live, believe that their own life has meaning in so far as they contribute to better lives for everyone in the community. They embody the fundamental values that bind leaders and their community together-stewardship.

Mihaly Csikszentmihalyi, the author of Flow: The Psychology of Optimal Experience (1990) and Becoming Adult (2000), writes, "Leaders who want to support creativity do not themselves have to be creative. But they have to become connoisseurs who can recognize good new ideas and good people" (in Bennis et al., (2001) p. 123).

Recognizing the truly creative worker is simply being sensitive to the competent, honest, intrinsically motivated person who works for the sake of the work itself. Csikszentmihalyi reminds us that the leader is a critical player in the field and more than a patron of the arts or the creative act, the leader must select the best people with the best ideas, and protect and nourish them. Great leaders share leadership. They educate and promote others.

Tara Church writes in Chapter Sixteen of The Future of Leadership that she believes as her teacher Warren Bennis, that leaders are made, not born. She states her position: "leaders are people who can express themselves fully- who they are, what their strengths and weaknesses are, and how to maximize their strengths while compensating for their weaknesses" (p. 228).

She acknowledges that her generation, born between 1965 and 1979, holds a vision of leadership that is much more local, voluntary, diverse and unwilling to wait for institutions to respond to human needs and at the same time, they are less likely to become engaged in political movements or serve institutional governments. There are 50 million people in her generation beginning their ascendancy to new leadership roles in the United States. Across the globe, many more young people belong to this generation of instant communication and they share aspirations, hopes and preferred style of working with others. Because they are members of, and creators of, the digital community where communication of shared values and beliefs, sorrows and failures, hopes and dreams, and private emotions and personal feelings appear like linen on a clothes line tenement apartment in the industrial age, they possess the boldness, if not the wisdom and values, to create a new world.

The generation born in the 1980s will be the merchants who demand the renaissance in leadership that we hope will transform competent individuals into leaders of caring communities whose members develop products and knowledge that benefit humans across the globe. Certainly, we have the communicative tools and we can acquire the competence and the values that will remake ourselves into groups dedicated to improve the lives of all children and adults placed in our care.

Our world that we have inherited as a gift from beyond our consciousness needs leaders who see us and themselves as we are, naked, bereft of pretense, hands open and reaching for opportunity. We are spirits in need of guidance to help us to do as little harm as possible and to contribute as much good as we can imagine.

In the Twenty-first Century, leaders who seek to develop social agencies that serve the interests of the least powerful will promote creativity and reward hard work. They will expand jobs and economic benefits across the globe. They will make a positive difference in the lives of those they encounter.

Democratic leaders who know and manage themselves appropriately will balance their own interests with those of their neighbors who share this global village that we call Earth. They will make our planet a better place to live much as village elders did eons ago. They will live in the present time, value every human being and see their mission in life as one of service and generosity towards everyone they encounter. They will balance all of their actions with a moderate level of self-interest and a large and profound desire to expand the quality of life for all citizens in the regions that they can touch through the actions of their enterprise.

Blackboard Discussion
1. Plato, the Greek Philosopher, presented a simple phrase to summarize Socratic thinking: "Know Thyself." In England, during the Sixteenth Century A.D., William Shakespeare, the playwright, offered within his drama, Hamlet, a guiding principle for any youth setting off on a career adventure. In the words of Polonius to his son, Laertes, Shakespeare offered: "Be true to yourself and it follows that you cannot be false to any man."
In the Twenty-first Century, how can you learn who you are and manage yourself better?
2. How should we prepare ourselves to lead global enterprises in a diverse world and be true to the highest principles of democracy?

References

Bushkirk, Richard H., Modern Management and Machiavelli.

Church, T. (2001) Chapter Sixteen Where the Leaders Are, *The future of leadership*, Bennis, W., Spreitzer, G. M., & Cummings, T.G., editors, San Francisco, California, Josey Bass & Company.

Csikszentmihalyi, M. (2001) Chapter Ten, The Context of Creativity, *The future of leadership*, Bennis, W., Spreitzer, G. M., & Cummings, T.G., editors, San Francisco, California, Josey Bass & Company.

Drucker, P. F. (March April 1999) Managing Oneself, *Harvard Business Review*, pp. 64-74.

Goleman, D. (1995). *Emotional Intelligence*. New York: Bantam Books.

Goleman, D. (2006). *Social Intelligence*. New York: Bantam Books.

Machiavelli, N. *The Prince (1513)*. Translated, W.K. Marriott (1908), London, Great Britain: Dent and Sons.

Stewart, T. (2001) Chapter Six Trust me on this: organizational support for trust in a world without hierarchies, *The future of leadership*, Bennis, W., Spreitzer, G. M., & Cummings, T.G., editors, San Francisco, California, Josey Bass & Company.

Sun-tzu. (500 B.C.) *The Art of War*. Translated by Lionel Giles

Related Readings

Bennis, W. (1999) *Managing People Is Like Herding Cats*. Provo, Utah: Executive Excellence Publishing.

Rebhorn, W. A. (2003) Translation and notes on the *The Prince and Other Writings by Niccolo Machiavelli*, (1512-1520). New York: Barnes and Noble Classics

Sawyer, R. D. (2001) Translation of *The Art of War by Sun-tzu* (500 B.C.). New York, MetroBook Edition.

Chapter Two
Technological Challenges for Leaders in a Global Economy
-Elsa-Sofia Morote

In the 21st Century, a communication revolution dominates the world. The Internet drives and determines the way people go about living. Politics and business thrive on the new technology and the winners are those who understand and can make successful use of the World Wide Web (Castells, 2009). The challenge for today's leaders is to focus on the new Advanced Information Technology (AIT) and how to use them to guide constituents in an ethical manner..

The AIT includes, but is not restricted to, email systems, message boards, groupware, management systems, and social networking systems (Avolio & Dodge, 2001). Furthermore, Advanced Information Technology means the tools, techniques and knowledge which can engage in a variety of ways the organizational activities of business using high-quality data collection, transmission and display (DeSanctis & Poole, 1994).

The AIT has grown tremendously in several countries, for example, the Indian information technology industry has played a key role in putting India on the global map. Thanks to the success of the IT industry, India is now a power to reckon with. According to the National Association of Software and Service Companies (NASSCOM) in India, the apex body for software services in India, the revenue of the information technology sector has risen from 1.2 per cent of the gross domestic product (GDP) in the FY 1997-98 to an estimated 5.8 per cent in the FY 2008-09 (India Brand Equity Foundation, 2009).

The Advanced Information Technology (AIT) creates a need for inspired leadership in this global economy. Key characteristics of an AIT enabled economy are real time information availability, greater knowledge sharing with stakeholders, and the use of information knowledge to build relationships (Avolio & Dodge, 2001). Leaders play a more proactive role in creating the social structures that foster the implementation of AIT.

Some researchers such as Susan Annunzio (2001) used the term "eLeadership" to refer to a leader who leads in an AIT environment and defined their actions as "shaking up your corporate culture and fostering an attitude of speed and flexibility in order to facilitate the internal transformation to an environment for the new economy." (p. 12).

In 2000, in the USA, the Alliance with Forrester Research conducted a survey with almost 600 business leaders from a wide variety of industries. The aim was to learn more about the skills and experience necessary to function effectively in an AIT. The results of the survey showed that the foundation skills traditionally associated with leadership – for example, retention, communication, motivation and direction setting, change even while they remain in use.

Technology is changing the context in which we work; it is accelerating ambiguity and the rate of change, and the need to work collaboratively across the borders. Consequently, many previous assumptions about leadership, teams and organizations must evolve (Pulley, Sessa, & Malloy, 2002). In addition, according to Annunzio (2001), eLeaders have the following qualities: honesty, responsiveness, vigilance, willingness to learn and relearn, sense of adventure, vision and altruism.

Pulley, et al. (2002) also used the term "eleadership", however several researchers, including myself, do not think that adding the "e" would make it a different leadership. Leaders have always dealt with several kinds of technologies in different eras. Technology has traditionally played a very important role in facilitating protest, for example; Xerox machines facilitated the early anti-communist protests in Poland, and now Iranian twitter users have used technology to protest. The devices and the technology changed. In the last decade, we have seen technology play a crucial role in helping people gather and, most importantly, be heard. To learn how leadership reacts to technologies or vice versa, we will have to examine the context in which the leadership process is emerging, and then define what a leadership role will be in this process.

The Adaptive Structuration Theory (AST) defines the contextual aspects of all human systems in terms interactions and exchanges. This theory is formulated as **"the production and reproduction of the social systems through members' use of rules and resources in interaction"**. DeSanctis and Poole (1994) adapted Giddens' theory to study the interaction of groups and organizations with information technology and called it Adaptive Structuration Theory.

AST criticizes the technocentric view of technology use and emphasizes the social aspects. AST considers that groups and organizations using information technology for their work dynamically **create perceptions about the role and utility of the technology** and how it can be applied to their activities. These perceptions can vary widely across groups. These perceptions influence the way technology is used and hence mediate its impact on group outcomes.

Figure 1 shows that a combination of structural features of the AIT (restrictiveness, level of sophistication, comprehensiveness) and spirit (decision process, **leadership**, efficiency, conflict management and atmosphere) [p1] enter into a social interaction. The attitude toward appropriation will occur during a decision process [p5] generating a decision outcome [p7] that could be but is not limited to efficiency, quality, consensus and commitment.

AST is a viable approach for studying the role of advanced information technologies in organization change and how technology shapes the role of leaders in this new structure. AST examines the change process from two vantage points: 1) the types of structures provided by the advanced technologies and 2) the structures that actually emerge in human action as people interact with these technologies.

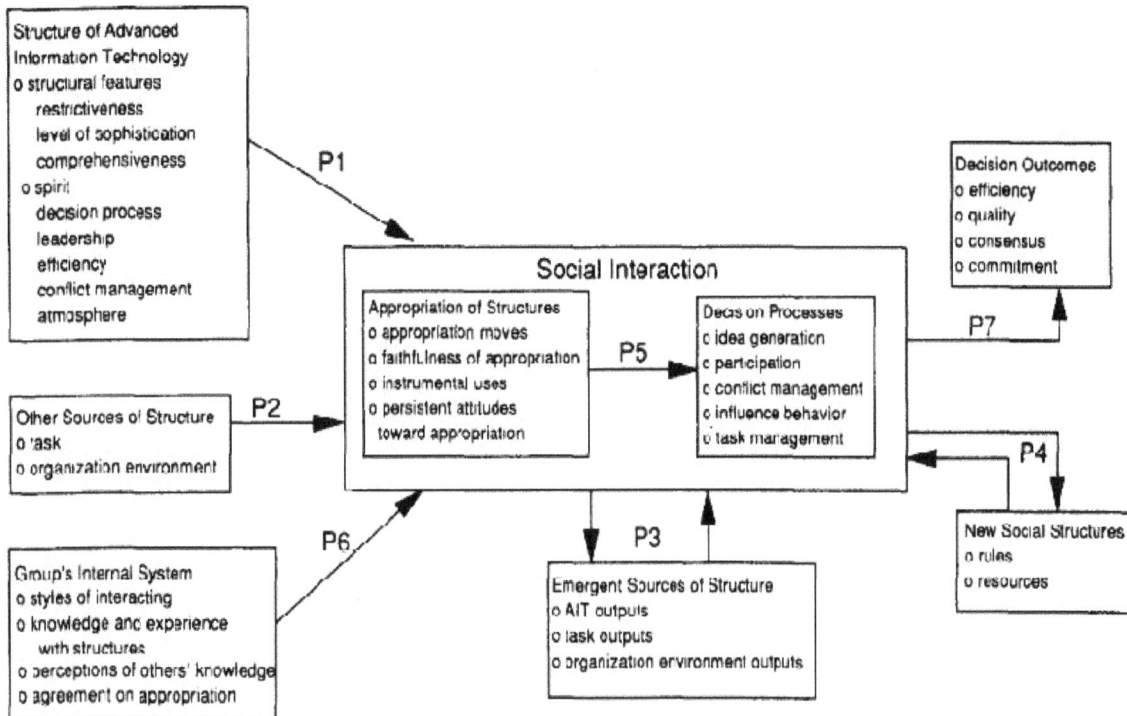

Figure 1. Capturing the complexity in advanced technology use
Source: DeSanctis, Geradine & Poole, Scott, M. (1994). Capturing the complexity in advanced technology use: Adaptive structuration theory. Organization Science, 5(2), 121

I believe there is a bidirectional causal relationship between leaders and their environment. Leaders respond to the environment, but they in turn can influence the environment. In this lecture, we will talk about [a] how technology as part of the environment challenges leadership in the global economy, [b] how leadership influences technology, and finally, [c] we will discuss the leadership balancing act for success. We will discuss all under the AST framework.

Advanced Information Technology Challenge Leadership

Technology affects our organizational environment and structure. Several empirical studies show how technologies challenge some industries and their leadership. Political leaders are also affected. Castells (2009) argues that in the new network society of instant messaging, social networking, and blogging-"mass self-communication"-politics is fundamentally media politics. This fact is behind a worldwide crisis of political legitimacy that challenges the meaning of democracy in much of the world.

Technological innovations can have important strategic implications for individual companies and yet, not all technological change is strategically beneficial. Technology challenges political leaders, as the individuals having access to it, and can challenge some policies or leaders' decisions. For example, on November 16, 2009 in Shanghai, China, President of the USA, Obama explained to a room full of Chinese students that the free-flow of information strengthens societies by allowing citizens to demand accountability from their leaders. He was referring to the use of Twitter banned in China. It seems that as of today, the Chinese authorities have blocked Internet access to Twitter, Flickr, Bing,

11

Live.com, Hotmail.com and several other sites. Wordpress, YouTube, Blogger are also blocked. Chinese authorities want to reduce or remove the entire major social networking and social media part of the web ahead of the 20th anniversary of Tiananmen massacre on June 4th. In this case, Chinese leaders felt that the use of the social networking technology challenges their social order. Chinese State media have alleged that social media "spread misinformation" and that outsiders used them to orchestrate the violence. In this case, considering the AST in Figure 1, the group's internal interactions (Chinese students–p6) use technology; meaning Chinese students appropriate technology or use it. Once the internal group that is using this technology enters into the [p5] social interaction area of Figure 1, it will interact with the leaders. But, instead of getting a consensus or commitment, [p7] they affect leadership with the intention of creating new social structures [p4].

Technology also affects the industry. For instance, Nobel Laureate Lawrence Klein examined the role of information technology on increasing productivity in the finance sector. IT is especially relevant in the financial industry in that it was one of the first sectors to use computer services on a large scale. By 1980, the finance industry incorporated electronic transfer, ATM machines, automatic accounting systems and other automated "back office" services to keep abreast of global markets and provide almost instantaneous services to customers (Lawrence, Saltzman, & Duggal, 2003).

New information technologies are rapidly unsettling well-established business models based on the services of third-party intermediaries in executing transactions. In addition to banks and brokerage firms, some of the traditional intermediaries adversely affected by new technology firms include postal services, retailers, real estate agents, auctioneers, and travel agents.

Meditation time - 15 minutes

Watch this video, and meditate how technology would challenge your area of work. This video is about Elizabeth Fugitt, Chief, Records Management Application Unit, Federal Bureau of Investigation in the USA. Presenting about Meeting New E-Discovery Requirements through Strategic Data Management.
http://www.youtube.com/watch?v=L_KM4HWVOSY

Leadership influences Advanced Information Technology

It is government and its policies that guide countries to reach AIT. Leaders and globalization affect technology. For example, due to the global economic crisis in Mexico on November 17, 2009, the congress cut its budget for science and technology by US$900,000 (Melesio, 2009). In this case, the government affects the level of money invested in science and technology assigning a specific budget to that area, but that decision was based on the current global circumstances.

The TAI, a composite index of technological achievement, reflects the level of technological progress and thus, the capacity of a country to participate in the network age. A composite index helps a country position itself relative to others, especially those farther ahead. Many elements make up a country's technological achievement, but an overall assessment easily made based on a single composite measure offers greater simplicity than dozens of different measures (Desai, Fukuda-Parr, Johansson, & Sagasti, 2002).

The TAI has eight indicators, two in each of these four dimensions:

- *Technology creation* measured by the number of patents granted to residents per capita and by receipts of royalties and license fees from abroad per capita
- *Diffusion of recent innovations* measured by the number of Internet hosts per capita and the share of high technology and medium-technology exports in total goods exports
- *Diffusion of old innovations* measured by telephones (mainline and cellular) per capita and electricity consumption per capita
- *Human skills* measured by the mean years of schooling in the population aged 15 and older, and the gross tertiary science enrolment ratio

As an example of how countries rate in this technology achievement index, Finland was rated number 1, the United States, number 2, Japan 4, Germany 11, China 24, Mexico 32, Chile 37, Islamic Republic of Iran, 50 and India, 63 of 72 countries analyzed. (Desai, Fukuda-Parr, Johansson, & Sagasti, 2002).

What happens if a country has an index 72? Am I at a disadvantage as a resident? Not necessarily, since political and economic leaders can push their country's needs for education and train people for new work. Leaders of social or business agencies should learn how to deal with their constituents and their environment. However, in the framework of a company, the true measure of **innovation is the ability to convert technology into products, services and solutions that increase efficiency, effectiveness and overall company performance** (Van der Does & Caldeira, 2009).

One of the main challenges leaders face today is how optimally to integrate human and information systems in their organization to leverage AIT (Avolio & Dodge, 2001). Leadership is likely to play an important role in the adaptation between AIT and its environment. As Figure 1 shows organizational members, especially leaders, play a major role in the creation and interpretation of AIT. AIT's interpretation determines its use and ultimately, its contribution to organizational performance (Avolio & Dodge, 2001).

The Thompson case offers an interpretation of AIT. In 2000, Thompson, formerly one of the world's greatest newspaper publishers chose in the all time best year for newspaper ad revenues, exited from newspapers entirely (Colvin, 2009). Thomson, now Thomson Reuters, adapted to the world it saw coming.

Leadership plays a key role in the AIT assimilation with several industries finding the way to learn what to use or not use about technology, and train their people to affect their adaptative structuration. The leaders see this need coming and act accordingly with examples being in several areas such as industry, health and education. For example, Xerox hired a consulting firm to create a leadership development program that would address technological and change issues in a practical way (Pulley, Sessa, & Malloy, 2002)

Balancing Act for Success

It is important to consider how AIT interacts with leadership to influence both the structure and effects of leadership and how leadership, in turn, might influence AIT's adoption and its effects on organizations (Avolio & Dodge, 2001). Barack Obama, President of the United States, believes in the power of the web and harnessed the Internet to help raise money and rally supporters during his historic 2008 election. In 2008, his website, managed by Hughes (co-founder of Facebook) mybarakobama.com, allowed Obama supporters to create groups, plan events, raise funds, download tools and connect with one another. The numbers speak for themselves because by the time the campaign was over in 2008, volunteers had created more than 2 million profiles, planned 200,000 offline events, formed 35,000 groups, posted 400,000 blogs and raised 30 million dollars. That is using technology for success!

Those working for would-be President Obama performed as and with virtual teams and consequently entered into a new field of endeavor for a leader. These workers were individuals who worked within and beyond boundaries, using the links of communication technology. Their skills complemented one another; and by having a common purpose and singular goals, they were accountable for the total effort. In today's global economy, each leader must adapt to and conquer the use of virtual teams.

This is a unique time in our history. Never before has there been such an essential need for leaders to have the ability to master new technologies, and in particular, developments in information technology.

There are advantages in knowing about evolving communication systems but knowing is not enough. Leaders must be able to turn this knowledge into successful action. As Frances Hesselbein from the Peter F. Drucker Foundation remarked in her interview, "the globalization of ideas is far more powerful than the globalization of business" (W. K. Kellogg Foundation Building Leadership Capacity for the 21st Century: A Report).

The most valuable items in global business today are information and knowledge. Great leaders of the future must be visionary and be able to consider both the big picture and the micro scene, combining the two to produce the best results. Leaders must be able to teach and lead groups and communities, showing them how to tackle complex problems that are interconnected and then solve them wisely and creatively.

The social, political, economic and natural environments of individuals and communities in today's world endure significant change. The communities are many and varied and so too are the changes. What they have in common though is the need for leaders to move with the times and show leadership skills that match the need for progress.

The best leaders share the same qualities. They know how to motivate people and garner resources to solve problems and face challenges effectively. The issues facing communities may be local, regional, national or even global. The key response is bringing people from all lifestyles together to improve the quality of life for everyone. AIT provides a gathering place for technological innovators to meet, share ideas and solve problems. Leaders have to understand the power of social media options within their own AIT systems.

We have discussed that technological innovations can have important strategic implications for individual companies and can greatly influence industries as a whole. Before we conclude what leaders can do in this new global world, watch the following video.

Meditation Time – 15 minutes

> Watch the video from minute 12 to 18, the presenter talks about patiently achievement consensus. The video is Chuck Harrington, Chairman and CEO, Parsons Corporation Visit UCLA Anderson School of Management, in his presentation "Leadership Skills and Style for a Global Technology"
> http://www.youtube.com/watch?v=cmNFVMMu39c

DeSanctis, Geradine & Poole (1994) described the power of adaptive structural theory (AST): "AST considers that it is useful to consider groups and organizations from a structuration perspective because doing so: (a) helps one understand the relative balance in the deterministic influences and willful choices that reveal groups' unique identities; (b) makes clearer than other perspectives the evolutionary character of groups and organizations; and (c) suggests possibilities for how members may be able to exercise more influence than they otherwise think themselves capable of" (page 14).

We should learn that our mental models of leadership must evolve to embrace the changes brought by technology. Leaders should consider the AST (a, b, and c) and follow Robson's steps 1-2-3 to achieve success in this globalization. As Robson (2009) provides advice in his article *Changing Systems, Changing Minds*, leaders should:

1. Build the will for change
2. Cultivate promising improvement ideas
3. Put those ideas into action through effective leadership and execution.

Blackboard discussion
1. Share your leadership and technology story. Describe a case in which technology challenged you in your field of work and how you dealt with it. (at least 200 words)
2. Act as consultant for your classmates, and review their postings, select one of the cases, use AST concepts (a, b, c) and steps 1-2-3 for achievement success to advise your classmates. (200 words)

References

Avolio, B. J., & Dodge, G. E. (2001). E-leadership: Implications for Theory, Research, and Practice. *Leadeship Quarterly , 11* (4), 615-668.

Castells, M. (2009). *Communication Power.* Oxford University Press.

Colvin, G. (2009, November 23). The same leadership problems come up again and again in a downturn. Solving them doesn't take fancy technology--just character and courage. *Fortune , 160*, p. 24.

Desai, M., Fukuda-Parr, S., Johansson, C., & Sagasti, F. (2002). Measuring the Technology Achievement of Nations and the Capacity to Participate in the Network Age. *Journal of Human Development , 3* (1), 94-122.

DeSanctis, Geradine & Poole, Scott, M. (1994). Capturing the complexity in advanced technology use: Adaptive structuration theory. Organization Science, 5(2), 121

Gopal, Abhijit, Bostrom, Robert P, & Chin, Wynne W. (1993). Applying adaptive structuration theory to investigate the process of group support systems use. *Journal of Management Information Systems, 9*(3), 45. Retrieved November 30, 2009, from Business Module. (Document ID: 1175081).

India Brand Equity Foundation. (2009, August 1). *India Brand Equity Foundation.* Retrieved November 27, 2009, from Information Technology: http://www.ibef.org/industry/informationtechnology.aspx

Lawrence, K., Saltzman, C., & Duggal, V. (2003, August 1). *Information technology and productivity: The case of financial sector.* Retrieved November 26, 2009, from Survey of Current Business: http://www.bea.gov/scb/pdf/2003/08August/0803IT-Prod.pdf

Melesio, L. (2009, November 17). *México reduce su presupuesto para CyT en 2010.* Retrieved November 28, 2009, from ScienceDev.net: http://www.scidev.net/en/news/scientists-lament-mexico-s-reduced-science-budget.html

Pulley, M. L., Sessa, V., & Malloy, M. (2002, March 1). E-Leadership: A two-pronged idea at Xerox, leadership development is via the Web and about the Web. *T+ D, Business Module* , pp. 34-47.

Robson, B. (2009, Nov/Dec). Changing Systems, Changing Minds : Improving Healthcare with IT. *Healthcare Executive , 24, Business Module* (6), pp. 72-74.

Van der Does, L., & Caldeira, S. J. (2009, May). Use the right technology, not just the latest gadgets. *Nation's restaurant news* , pp. 18,34.

Waldman, D., Ramirez, G., House, R., & Puranam, P. (2001). Does Leadership Matter? CEO Leadership Attributes and Profitability under Conditions of Perceived Environmental Uncertainty. *The Academy of Management Journal , 44* (1), 133-144.

Chapter Three
Financial Ethics and Leadership
-Carlos Omar Trejo-Pech

Firm Misconduct

The high number of firms in the U.S. that have recently engaged in unethical behavior is alarming. A study published by Clement (2006) in *Business Horizons*, a leading U.S. journal in management, reports that 40% of firms listed in *Fortune 100* have recently engaged in behaviors that can be considered unethical. Among the actions Clement considers unethical are accounting fraud, securities fraud, consumer fraud, discriminatory practices, undisclosed executive pay, antitrust activities, patent infringement, and other violations of the law.

More than 70% of the unethical cases reported in Clement (2006) related to frauds. More specifically, 54% (33 out of 61) of those cases were related to financial frauds, either in the form of misrepresentation of financial results to improve sales or net income (i.e., accounting fraud) or by lying to shareholders or other investors, usually to falsely promote the firms stocks (i.e., securities fraud). Further, consumer fraud in this study included not only actions misleading customers about quality or safety, but also misrepresentations of the actual risks (perceived by the selling firm) involved in financial products. Thus, *at least* 54% of the unethical cases presented in the study by Clement related to finance. Hence, the responsibility that finance students and finance professionals have in relation to ethics is enormous.

While unethical behavior seems to more closely related to finance than to other functional areas of the firm (according to the frequency of cases), unethical actions by managers in other areas can have an even worse impact on third parties. For instance, Clement (2006) reports that Phillip Morris, Lorillard, Merck, and Ford Motor Company promoted products that led to multiple deaths. MCI WorldCom and Enron, other firms cited in this study, recorded $11 billion in false income and caused the highest level of accounting and securities fraud respectively.

The financial frauds by those two firms received broad coverage in the media, so that they probably come to mind when one thinks of a lack of business ethics in finance. Case studies on these firms have been widely written by scholars ("*Accounting Fraud and WorldCom*" and "*The Enron Collapse*" by Kaplan and Kiron (Rev. 2007), Hamilton and Francis (2003) are examples).

Unethical behavior leading to disastrous consequences is common in areas other than finance. It is plausible that the temptation to engage in financial frauds may appeal most to managers because of the *immediate* effects it has on net earnings, or as Michael Jensen, one of the most important researchers on firms behavior, put it: "*even more silly, [on] earnings per share*" (Jensen (2002), p. 245). Jensen argues that one of the most important drivers of the temptation to engage in unethical actions is the urgency of managers to accomplish short-term rather than long-term results. Further, as the financial function is very closely interrelated to other functions of the firm, simply "because the objective of business firms is stated in financial terms, i.e., to maximize profits" (Bauman, S., in Ang (1993), p. 47). Many corporate conflicts of interest involve the handling of funds; hence, the discipline of finance requires extensive moral character. Because of these reasons, in this article the term "business ethics" and "financial ethics" are used interchangeably.

The HBR Debate on MBAs Ethics

In the middle of the current financial crisis, *Harvard Business Review* organized a debate on *whether business schools contributed to the global financial crisis by selecting the wrong kind of students and teaching them the wrong things*. This debate, which lasted 5 weeks in April-May 2009, was open to business school professors, business leaders, MBAs, and the public at large. The debate about the role of business schools in the financial crisis seemed necessary given that there was plenty of blame pointing especially to the giants of finance, many of whom held MBAs from top business schools. The complete debate was published by *Harvard Business School Publishing* (Podolny, Hemp, Kerr, Sutton, Kaplan, Martin, McCabe, Donovan, Fernandez, Korten, Gratton, Cabrera, McGrath, Mitnick, Khurana, Snook and Light (2009)).

As dean of the Harvard Business School, Jay O. Light states at the end of the debate: "…to suggest that business schools and the MBA are the root cause of the global financial crisis is simplistic nonsense that ignores the obvious reality of the many complex and interrelated factors that underlie the problem," (Light (2009), p. 72).

A serious discussion and valuable insights on business ethics are worth sharing in order to ignite a community conscience among business students and business professors in this sensitive topic. To motivate this conscience, I included selected excerpts from that debate below. Because of the very nature of debates, questions rather than conclusive answers appear. I hope that answers to those questions, raised by the readers of this chapter, will emerge from reflections this discussion initiates.

Cheating - In Don McCable's participation in the debate (McCabe (2009)), there was no consensus on issues related to cheating and honest-dishonest conducts by MBAs. While some of the discussants pointed out that MBA students tend to cheat more and are more money-oriented than students from other disciplines, suggesting that future business leaders may be more prone to ethical problems, others argued that MBAs share the same quality of honesty as the general public. Further, the latter group argued that if MBAs cheat while they enrolled as students, it is because the experience of business school may be corrupting, and not because business students are dishonest people.

One counter argument was that being part of an MBA program is the best cheating-prevention program since an MBA is like a small town in which everyone knows everyone else's business and everyone has long memories. In such an environment, no one would like to corrupt their reputation because of the high likely social and economic consequences in their future as graduates.

In relation to this I bring part of a speech by Warren Buffet, frequently referred to as one of the wisest investors of all times, delivered to University of Florida's business and economics students.[1] Mr. Buffet asked the audience to play the following exercise, from which I extract some parts that I considered relevant:[2] Mr. Buffet asked students to pretend they have to "go long on" or "buy" 10% of one of your classmates for the rest of their lives. "What would the qualities of your chosen classmate be –asked Mr. Buffet?" Most probably, he continued, students would choose neither the one with the highest IQ, nor the one with the best grades, and not even the more energetic one. He guessed that students would probably pick the one to whom they respond the best, the one with leadership qualities, and that person would most probably be generous, honest, and a person who gives credit to other people's work. Mr. Buffet continued the "game", asking the audience to choose one of their classmates to "go short" or "sell" that 10%.[3] Again, he argued, one would not pick the person with the lowest IQ, but rather one would choose the person who turned one off for one reason, and that person most probably would be an egocentric, selfish, and dishonest person.

Mr. Buffet concluded this section of his presentation saying that all of these positive qualities are all achievable if one wants to have them –as they relate to character, behavior, and temper. The negative characteristics, on the other hand, could be eliminated from your personality with a little effort.

Can Ethics Classes Cure Cheating? – Aine Donovan, executive director of the Ethics Institute at Dartmouth College, and adjunct associate professor at Tuck School of Business, reflected on this question (Donovan, 2009). Donovan supports the idea that the only way to counter cheating among MBA students (and its consequences in business ethics) is with an honor code that instills and reinforces a sense of right and wrong. She further proposes that in schools with a very strong value structure like military and religious schools, an honor code is intrinsic and firmly established in the curriculum. In her opinion, *teaching* ethics in business schools by itself would not alleviate the cheating problem, if any. She rather advocates for a culture of ethics in organizations and schools.

Others, in response to Donovan's reflection, claim that schools have the responsibility to *teach* ethics in order to draw the landmarks students should follow. In this view, schools would lay out the fundamentals of ethics and the consequences of both honoring the boundaries and one's vows and going beyond the limits.

Ethics and Business Schools Admission Requirements – Fernandez-Araoz, a senior adviser of a global executive recruiting firm, suggested that admissions committees in business schools should ensure that they admit individuals with the right values in the first place (Fernandez-Araoz, 2009). In particular, admission committees should check to see whether applicants have demonstrated altruistic values in practice.

A counter argument to Fernandez-Araoz's suggestion from one of the participants in the debate was that it is not possible to judge character adequately on an application for a school. She says, "Students have mastered the tricks for gaining entry." In her opinion,

---

[1] A video clip of this presentation has been widely spread and could be easily found on the internet (for instance, in www.youtube.com)

[2] These excerpts do not intent to be a textual transcription of Mr. Buffet's presentation.

[3] It is common in finance to use the terms "go long" to buy stocks and "go short" to sell them (without necessarily holding them) to profit from this trading activity.

the task of schools is to saturate their experience with moral meanings during the time the students are in classrooms.

Is Leadership Related to Ethical and Unethical Behavior?

Leadership and ethics are very closely related. The business ethics literature indicates that ethical and unethical behaviors within firms permeate an enterprise from top management to the rest of the organization. The single most important factor in achieving ethical behavior in an organization, is top management commitment to that objective.

There is something to be aware of, however. Recent research by Treviño, Weaver and Brown (2008) presents empirical results showing that the perception of organizational ethics by senior managers are more positive than the perception of low level employees. This happens because of the corresponding identification by senior managers with the organization. It is possible that top managers believe they lead ethical organizations, and unethical problems may actually be reigning in the organization. One of the implications of this finding by Treviño, Weaver and Brown (2008) is that senior managers should seek out the perception of lower level employees about ethics in the organization -not the perception of mid level employees. Further, managers are warned not to trust responses from surveys about ethics to lower level employees, but rather they should carefully review organizational structures of their firms (i.e., how functional are the structures to foster or discourage employees' interactions across multiple hierarchical levels).

Does It Pay to Behave Ethically? What is the Cost of Dishonesty?

Some companies that incur dishonest business practices have executives who do this as a means to increase their profits in the short term. An argument that supports short-term profitable goals would be, I have heard this from a prominent professor of finance, that a sense of urgency is necessary for executives to reap their best efforts. This is a practical argument if one considers the following: is it possible to maximize profits in both the short and long-term? Is there any conflict on the timing of future benefits for a firm? It has been documented in an article published by *MIT Sloan Management Review* that firms that deploy dishonest practices do it as a means of increasing their short-term profits (Cialdini, Petrova and Goldstein, 2004). This misconduct, Cialdini, Petrova and Goldstein state, is likely to fuel a set of psychological processes with the potential for ruinous financial outcomes.

The main argument of these authors is that a firm that encourages unethical behavior in its external dealings will experience a series of internal consequences driven mainly by the psychological aspect of human beings. These consequences, called malignancies by the authors, are very costly and damaging to the firm mainly because: *a)* like tumors, these malignancies grow and spread quickly in detriment of the firm's health and vigor, and *b)* it would be difficult to trace and identify them by the financial analysis firms typically perform to measure productivity. The authors present a self-explanatory chart of the long-term economic consequences of misconducts by firms. I briefly emphasize some points here.

The first malignancy, what they call "reputation degradation," refers to the fact that once stakeholders (customers, financiers, etc.) perceive a firm as dishonest, the fallout for the firm could be devastating. Surveys in the US show a high likelihood that customers would stop buying the firm products or services, and investors would stop buying this firm's stocks when they perceived misconduct by firms. As it happens with personal reputation, while it takes long to build a respectable reputation, a false move or wrongful judgment can destroy a reputation overnight. The authors cite past research in psychology supporting this: "...by nature, people react more adversely to deceitfulness than to any other attribute" (Cialdini, Petrova and Goldstein (2004) p. 68).

The second malignancy refers to mismatches between values of employees and the organization. Some employees would feel uncomfortable with ethical misconducts and this would have consequences such as increasing stress, absenteeism, low job satisfaction, and high turnover with the consequent increase in costs. Past research has documented a high correlation between low job satisfaction and low productivity, especially for high skilled employees, those who contribute the most to a firm otherwise. In addition, highly skilled workers would find it easier to leave the firm and get another job, with the consequent increase in hiring / training costs for the firm.

There is also the possibility that some well-behaved employees will change over time and act unethically. This is usually the consequence of peer pressure or a supervisor's direct request (the latter was a common practice on *WorldCom*, in Kaplan and Kiron, Rev. 2007). The authors document that those "converted" employees start cheating their own firms (i.e., pilferage, kickbacks, and inventory shrinkage). After all, they rationalize their misconducts as routine, and if they are "benefiting" the firm by their acts, why not benefit themselves? These authors document that fraud perpetrated by employees is the most common type of fraud that afflicts firms in the US.

A third malignancy the authors identify is increased surveillance or very close supervision by the organization over employees. Despite the high direct costs incurred by firms on surveillance software, the indirect costs could be more harmful for firms. Employee monitoring relates to high levels of tension, anxiety, and depression among employees. Further, increased surveillance reinforces the lack of trust on employees, creating an "us versus them" environment with the negative consequences that this carries.

There is also a natural tendency for those employees in increased surveillance environments to cheat whenever they can bypass the surveillance system. Other less obvious, psychologically embedded negative attitudes develop as the result of increased surveillance by firms. Managers should be aware of advice given by these authors: management tends to overestimate the power of surveillance systems. Those in charge of the implementation of monitoring systems are too fixated on the belief that those systems are more effective and more vital that they actually are.

Final Thoughts

Ethics is a difficult proposition especially for pragmatic businesspeople. Hartman (2008) states "... many businesspeople and some business scholars [feel] discomfort about speaking a language in which ethical terms have a significant role" (p. 257). That discomfort may have its roots in the disconnection between *positive*, empirically testable propositions (i.e., the way things are, independent of any normative value judgments about its desirability or undesirability) and *normative* propositions (i.e., derived from a standard or norm that specifies desirable or undesirable conduct or behavior, what ought to be (Erhard, Jensen and Zaffron, 2008)).

From a purely pragmatic point of view, even beyond normative or ethical reasons, persons and organizations should act guided by universal principles. There are positive and legitimate economic reasons for firms to act ethically. But there is a more profound model currently under development by Erhard, Jensen and Zaffron (2008). In a recent interview with Michael Jensen (Jensen, 2009), he emphasizes the importance of integrity, which is defined as what it takes for a person to be whole and complete. Individuals, according to Jensen, "are whole and complete when their *word* is whole and complete, and their word is whole and complete when they *honour* their word" (Jensen (2009), p.16).

Further, individuals honor their word in one of two ways: first, by keeping their word, and on time as promised; or second, as soon as they know that they will not keep their word, they inform all parties involved and clean up any mess that had been caused in their lives. Jensen distinguishes integrity from morality and ethics. In his proposition, integrity is a purely positive proposition as opposed to normative ethics and morality. What is novel in this model is the fact that integrity is considered a factor of production as important as technology according to its impact on performance (i.e., integrity is a *necessary* condition for maximum performance). Integrity, closely related to trust, becomes an indispensable ingredient on the well-being of organizations and individuals in this model.

The aim of Erhard, Jensen and Zaffron (2008) is to "lay the foundations for the positive analysis of normative values." In their view, different judgments about normative values are the root of tensions and conflicts among human beings (i.e., the deeply held personal beliefs about what is good or bad behavior has caused among humans beings the most horrific crimes). As the authors put it, they look forward to see the creation of an entirely new field of inquiry that "...goes beyond a discussion or debate about what are better or worse values to a discussion of what are the effects of differing values, and how intentions differ from actual effects or results. And a great start for this lies in creating a rich body of knowledge of how the values reflected in moral, ethical and legal codes for standards of good vs. bad behavior affect human interaction in families, groups, organizations, social cultures, and nations. That is a purely positive question for philosophy, economics and the rest of the social sciences, and separating out the concept of integrity from these normative concepts and seeing integrity as a purely positive phenomenon that plays a foundational role in performance is an important milestone on the road to the creation of such a science" (Erhard, Jensen and Zaffron, 2008, p.105-106).

This modeling of integrity has its origin in the theory of the firm, particularly in the stockholder and stakeholder theories of agency that address authenticity and integrity mainly. Interested readers could refer to Jensen (2002), and Agle, Donaldson, Freeman, Jensen, Mitchell and Wood (2008).

Discussion Questions:

How does ethical behavior benefit an enterprise?
In Jensen's Proposition, integrity is purely positive as a disposition in contrast to normative ethics and morality that have contextual issues. Should Leaders make a distinction among integrity, ethics and morality?

References

Agle, B, T Donaldson, E Freeman, M Jensen, R Mitchell, and D Wood, 2008, Dialogue: Toward Superior Stakeholder Theory, *Business Ethics Quarterly* 18, 153-190.

Ang, James, 1993, Forum On Financial Ethics, *Financial Management* Autum 1993, 32-59.

Cialdini, Robert, Petia Petrova, and Noah Goldstein, 2004, The Hidden Costs of Organizational Dishonesty, *MIT Sloan Management Review* 45, 67-73.

Clement, Ronald W., 2006, Just How Unethical is American Business?, *Business Horizons* 49, 313-327.

Donovan, A, 2009, Can Ethic Classes Cure Cheating?, in Harvard Business Review, ed.: *The HBR Debate: How to Fix Business Schools* (Harvard Business School Publishing).

Erhard, Werner, Michael C Jensen, and Steve Zaffron, 2008, Integrity: A Positive Model that Incorporates the Normative Phenomena of Morality, Ethics and Legality *Harvard Business School NOM Working Paper No. 06-11; Barbados Group Working Paper No. 06-03; Simon School Working Paper No. FR 08-05. Available at SSRN: http://ssrn.com/abstract=920625* 1-124.

Fernandez-Araoz, C, 2009, Make Ethics a B School Admissions Requirement, in Harvard Business Review, ed.: *The HBR Debate: How to Fix Business Schools* (Harvard Business School Publishing).

Hamilton, Steward, and Inna Francis, 2003, The Enron Collapse, *The International Institute for Management Development Case Collection* IMD164.

Hartman, Edwin, 2008, Reconciliation in Business Ethics: Some Advice from Aristotle, *Business Ethics Quarterly* 18, 253-265.

Jensen, Michael C., 2002, Value Maximization, Stakeholder Theory, and the Corporate Objective Function, *Business Ethics Quarterly* 12, 235-256.

Jensen, Michael C., 2009, Integrity: Without It Nothing Works, *Rotman Magazine: The Magazine of the Rotman School of Management* Harvard Business School NOM Unit Working Paper No. 10-042, 16-20.

Kaplan, Robert, and David Kiron, Rev. 2007, Accounting Fraud and WorldCom, *Harvard Business School Publishing, Case Collection* 9-104-071.

Light, J, 2009, Change Is in the Offing, in Harvard Business Review, ed.: *The HBR Debate: How to Fix Business Schools* (Harvard Business School Publishing).

McCabe, D, 2009, MBAs Cheat. But Why?, in Harvard Business Review, ed.: *The HBR Debate: How to Fix Business Schools* (Harvard Business School Publishing).

Podolny, J, P Hemp, S Kerr, R Sutton, R Kaplan, R Martin, D McCabe, A Donovan, C Fernandez, D Korten, L Gratton, A Cabrera, R McGrath, B Mitnick, R Khurana, S Snook, and J Light, 2009, The HBR Debate: How to Fix Business Schools, *Harvard Business Review* 1-74.

Treviño, L, G Weaver, and M Brown, 2008, It's Lovely At The Top: Hierarchical Levels, Identities, And Perceptions of Organizational Ethics, *Business Ethics Quarterly* 18, 233-252.

Chapter Four
The Challenge of Change in Higher Education
-Deepa Sharma
-Gita Patil

Change in Higher Education

Change — that is the only constant in life!!

(Diogenes Laertius in Lives of the Philosophers)

Although it is universal knowledge that change is inevitable, change is the most complicated thing to accept. Change and confrontation to change is a dilemma that we face every day. And the key to manage change appears to be in not learning to resist, but to take it head on!

The challenges to the higher education sector are to create an environment in which trust and truth can flourish and thereby, lead to a productive process of change. Further, for change to be successful, one must be willing to challenge some of the conventional ideologies we have built for decades into our work situation and have come to recognize as "the right way" to do things.

There appears to be no readymade recipe for managing change. The key is to believe in the philosophy of continuous improvement. Dr. Edward Deming's philosophy (Deming, 1997) and his 14 points for management have significant implications for the reforms in education. His resolute, single-minded and profound belief in the power of people has brought miracles in industry and education.

Higher Education- On Threshold of Revolution

Education is a complex concept and refers to a process, as well as product. Education as a product is viewed as the sum total of what is received through learning, i.e. acquisition of knowledge, skills, attitudes, values and development of personality. As a process, education involves the teaching/learning process, the process of social interaction and the transmission of culture that develops these characteristics in individuals. Higher education has been changing subtly and gradually over the last decade. It must gear up and face the challenges of a changing world. The key change agents or trends that higher education sector needs to be mindful about are:

Emerging Technologies- It is safe to say that the biggest change to hit the world within the last decade with immense implications for education, is the information and communication revolution. The internet and the social networking sites are the biggest challenges to the traditional educational setup. Education sector and its stakeholders must gear up to face the changed scenario and take advantage of the emerging technologies.

Globalization- The education system does not operate in a vacuum, but is a part of the larger societal system and sociopolitical and economic policy changes like liberalization and privatization and their impact on the education system. With the globalization of economy and globalization of education, the world has already become a smaller place. Globalization brings challenges like dealing with multiculturalism and cross-cultural issues among others. Any education system, including the ones where there is less face to face interaction, for example the online ones, essentially must address these issues.

Era of knowledge- The twentieth century is known as the knowledge era. The teachers must take care that they do not become obsolete. The information and the data is available everywhere- in fact, no teacher can keep up with the available body of information. It is the teachers' job to transform the available information into relevant knowledge. The teachers' must now change from being simply an information provider to facilitators of analytic thinking.

Enhanced access to higher education- Education is seen as one of the ways to upward social mobility. According to University Grants Commission (2011), India's number of students enrolled has risen from 9.95 million in 2004 to 13.6 in 2009. Although more and more number of students are enrolling in higher education, the education system in India currently represents a great paradox. On the one hand, there are IIMs & IITs that rank among the best institutes in the world and on the other hand, there are a number of schools in the country that do not even have the basic infrastructure. Even after 50 years of independence, the nation is far away from the goal of universal literacy. The high number of enrollments in countries like India means catering to a vast quantity with a quality education.

Resource crunch-With economic fluctuations comes the need of judicious utilization of resources. Governments in recent times have responded to fiscal deficits by withdrawing and cutting support to education. Rising costs have highlighted the need for emphasis on value for money and focus on issues like transparency in the system, accountability and cost effectiveness. It is imperative to chalk out a planned strategy that helps in team building, brings out the best in people and develops right attitudes.

Taking the Challenges of Change Head On

The challenges of change that higher education is facing are enormous, but can only be dealt with when diligent and cooperative efforts addressing the immense education system are undertaken with full vigor.

Focus on the core educational mission-The question today that is foremost in the minds of all academicians is: "What is the real purpose of education?" In his path breaking book *"Excellence Without a Soul: How a Great University Forgot Education,"* Harry Lewis, a Harvard professor for more than thirty years and Dean of Harvard College for eight, draws from his experience to explain how the great universities have abandoned their mission. He laments the "loss of purpose" in higher education. Universities must remember that the fundamental purpose of undergraduate education is to turn young people into adults who will take responsibility for society.

Education must produce good citizens and above all, good human beings who can take up the challenges of life. Universities can offer courses on value education either as a separate course or as a part of the existing curricula. It has to force the students to think, to rationalize, and to take decisions with full responsibility.

Adopting student–centric measures-Classroom activity should become highly interactive and Learner-centered as the teacher assumes the role of a facilitator. The teaching-learning activity should emphasize proactive relationship building and assessment should become a continuous evaluation process using varied methods of assessment. Instead of chalking out "lesson plans" and "study plans," the teacher must have "student learning sessions" and "student learning methods." The entire thrust has to be on the "learning" rather than "teaching." The curricula can allocate some specific guided hours for student-self-study, discussions, projects and presentations.

Focus on Enriched Faculty

Every employee needs to be encouraged to take up new challenges. The staff should be motivated to take up multidimensional roles in addition to the conventional roles - multiple roles as leaders in different areas of institutional development like health, extension work and overall development of students. In this journey the emphasis should be on co-ordinated work and transparency.

Contact with community-Educators need to be in direct contact with students, parents and the public to make them aware of the quality standards. Internal and external stakeholders need to be involved in the policy making process. More in the involvement of community, means lesser the resistance towards any new concept and greater the success of new ideas!

Organizational walls-Organizational walls need to be torn down and cross-departmental teamwork should be emphasized. Networking, the need of today's age, is experimenting and implementing methods that brings out the best in individuals and develops new attitudes that focus on leadership, teamwork, co-operation, accountability and recognition. A low cost and very effective way to exchange information and ideas could be to initiate administrator controlled social networking groups. It helps to break down the traditional walls and gives a lot of flexibility to the participants.

Innovation-Cristensen and Eyring (2011), in their book "The Innovative University," wrote "*if the* traditional universities *cannot find innovative, less costly ways of performing their uniquely valuable functions, they are doomed to decline, high global and national rankings notwithstanding. Fortunately, such innovation is within their power*" pp.xxv. The authors emphasize the virtues of "disruptive innovation"- which they explain as "more affordable and easier to use," for example online learning. Thinking out-of-the-box is not a matter of genetics or either-you-have-it-or-not, it is a result of sustained efforts that emancipates the energies of the people to release their creative power and prepare them for the world of tomorrow.

Distance, Collaborative and Flexi-learning

A very fine illustration of collaborative, low cost and student-centric learning is the course on International Leadership Studies (16 weeks) which was the initiative of Dowling College Leadership Research and Learning Center, Oakdale, New York: Shri M. D. Shah Mahila College of Commerce and Arts, Mumbai, India; Universidad Panamericana, Guadalajara, Mexico and Iona College, Hagen School of Business, New Rochelle, New York. Each institute enrolled ten students participating in the seminar series to produce a community service project that tracked the leadership challenges, plans, implementation issues and achievements. The students interacted with students of other colleges on a common virtual platform. All work and commentary was presented on an open access Blackboard program sponsored by Dowling College.

The leadership lecture series was a great success, with absolutely no cost for the students. The students from the four institutes across the world gained extensive experiences when they interacted with their peers and faculty from across the globe.

While we move forward to reinventing ourselves, it is important to remember: "Change has considerable psychological impact on the human mind. To the fearful, it is threatening because it means that things may get worse. To the hopeful, it is encouraging because things may get better. To the confident, it is inspiring because the challenge exists to make things better" (King, Whitney, Jr.). As Charles Kingsleigh says in Alice in wonderland – "Precisely, Gentlemen, the only way to achieve the impossible, is to believe it's possible."

Blackboard Discussion

What are the challenges that teachers of higher education are going to face in the future? What measures should you take to keep up with the challenges of change in the future? What challenges do you face in the job scenario? How does higher education prepare you to face those challenges?

References

Christensen, Clayton M. and Eyring, Henry J. (2011) The Innovative University: Changing the DNA of Higher Education from the Inside Out, Jossey-Bass Higher and Adult Education Series

Deming, Edwards W. (1986) *Out Of Crisis.* Massachusetts Institute of Technology, Center for Advanced Engineering Study, U.S.A.

Deming, Edwards W. (1997) *The New Economics for Industry, Government and Education* Massachusetts Institute of Technology 2nd edition, 4th printing, U.S.A.

Harry Lewis (2006) Excellence Without a Soul: How a Great University Forgot Education (New York: Public Affairs)

Higher Education in India strategies and schemes during XIth plan period for universities and colleges 2011. Ugc.ac.in

Chapter Five
Leadership in Business
-Edward F. Lyons

The term leadership is not defined easily because of the many types of leaders and the different characteristics of leaders. One person's leader may be another person's tyrant. Leadership may not be easily defined, but you know it when you either see it or do not see it.

Objective

This Chapter describes the responsibilities of a leadership position (COO, CEO, President or Chairman) and the skills and attributes necessary to be a successful business leader in an ever-changing marketplace.

Although there are many desirable skills of a leader, there are several that I view as essential; they include:

1. Develop a strategic perspective, be a <u>visionary</u>
2. Establish and manage a high <u>performance team</u>
3. Relate to others, integrate <u>Emotional Intelligence</u>

We explore these topics in detail later in this segment.

Scope

The bounds of this discussion include:
- Businesses include manufacturing, distribution and service
- Characteristics common to being either a manager or a leader
- The topic applies to companies and business units or departments within a company; ideally there are many leaders within an organization

Definition

To paraphrase the Mad Hatter in Alice in Wonderland, 'the word means what I want it to mean, nothing more or less.' There are many definitions for leaders and leadership:
- To lead is to guide or conduct by showing <u>the way.</u>
- "Ultimately, it is the responsibility of the leaders to provide the impetus necessary to establish and maintain an <u>excuse-free culture</u>" (Bleech, p. 88).
- A leader is a <u>visionary</u> whom employees will follow.

- A leader establishes the business <u>culture.</u>

Leadership is distinct from management; the focus is on the <u>future.</u>

According to M. Buckingham, "Great leaders tap into the needs and fears we all share." A definition more in line with my thinking is from W. Imberman who believes that leadership is "the ability to discern what needs to be done, what goals must be met, and how to motivate associates and subordinates to make those needs and goals their own priorities" (p. 32).

He goes on to state, "Leadership is not the result of consensus, does not necessarily produce popularity, but does generate a sense of achievement."

A definition that suits me: a leader is someone with a vision of where he or she wants to go and gains support and allegiance from those individuals and groups that are necessary to achieve that vision. The individuals and groups refer primarily to employees and financial backers, and to a lesser degree, they should also include customers and vendors. Further, a leader is someone who makes difficult choices and accepts responsibility for actions.

Business Leadership

The common thread among leaders is their ability to lead a diverse group of individuals. A list of successful global business leaders would include:

Henry Ford	Bill Gates	Steve Jobs
Ingvar Kamprad	Mr. Toyoda	Mr. Tata

These are business leaders that provided innovative products, manufacturing enhancements, and who developed new markets and took advantage of innovations that others designed.

Types of Business Managers

There are many types of business managers. They may be described as:
- Authoritarian - taskmaster
- Participative
- Team builder
- Benevolent dictator
- Avoidance – defer decisions
- Shoot from the hip – avoid analysis
- Indecisive – paralysis

The first four types of managers can be LEADERS in business. The last three do not make 'effective' leaders in business. The appropriate leader may depend on the circumstances. If the business is in dire straits, an autocratic leader may be the best option. That same leader may transition into a participative leader as circumstances change or depart the company.

Shared Attributes - Managers and Business Leaders

Respected managers and leaders share many attributes; a partial list includes the following:

- Ethical/professional
- Accountable
- Understands personal limits
- HR – legal, benefits, employee rights
- Continuous improvement
- Lean initiatives

· Decision maker
· Metric focused
· Basic skills in finance/accounting
· Knows the business – process
· Best practices

A Leader is generally a good Manager; a good Manager may not be a Leader.

Measurements – Metrics defining a Business Leader

How should a leader be measured? The metrics often linked to the attributes sought in a business leader include:
- Financial metrics
    - ROCE - Return on Capital Employed – over a number of years
    - Shareholders' equity growth
    - Market capitalization
- Success over a period of years (minimum of five), at least managed during a complete business cycle
    - Market share improves over time
    - Five year sales and profit growth trend
- Performance compared to competitors is positive
- Turnover of key employees is minimized
- New product and system introductions
- Strength of management team – flexibility
- Turnaround of operation(s) – product, division, company
- Customer assessments based on surveys and position with major customers improve

The performance of a business leader must be assessed within the context of the operating environment. With good luck, a leader might have terrific financial results because of incompetent competitors, favorable economic environment, unique technology or other reasons that have little to do with his or her leadership capabilities.

A litmus test of effective leadership is how well the leader manages the business through adversity. A crisis in my experience was the loss of 30%+ of our workforce because of immigration related problems. Although the company followed all the appropriate governmental protocols, we were left with the challenge of satisfying customers' requirements with a significant shortfall of employees. The importance of having a talented team focused on a single objective guided us through the crisis.

As discussed later, the leadership of Jim Burke in handling the Tylenol tampering case is an excellent example of crisis management. There are many negative examples including Toyota's late recall of cars with "sticking gas pedals" or "acceleration issues" (February 2010).

A Business Leader – A Case Study

Jack Welch, as CEO of General Electric, I consider Jack Welch, the former CEO of General Electric, to be one of the most successful business leaders in the past 50 years.
- His Track record is impressive:

- He was elected CEO of GE in 1981 – market capitalization at that time was $13 billion.
- 15 years later, the market capitalization was $162 billion.

His approach to leadership can be summarized as follows:
- Start with establishing a sound foundation
- Reinvent the business – continuously
- Customer focused – clear direction
- GE should be a problem solver
- View problems as opportunities
- Strive to be number 1 or 2 in market share by business sector
- Gain competitive advantage through quality initiatives – Six Sigma, Lean and in general continuous improvement
- Define "work out" programs to improve productivity
- The options are either improve or divest businesses
- Build a strong management team – invest in people
- Training
- Good compensation/high productivity

I know two individuals who worked at GE - one as a division president and the other as a general manager of a business unit. Both had attended training and management meetings under the tutelage of Jack Welch. Both were impressed by his knowledge of their businesses, the questions asked, the support given and the ability to address challenging issues with sound analysis and excellent communications.

Another business leader I admire is Jim Burke of Johnson & Johnson who has been ranked by Fortune magazine as one of the top ten executives of all time. He is remembered for his ability to address rapidly the tampering of Tylenol medication. He recalled all of the Tylenol product immediately and communicated effectively what the company would do to protect consumers. He addressed a crisis. Earlier in his career, he was asked to develop a drop and nasal medication for children. The initial product was a failure. General Robert Wood Johnson, heir to the family fortune, rather than being upset with Burke, congratulated him for the effort.

In addition to the characteristics already mentioned, there are two additional lessons of leadership that are important:

1. In time of a crisis, act decisively and communicate effectively
2. If a person works diligently, follows a disciplined analytical approach, examines alternatives and still fails, congratulate the person. Allow room for error; if you don't, risk avoidance will be the goal. How a business leader handles a crisis is the ultimate test of leadership.

"The skills required to conquer adversity and emerge stronger and more committed than ever are the same ones that make extraordinary leaders" (Bennis, p. 40).

Managing for the Future

The ability to handle adversity and change will often define a leader. Consider some likely drivers of change over the next five years:
- Dispersed workforce – locations, home offices
- Workforce adaptation

- Technology – IT, automation, new materials, enterprise resource planning
- Financial instruments – new, not well understood
- Resilience to market shocks
- Legislation – individual countries and blocks of countries
- Global perspective – trend toward 'de-globalization'??
- Environmental pressures – View of future opportunities and challenges
- Acceleration in technological advancement
- New global industrial powers
- Competition for limited resources: oil, water, minerals, power, quality personnel.
- Demographic changes
- Climate change
- Communication – accelerating IT changes
- Energy limits
- Water and food crises
- Currency – basket rather than the US dollar
- Aging workforce in some regions
- Educated workforce needed for the modern world
- E Business

To paraphrase Will Rogers, even when you are on the right track if you stand still you will get run over. Change is accelerating. A leader must anticipate change, have the organization in place to address change and have the insight to take advantage of change. If that person does not and the competitors do, the business is very vulnerable and likely to lose market share or worse.

Global Management

The past decade has been an exciting time with the transition from a period where the USA, Europe and Japan ruled the business world to where the BRIC (Brazil, Russia, India and China) countries must be added to the list of major participants. The developing BRIC nations and Indonesia represent 45% of the globe's population.

In the early 1980s, companies from developed countries assumed that they could replicate their business model in other regions of the world, especially the highly populated developing nations with very large potential consumer bases. The opportunities for increased sales in emerging economies such as China and India continue to be, very attractive.

In today's rapidly changing marketplace, the question is whether the skills of a global leader are different from those skills required of a leader who focuses on the domestic market. The essence is the same although there are additional traits, experiences and knowledge that are desirable. A partial list would include:
- Local managers must understand and share the vision – this can be challenging given different cultures
- Leaders must understand the local culture
- Leaders must assure that a management team is in place that is knowledgeable of the financial, taxation, repatriation of profits, human resources (benefits, workers' councils, closures) and legal issues and nuances of different countries
- A must is to understand the local markets and the manner of doing business. Do NOT assume the foreign market, supply chain, financing, terms of trade, etc. are the same as found in the domestic market. McDonalds has adjusted to

the Indian market by offering veggie burgers; in some regions it attempts to modify the architecture of the restaurant to fit in with the local environment.

Characteristics/Traits of Successful Leaders

The traditional view of leaders, "special people who set directions, make the decisions, and energize the troops- are deeply rooted in an individualistic and nonsystematic worldview…new view of leadership in learning organization …leaders are designers, stewards and teachers" (Senge, p. 34).

Leaders focus on three essential skills:
- Ability to envision, define, communicate, gain commitment from the management team and implement the programs to achieve the vision
- Form and develop a 'high performance' management team
- "Emotional Intelligence" is the academic term that describes empathy, motivation and a host of other interpersonal traits.

Each of the characteristics discussed below, in my experience, are fundamental ways that leaders define themselves.

1. **Vision Statement and How to Achieve the Defined Vision**
   There are conflicting thoughts on establishing a vision or goals for a business:

   "A goal without a plan is just a wish." -Antoine de St. Exupery
   "Goals create limitations on the imagination and inhibit innovation." -Kriegel
   "We can't solve problems by using the same kind of thinking we used when we created them." - A. Einstein

   In contrast to most literature dealing with business planning, I view the vision as more than a statement. Rather, my vision is a description of the business in some future time period. It can be quite detailed. It can include topics such as organization structure, products, target markets, sales regions, production capabilities, market position, sales and margin levels, and so forth.

   If you want your vision statement to be meaningful and believable to your management team, avoid a catchy cliché. If you are going to say that the company will be such a size in five years, provide a road map. Otherwise, consider a Jack Welch statement that each business sector will be number 1 or 2 in market share. A leader must be credible – a leader should define a challenging vision, but one that is achievable.

   It is my belief that a vision without a plan on how to achieve the vision is of little or no value. Defining a vision is not wishful thinking, but rather a disciplined assessment of the company, its strengths and weaknesses, the business environment and competitive environment. I have used a 'Plan Format' chart as a tool in creating the goals of the business. My chart depicts the relationships among those factors that affect the business. Assessing the internal and external factors is helpful in defining a vision. What steps are necessary to be successful in achieving the vision beyond the planning horizon are related to execution, training and feedback.

Once the vision is defined, the role of the leader (with the support of the management team) is to translate that vision into a series of specific goals. For each goal there should be a series of programs to assure the success of each goal. For each program there should be:
- Objective of the program
- Planned timing
- Person responsible
- Metric to measure when and how well it was accomplished
- Budget

In defining visions and goals there are often objections and resistance to change. A role of the leader is to address the objections. A leader should listen to concerns and appropriately address them; however, this is not a popularity contest and once all concerns are addressed, the leader must state and implement the plan.

2. Build a 'High Performance' Management Team

The most important step of an effective business leader is also a self-serving goal where the leader builds a team of high performing managers that simplifies a leader's life. He or she can take vacations, have a family life and be confidant that subordinates can handle responsibilities effectively. Strong teams assist in generating ideas (products, technologies, finance and so forth) and help to build a first class operation. The top person in a business is known by the quality of the management team.

There are business owners and managers who believe they only need implementers - those employees that follow orders and leave their creativity at home. I had the unfortunate experience of investing in a company that had an exciting technology and excellent business prospects. The self-anointed leader was the inventor of the technology and wanted to manage all functions: general manager, sales and marketing, production, purchasing and so forth. He could/should have been a leader in product development utilizing his skills (he has a PhD in Chemistry and 90 patents).

The business failed several times with different groups of investors. The inventor had a reasonable (albeit overly optimistic) vision of what the business could become. His estimates of applications, markets, sales and margins were unrealistic. His failure was not building a professional management team; in his case, he failed to add a general manager.

Building a Team

So how do you go about building such a team of professionals? The first step is to 'know thyself.' An objective assessment of the leader's personal and professional strengths and weaknesses provides a clue to the qualifications of the management support required.

An example concerns a former business partner who has a service company. His strength was dealing with people; he was outstanding in relationship building. He was the 'front man' responsible for sales, marketing and new business. He understood his limitations and strengths. He was not the operations or finance person; he hired very competent managers to oversee those functions. Today the business is very successful with over 500 employees.

Twenty years ago, as a middle manager, I participated in a 360-degree feedback program. The goal was to develop competencies in topics that are important to the organization in achieving its VISION. In my case, the 360-degree program consisted of a lengthy questionnaire covering a broad range of topics from ethics to managing people.

To each question a grade was given from 1 to 5 (from poor or disagree to excellent or strongly agree). I completed the questionnaire, as did my supervisor – the president of the company, three peers and three subordinates. It was very helpful to me in understanding my strengths and weaknesses. It provided an objective assessment by looking where my opinions differed from my boss's understanding of how I was perceived by my peers and how successful or not I was in managing subordinates.

A consulting firm managed the program and the results were interpreted by a psychologist trained in management development. I received a report defining areas of personal development. It fulfilled my need to 'know myself'.

Having formulated a vision and completed an objective assessment of strengths and weaknesses, the next step is the assessment of the organization. Develop the organization's structure first and then assign the best people into that organization, and not the other way around. A rule might be 'hire slowly and fire quickly.'

A business leader is evaluated by the quality and professionalism of the individuals that are part of the management team. A separate subject is how to motivate key employees over time. If you have to select one path, then focus on recognition.

Motivating a Team

Accepting responsibility for actions, managing a team (sport or business) and recognizing performance.

Bear Bryant, football coach, University of Alabama, stated, "I'm just a plow hand from Arkansas, but I have learned how to hold a team together. How to lift some up, how to calm down others, until finally they've got one heartbeat together as a team. There are just three things I'd say:
- If anything goes bad, I did it.
- If anything goes semi-good, then we did it.
- If anything goes real good, then you did it."

One purpose of a business plan is to ensure that the management team understands and accepts responsibility to achieve the vision. If there is not a direct linkage between the business plan (vision-goals-programs) and acceptance by managers of responsibility for achieving the plan, you might as well leave the plan in a drawer and vow not to waste time creating a plan next year.

An approach that I have found to be effective in linking the goals of the business plan to the individual's goals is to include these goals in the individual's performance review. Linking the business plan and the individual's goals in the performance review allows the supervisor to hold the individual accountable."

3. **Emotional Intelligence**
The third characteristic of an effective leader is the ability to relate to people. Showing interest in individuals beyond their work, listening, admitting errors and altering a course of action helps validate the intrinsic worth of subordinates. Acknowledging personal weaknesses, building a team that complements one's strengths and accepting the consequences of taking risks, empowers subordinates. Knowing how to listen and motivate people is referred to as "Emotional Intelligence". According to Daniel Goleman, there are five components:

1. Motivation – a drive to achieve success, abounding enthusiasm for work and not driven by compensation but rather a commitment to the future
2. Self-awareness – realistic in assessing personal strengths, willing to acknowledge weaknesses
3. Self-regulation – manage moods and assesses before judging and therefore open to change
4. Empathy – understanding of others, sensitive
5. Social skills – builds relationships and effective persuader

To quote Goleman, "I have found …most effective leaders are alike in one crucial way: They all have a high degree of….*emotional intelligence*. It's not that IQ and technical skills are irrelevant. They do matter, but mainly as 'threshold capabilities'; that is they are entry-level requirements for executive positions."

Situations

One might ask if the leadership concepts presented are geared only for larger businesses that have management teams. The concepts related to vision are applicable to any business of any size. Remember the famous statement that Lewis Carroll penned in Alice in Wonderland, "If you don't know where you are going any road will get you there."

Whether one leads a large complex or a small entrepreneurial business, the leader (who might be the owner) should know where he or she wants the business to be in the future. The actions of the leader will vary depending on the circumstance. If the business is in trouble, the focus is to reduce costs and remain viable. A different challenge might appear if the business is stable and not growing. Yet, a business might be at risk from newer technologies or improved competitive production techniques. In each case, different leader behaviors and teamwork will be required.

In some instances, the management team may be comprised of the owner and a supervisor. Here, one option is to seek management support from outside sources, for example: banker, accountant, and attorney or perhaps members of the local chamber of commerce, suppliers and customers. There are organizations for small businesses where a facilitator brings together CEOs of small companies to share experiences and learn from each other. One such group is The Executive Committee (TEC). The various skills of 'emotional intelligence' apply to all leaders regardless of the size or type of the business.

Closing Comment

Steven Ballmer, the CEO of Microsoft since 2000, was asked the question if he could teach any business school class what would it be. He responded, "Leadership. I've come to believe that to be a great leader, you have to combine thought leadership, business leadership and great people management….the truth is great leaders have to have a mix of those things."

Discussion Questions

Describe your personal career vision: that is, what would you like to be doing in 5 to 10 years? Assess your anticipated strengths and weaknesses. In order to achieve your vision, what steps (training classes, internships. jobs, volunteer work and other pursuits) would you take to achieve your vision and be seen as a leader by your peers?

Select a leader of interest to you and describe this person and his or her primary characteristics. Explain why he or she is a leader, what weaknesses the person exhibited and how that person overcame or failed to overcome those weaknesses.

References

Ballmer, S. May 17, 2009. "Corner Office". The New York Times

Bennis, W. September 2002. "Crucible of Leadership". Harvard Business review

Bleech, J and D. Mutchler. 1995. Let's Get Results Not Excuses. Leadership Development Center

Buckingham, M. March 2005. "What Great Managers Do". Harvard Business Review

Giuliani, R. 2002. Leadership. Miramax Books

Goleman, D. Jan. 2004. "What Makes a Leader?" Harvard business Review (page 82)

Hesselbein, F. et al., Editors. 1996. The Leader of the Future. The Drucker Foundation

Imberman, W. June 2009. "Business-as-Usual is No Longer an Option". Foundry Management & Technology

Johnson, S. 1998. Who Moved My Cheese? G.P.Putnam's Sons

Kriegel, R. 1991. If it Ain't Broke…Break IT! Warner Books

Senge, P. 1994. The Fifth Discipline. Currency Doubleday

Slywotzky, A. and D. Morrison. 1997. The Profit Zone. Times Business

Chapter Six
Leadership in the Not-For-Profit World
-Jean C. Sussman

Introduction

In this Chapter, we will examine attributes, roles and responsibilities of leaders in a not-for-profit organization.

You have just finished a segment on leadership in business. In that segment you learned about the key attributes of being a leader. The three top attributes discussed were:
- Developing a strategic perspective, a vision
- Establishing and managing a high performance team
- Being able to relate to others, "Emotional Intelligence"

I would add one more key attribute – the drive to excel.[4] The commitment to being the best and to seek constantly to improve is an important defining characteristic of a leader.

At this moment you might be saying to yourself that these four attributes are essential to leading all types of organizations -- so why should we go any farther and talk about leadership attributes specific to not-for-profits?

You are partially correct. These four attributes are essential for general leadership. In addition, leading a not-for-profit organization has additional challenges. In this segment we will:

I.   Look at three ways to examine *styles* of leadership

II. Take a look at building a mission for a not-for-profit

III. Discuss four important leadership attributes necessary for leading a not-for-profit organization:
     A. Fundraising, including leading the organization through an economic crisis
     B. Board development
     C. Staff hiring and retention
     D. Dealing with volunteers

IV. Reexamine measurement from the perspective of leading a not-for-profit organization.

---

[4] See Collins

I. Leadership Styles Vs. Leadership Attributes

Let's start by distinguishing between leadership *styles* and leadership *attributes*. The former addresses the individual's approach or technique in dealing with the organization. The latter deals with the individual's core beliefs on what is important to that organization's success.

In this section we will be looking at leadership *attributes* for not-for-profits. However, I want to make a quick comment about leadership *style* in case anyone is interested in pursuing this topic. There are a great number of paradigms that examine *style*. I am presenting just three here -- in no way is this meant as a survey on the subject. Using these paradigms as a starting point will lead you to a wealth of information and additional models on the topic. You might even see yourself in one of these paradigms – or see someone you would like to be. Understanding leadership style is important because it gives you insights on how work gets done and how others in the organization are treated.

<u>Max Weber</u>: Max Weber, in 1947, was one of the first to write about leadership styles. He characterized leadership styles as:
- ➢ Bureaucratic: where leadership stems from knowledge
- ➢ Traditional: where leadership is based on some arbitrary exercise or history of power (such as a king), and
- ➢ Charismatic: where the individual is seen as a hero, or as someone with uncommon skills (superhuman)

<u>James McGregor Burns</u>: Burns, in his 1978 book <u>Leadership</u>, argues that morality is essential for leadership. He distinguishes between transactional and transformational leadership. Transactional leaders focus on the exchange of goods and services, on a chain of command and on subordinates meeting clearly defined expectations. Transactional leaders expect rules to be followed, deadlines met and procedures in place. Likewise, people are rewarded by following the rules established by the transactional leader.

Transformational leaders are concerned with the collective well being of those who follow them. Transformational leaders use charisma and seek to appeal to the values and ethics of people. The followers of transformational leaders are rewarded in part by feeling that they are a part of a highly motivated and passionate organization. Transformational leaders lead by example, rather than by rules.

In reality, most leaders are both transactional and transformational. However, an individual who is not moral (and Burns defines this in his book) cannot be a leader, even if he/she has traits identifiable with transactional and transformational leadership. Burns' theories form the basis for subsequent academic research.

<u>Contingency Theory</u>: This more recent theory advocates that the best leaders are those who can adapt to a specific situation -- that the style will change depending on the circumstance and that there is no "best" leadership style. Two of the foremost advocates of this theory are Paul Hersey and Kenneth Blanchard, authors of <u>Management of Organizational Behavior: Utilizing Human Resources</u>. They postulate four types of leadership styles: 1) telling: where subordinates need to be told what to do; 2) selling: where subordinates accept the idea of what they need to do and figure out how to accomplish it on their own; 3) participating: where the group makes the decision on how

to proceed, with the leader being present; and 4) delegating: where the leader walks away from decision-making and leaves the responsibility to a subordinate.

A large body of material used in leadership development programs is based on Contingency Theory, Transactional and Transformational Leadership and the work of Weber.

Now let's look at developing a core mission.

II.   Development Of A Core Mission

In the last chapter, you learned about the importance of creating a vision or mission in the business world. It is equally important in the not-for-profit world, and is worth examining from this perspective.

In the for-profit world, the mission typically is related to financial results. But in the not-for-profit world money is likely not the primary measure of success. A mission is extremely important in the not-for-profit sector because it helps build a brand in which donors will invest. Moreover, it provides psychic rewards to staff and volunteers.

Because the development of a mission is so important, let's review key guidelines necessary for developing a mission in the not-for-profit world:

➤ Your mission statement should "accurately describe what your organization does, the people it serves, and where it does its work." [5]
➤ It should describe what you can or will do best.
➤ It should be written with a passion that you and your staff feel.
➤ It should be easily explainable to the board of directors, donors, staff and volunteers.
➤ Use your community and your key funders (those who have been with you for years, who understand your current mission and support capacity building) for input through focus groups or through questionnaires to develop the mission.
➤ Your mission needs to be translatable into goals that can be measured. If not, how will your investor know that you, as the leader, have been successful? How will you know if you have been successful?
➤ Think about your mission statement as a way to lure investors.
➤ Adapt the private sector focus on customer satisfaction, continuous improvement and a market driven mission.

Now let's turn to the four leadership capabilities in the not-for-profit world

III.   Four Capabilities Required-For-Not-For-Profit Leadership

A.   Fundraising

The fundraising role is very important. In the private sector, investors expect a competitive financial return. In the not-for-profit world, the reasons for investing – for donating – are more complicated. A financial payback is not necessarily the reason for donating money. An exception to this is when a loan is made. But even then the return will be less than that available in the private sector – and the lender knows that.

Fundraising can make or break an organization. Fundraising provides the capital for the not-for-profit to accomplish its mission. Fundraising also can help attract and retain

---

[5] Brinkerhoff p. 17

key members of the organization, including the management team, staff, board members and volunteers. More specifically, let's look at:

1. The mission statement's importance to fundraising
2. The relationship between funders and the not-for-profit
3. The importance of funding for capacity building
4. Turning down a donation, and
5. Economic crisis, fundraising and financial management.

1.   The mission statement's importance to fundraising   In order to raise money, the not-for-profit must have a clear and compelling mission. The articulation of the mission, and the demonstrated commitment to it, provide potential donors the reason for giving money. The mission also helps the leader of the not-for-profit focus on which donors most support the mission. The importance and difficulty of fundraising underline one of the key attributes of a leader: the ability to articulate a core mission, to be passionate about it, and to bring others along with you.

2.   Relationship between funders and the not-for-profit   The relationship between funders and the not-for-profit receives a lot of attention in the literature and a lot of attention in training programs for not-for-profits. Many funders – especially smaller ones – want to have a personal relationship with the not-for-profit. They need to feel that the not-for-profit is meeting their own need.

Funders have every right to ask for information on how their contribution is used, to visit the organization and to volunteer. However, the donor does not have the right to meddle in the day-to-day operations of the not-for-profit. The leader, through the establishment and regular sharing of appropriate performance measurements, should be able to provide the donor with the information needed.

Some oversight by the funder is just a part of doing business. If the organization has established a good set of performance measurements, additional ones that require large amounts of staff time should not be needed. If additional oversight is absolutely required by the funder, then it should be paid for by the funder.

3.   Leadership and capacity building   An important component of fundraising is raising money for institutional capacity building. Capacity building refers to money set aside for staff development, training, research, etc. In other words, capacity building is development that spans the organization – that crosses all programs and prepares the not-for-profit for the future. Capacity building also refers to the ability of the organization to grow its cash reserves – to save for a future need. Unfortunately, funders typically support (buy) services – rarely are funds allocated to capacity building. Funders may try to force the not-for-profit to account for every cent spent on the specific program without allowing any of the money to add to the reserves of the not-for-profit (to the balance sheet) for future growth, research and risk-taking.

Convincing funders to alter how they look at donations is a key role of the organization's leader. Why should a not-for-profit always be strapped for cash? Why should a not-for profit not be able to develop its staff? Changing the paradigm of giving to support capacity building is an important role of the leader.

A good way to be able to focus on capacity building is for the leader to seek unrestricted funding. This means that the donation is not tied to a specific program.

42

Unfortunately, in the not-for-profit sector, the donations frequently are tied to a specific program. The donor may believe that if he/she gives you money then he/she has the right to tell you where you can spend it. Restricted giving misses a fundamental point: "to make the greatest impact on society requires first and foremost a great organization...and a disciplined organization that delivers exceptional results..."[6] And building such an organization takes time and resources for general development work. If the donor is a private company, these programs frequently are linked to that company's business. If the donor is a foundation, that foundation may have its own list of priorities that may or may not line up with the priorities of your not-for profit.

4. **Turning down a donation** This is a difficult question and one that would seem unimaginable to many organizations. It is tied to restricted giving. "Donor restrictions on either assets or income... create risk and expense because they are more likely to create demands on capacity and programs beyond what the donor originally envisioned..."[7] That is because the restricted donation may not cover ancillary costs – such as infrastructure, management time, training or required cash reserves. Donors, and the leadership of the not-for-profit, need to be aware of the unintended consequences of accepting and giving restricted funds. The leader needs to work closely with the donor to ensure the money can be used to meet the needs of the organization, not just the objectives of the donors.

Several questions should be answered before restricted money is accepted. Are there stipulations tied to the use of the money? If the answer is yes, then will the money still go to the core mission of the not-for-profit? If the answer is yes, then does the donation cover the *full* cost of the program for which it is intended?

If these full costs are not covered, then there will be a drain on the organization. The leader of the not-for-profit needs to ask whether the acceptance of the donation, with the accompanying stipulations, will drain the resources of the not-for-profit such that its core mission cannot be met. If that is likely, and the donor will not increase the funding, then the donation should be declined, as difficult as that may seem.

Let's look at an example. Organization "X" is a not-for-profit that provides free meals to the poor. A donor wants to give money to double the number of meals provided. The money only can be used for food. All of a sudden the not-for-profit finds itself without adequate space for cooking and serving the food. It needs to go out and purchase more equipment and perhaps even find a larger facility. But because the donor requires all money go to food, the not-for-profit has to use its cash reserves, or take money from other programs in order to do this. So should the money, with its stipulations for use, be accepted? "X's" leadership should have thought through the unintended consequences (and perhaps renegotiated the restrictions) before accepting the donation.

A disciplined leader with a concrete mission (and a good financial manager) must take the time to understand whether a donation will force the not-for-profit to expand beyond its capabilities. One of the most difficult fundraising decisions is determining whether or not your organization can fulfill the stipulations attached to money. And even more difficult is deciding that the money – with its restrictions – cannot be accepted.

5. **Leading the organization through an economic crisis** Given the current economic climate, this discussion is appropriate. Discipline and focus are key to the success of any organization. When funding and resources become scarce, these attributes

---

[6] Collins p. 25
[7] Miller p.5

become even more important. Good leaders will take charge to ensure the organization is positioned to weather difficult times. The work that needs to be done is work that you will want to periodically tackle, regardless of the external environment. As such, much of what we talk about can be viewed as opportunities to ensure your not-for-profit is optimally aligned and headed in the direction you need it to be. And after all, isn't that a key role of a leader?

Underlying this work is the importance of communication. In fact, during challenging times communication with all stakeholders should be expanded. As a leader, you already are a skilled communicator. Now is the time to increase that communication. Use your employees, your board of directors, your volunteers and your clients in creative brainstorming – you never know what new ideas are out there until you ask.

- Take yet one more look at the core mission of your organization[8] . If you cannot articulate it clearly and succinctly, than it is unlikely that your donors, staff or board will understand
- Ask which activities are essential to meet your core mission. Consider narrowing your scope if necessary – go deep rather than broad
- Consider cutting programs that are not related to your core mission. If necessary – and I know this is very difficult – considering letting staff go (even if this is a temporary layoff)
- Work with your financial supporters to ensure funding is focused on your core mission, and that funds support your need to deepen and sustain your programs, not to expand them
- Ensure you are implementing and institutionalizing the best budgeting and financial planning practices.
  - o Always quantify your options. As you think about the future of your organization, about your resources and about your donor pool, you should be prepared to develop several budgets. Each of these budgets will represent a different financial scenario based on a different set of organizational objectives. I am not saying that you need to have multiple core missions – only a different set of objectives and plans based on different financial outcomes. And make sure you have planned for a worse case scenario. Have implementation plans that are aligned with the different budget scenarios. The implementation plans should be ready to go – but not until the funding is available.
  - o During recessions demand for the services of not-for-profit organizations can increase. Do you have a quantifiable plan for dealing with the possibility of demand increasing?
  - o Test yourself to ensure you have identified which items in your budget are essential – are nonnegotiable. And make sure you can articulate why that is the case/
  - o Ask yourself which of the activities your organization is engaged in provide positive financial results and which require financial infusions from other activities. Then ask yourself if those that produce deficits are really essential.
  - o Is your financial information easy to understand and transparent to those who need to see it?
- Create a greater reliance on volunteers and in-kind donations.
- Consider working strategically with other organizations. You might do this in small and large ways. For instance, if one of your core programs overlaps with that of another organizations, consider writing a joint proposal for funding. Or if

---

[8] See Guthman and LaBarbera

several organizations purchase the same goods (anything from office supplies, to phones to even vehicles) consider setting up a purchasing pool where you can bundle the items you purchase with the objective of achieving economies of scale. This approach will force you to streamline your purchases and ask whether or not you are purchasing and using the appropriate goods.

B.   Board Development and Leadership[9]

In the broadest terms, the role of a board is to help set the vision/mission for the organization and to ensure that the organization is well governed. This role should include approving and monitoring the budget such that financial targets are met, approving and monitoring key legal and organizational policies, and holding the head of the organization accountable for implementing the mission and meeting key performance targets. The board will not need to get involved with the day-to-day operations if the not-for-profit is a well run organization. By providing the board with a well run organization, the head of the not-for-profit can utilize the board's expertise to plan for the future.

To summarize, the President of the Board and the CEO share responsibility for board development, and the roles and responsibilities of board members include visioning, financial oversight, fundraising and providing expertise and mentoring to key staff members...

Visioning: The board should be engaged in finalizing the vision for the organization, while the process of setting the vision should be managed by the organization. The leader of the organization needs to focus the board's attention on long term goals and policies– not on involvement in the near term operations of the organization. The leader should ensure that board members have the mission statement top-of-mind at all times. This ensures decision making is based on the mission. If it needs to be changed do so in a systematic way.

Financial oversight: The board should be engaged in discussing the financial future to ensure that there is a concrete link between the long run vision and the specific financial goals for attaining it. The board also should serve as the financial oversight authority, ensuring rules and regulations are in place and followed.

Utilizing board expertise: A well rounded board should include members with expertise in the areas important to the not-for-profit, including finance, marketing, and personnel, governance, and staff development -- all at the strategic /policy level. Board recruitment and review needs to be a priority – think through the skills and attributes that would be useful on your board and select accordingly. For instance, board members should include representatives from the community served. Board members also should represent future leaders of your organization (or related organizations). What better training than to serve on the board. Board members should serve as mentors, and should ensure that they are providing the support and growth opportunities needed by the not-for-profit's leadership. Professional expertise is also important, such as finance, marketing, and legal experience.

The board president should be capable of leading the Board. A key characteristic of this individual is his/her ability to mentor and serve as a sounding board for the leader of the not-for-profit.

---

[9] See Lorsch and Clark

<u>Fundraising</u>: Board members must be fundraisers. They need to understand that they are expected to give from their own pockets, as well as raise money from outside sources. The most successful board fundraisers are those who write a meaningful personal check – they can talk from the heart about what drives them to support the organization. In addition, members of the board understand that they must serve as advocates for the not-for-profit with potential funders.

Board involvement in fundraising is also important because it helps relieve the responsibility felt by the leader of the not-for-profit. The nonstop pressure to raise money is a major cause of burnout in the not-for-profit sector.

<u>Performance expectations of the organization's leader</u>: The board must set concrete and measurable long term expectations for the organization's leadership. This is a key responsibility of any board of directors. The leader of the not-for-profit reports directly to the board of directors – and it is the board's responsibility to provide feedback, help where needed, and formal and informal training and mentoring.

C.   Leadership and Staff Hiring and Retention

Ask your friends and colleagues what they like most about their bosses. Then ask them what the key attributes of a leader are. You will find that there is a lot of overlap. What do you think are the key attributes of a leader with respect to staff development? They include:

- Encouraging learning;
- Encouraging taking risks and making mistakes (with the manager as a safety net);
- Encouraging independent decision making (with the manager as a safety net);
- Accepting responsibility;
- Sharing visions and goals and helping you to understand them;
- Excellent communication skills;
- Recognition of a job well done.

In the not-for-profit world a leader often is more involved with managing staff than in a typical business situation. This is because people work for a not-for-profit for different reasons than they work for a for-profit organization, and money is probably not one of the key reasons. The pay scale at a not-for-profit is typically less than that at a for-profit. Given this, discovering what motivates your staff and what is required to keep the best of the best engaged is important. For instance, you may have leeway with vacation, with working from home, and with work schedules. Be on the lookout for burnout, boredom and a loss of focus on the mission – and do something about it. Perhaps you need to meet with the individual and re-engage him/her. Or perhaps your vision is stale and you need to address that.

As a leader you also should facilitate your staff's involvement in decision-making, in interacting with your board, in working with donors, in networking outside your organization and in other aspects of the business. Set up a mentor for key staff using board members or outside resources. Share your succession plan and discuss professional growth opportunities. As the current leader, provide a good role model: balance work-life.

These "psychic" rewards can go a long way toward compensating a person for income, especially if the passion for the work is there.

Recruiting: As the leader, you also need to ensure that you hire the right staff in the first place, because staff members are the foundation of your organization. Hiring self-motivated, passionate, creative and hard working staff – and providing them with incentives to stay- is the key.[10] You can do this by:

- Ensuring whoever recruits for your organization is as passionate about the work as you are. People want to work for not-for-profits because they believe in your cause;
- Being selective about whom you bring in; and that those applying know that you are selective;
- Taking the time to really understand what drives your key people (you will find it is not money);
- Hiring those who will thrive in the culture of your organization;
- Developing a culture of openness which allows the best of your staff (and volunteers) to rise to the top and results in improvement in the performance of your organization;
- Ensuring you have a culture in place that stimulates change. What signals do you listen to about the need to change a key aspect of your organization?

How to Ensure Retention of Leaders of Not-for-profit Organizations: Strong leaders are to be cherished. Just like all of us, they need to be praised, recognized, challenged, offered opportunities for professional and personal growth, and compensated fairly with monetary and psychic income. The heads of not-for-profit organizations often leave their positions because of inadequate compensation and concern about life-long earnings potential, overall burnout, lack of mentoring and career advancement, and the intense focus on fundraising. Many report that they are not able to find a good work-life balance.

The challenge is how to retain good leaders. Whenever possible, boards need to ensure that leaders and management are not undervalued. "Even those...who should know better sometimes fall prey to the notion that important charitable work should happen at a discount. The same idea reinforces the view that professionals at nonprofits ought to work longer hours and for less pay than their for-profit counterparts."[11] Leaders of not-for-profits believe in their work – but that does not mean they should be taken advantage of.

Some of these issues need to be addressed by the board of directors, such as compensation, vacation, and even work-life balance. The leader, in conjunction with the board, might want to try some of the following, as well:

- Create a leadership forum for heads of not-for-profits: Invite speakers from the for-profit and not-for-profit worlds, to speak.

  o Allow for structured and unstructured time. In addition to a formal presentation, allow time for networking through informal conversations. This can provide invaluable ideas and contacts.

  o Create the opportunity for leaders to speak about serious issues at these forums. The leader could:
    - Share best practices
    - Explore new perspectives
    - Explore possibilities for collaboration

---

[10] And finding and keeping volunteers with the same personal attributes can be equally important
[11] Collins, p.20

- Increase the opportunities to introduce new ideas and practices into the organization. This would:
  o Allow the opportunity to pick and choose among best practices
  o Allow a safe forum for taking risks
  o Help create links among organizations

- Create a mentorship program with experienced leaders from the community (this is something the board should do):
  o Recruit colleagues of board members to mentor leaders
  o In small organizations with limited resources creating external networks is a way to provide fresh ideas. These relationships provide external perspectives and a safety net for leaders to test ideas and take risks

D. Dealing with Volunteers

Many not-for-profits rely heavily on volunteers. Volunteers can be essential in raising funds, administering programs, manning physical facilities and serving as general goodwill ambassadors for the organization. They can also be an important source of in-kind and cash donations. Not only do these individuals need to be managed in the traditional sense, but they also need to share the vision of the organization. This is where leadership skills are very important.

Volunteers who do not share the vision – who are not passionate about the not-for-profit – will not be advocates for the organization in the community, with potential donors, nor even with the not-for-profit's clients.

Volunteers are not cost free -- they need to be inspired, trained, supervised and evaluated, just like the rest of the staff.

Now let's return to one of the leadership attributes discussed in the previous segment of this class -- establishing performance measurements.

IV. Measurement In The Not-For-Profit World

In the for-profit world the key measurement of performance is the achievement of financial goals. Other measurements also are important, but ultimately financial results are what determine the staying power of the company. In the not-for-profit world financial results typically are not the most important measurement of success.

Measurements always must be tied to the overall mission of the organization. Thus, the leader must develop these measurements to ensure this linkage with the mission and with the overall performance of the organization.

Whenever possible, these performance measurements should be quantifiable. For instance, if a goal is to reach 100 clients a week, then you need to be able to measure clients served. In many instances, quantifiable measurements may not be so straight forward and proxies must be utilized. Ask yourself how you would define "great results" for your organization and then find a way to measure these results. For instance, if you run a not-for-profit art school, what would you like your funders and the public to know about the school?

- That a certain percentage of your students go on to college and major in art?
- That a certain percentage gets scholarships to do this?
- That a certain percentage of your students are invited to participate in exhibitions?

- That a certain percentage receives commissions or sells their work?
- Qualifications of teachers?
- Number of volunteers across time?
- Donations?

And
- Did you meet your financial objectives? This is important -- do not forget to measure it in as many ways as make sense

If you think about how you define success and excellence, you will be able to come up with quantifiable measurements. Lastly, make sure you spend time developing these measurements. They need to be put in place for a number of years. Measurements that cannot be tracked across time are not very useful. In addition, they should be useful to all constituent groups, especially funders. By carefully crafting your measures you should be able to satisfy the monitoring needs across all interested parties.

Concluding Comments

In this segment we focused on leadership attributes in the not-for-profit world. While acknowledging that many of the same attributes are needed across both the for-profit and not-for-profit organizations, we took a look at four attributes that are especially important in leading a not-for-profit organization: fundraising, board of directors' management, staff development and volunteers. We circled back and talked briefly about developing a mission and putting in place measurement tools.

Leading a not-for-profit organization can be a very rewarding experience. Successful leaders believe in the mission of their organization, are passionate about their work, and inspire dedication, enthusiasm and top performance in their donors, board, employees and volunteers.

Discussion Questions

Think about what it would be like to have leadership responsibility for a not-for-profit organization.
A. What do you think would be the hardest parts of the job, and why? Please give two examples.
B. What do you think would be the easiest parts of the job, and why? Please give two examples.
If you were ready to explore a change in career to a for-profit enterprise, how would you convince the for-profit company executives that they should hire you?
A. What specifically will you be able to tell them about your strengths and weaknesses as they relate to your working for the not-for-profit organization?
B. What specifically will you say about why you want to change careers?

References

Brinckerhoff, Peter C. Non-Profit Stewardship. St. Paul: Wilder Publishing Center. 2004

Burns, James MacGregor. Leadership. New York: Harper & Row. 1978.

Collins, Jim. <u>Good to Great and the Social Sectors</u>. Boulder: www.JimCollins.org. 2005.

Coltoff, Philip. "Lessons in Leadership." <u>Children's Voice Magazine</u>. 16-3 (5-6, 2007). P. 30-34.

Cornelius, Marla, Patrick Covington, Albert Ruesga. <u>Ready to Lead? Next Generation Leaders Speak Out.</u> Copies available through www.compasspoint.orc. 2009.

Gardon, Anne. "Critical Conversations in Times of Crisis." Strategies for Change. Westchester, NY: Paper presented at <u>The Not-for-profit Leadership Summit,</u> paper on line (http://www.uwwp.org/summit.htm). 5/11/09.

Guthman, Emily and Jessica LaBarbera. "The 2009 Nonprofit Economic Climate: Managing through a Downturn". Presented at The <u>Not-for-profit Leadership Summit,</u> Westchester, NY: The Nonprofit Finance Fund.org. Paper on line (http://www.uwwp.org/summit.htm). 5/11/09.

Hersey, Paul and Kenneth Blanchard. <u>Management of Organizational Behavior: Utilizing Human Resources</u> (3rd ed.) New Jersey: Prentice Hall. 1977.

Kouzes, James M. and Barry Z. Posner. <u>The Leadership Challenge</u>. (4th ed.) San Francisco: John Wiley & Sons. 2007.

Lencioni, Patrick. <u>The Five Dysfunctions of a Team</u>. San Francisco: John Wiley & Sons. 2002.

Lorsch, Jay W. and Robert C. Clark. "Leading from the Boardroom." <u>Harvard Business Review.</u> HBR.org. April 2008

Miller, Clara. "Hidden in Plain Sight --Understanding Nonprofit Capital Structure". <u>The Nonprofit Quarterly</u>. Spring 2003. 8 pages.

Weber, Max <u>The Theory of Social and Economic Organization</u>. Translated by A. M. Henderson & Talcott Parsons. New York: The Free Press. 1947.

Chapter Seven
Financial Challenges in the Global Economy
-John F. Manley

Introduction

As we enter into the second decade of the 21st Century, the events of the recent past provide insight into the financial challenges facing Multinational Enterprises (MNE), both multinational financial institutions (MNFI) and multinational corporations (MNC). Within finance, a distinction is sometimes useful concerning the degree of multi-nationality of the organization. Firms are referred to as international institutions if these firms simply have sales overseas, whether directly through their own efforts or indirectly through exporters or by their products being included as inputs within products of other firms whose products are then exported. Those firms with foreign sales through distributors or production centers located in several other nations are referred to as multinational; but if the firm has foreign sales with decision centers located in several nations and operations on several continents, then these are referred to as global institutions. For the purposes of this discussion, we will consider two broad areas of financial management concerns among twenty-first century financial challenges. For the first, we will discuss the issue of governance; while for the second, we will refer to a recent Brookings study to guide us. One of the two discussion board questions will come from each of these two broad areas of concerns.

Challenge Area One: Governance

Recent trends in globalization, technological applications, increased competition, and government solutions to financial crisis raise the need to discuss the relevant role and problems inherent in the governance system. From the textbook viewpoint within the United States of America, the primary goal of Financial Management is stockholder value maximization. This is achieved through the concerted efforts and managerial skills of senior firm management and the Board of Directors. As such, a critical discussion should involve the challenge associated with providing the appropriate structure within, characteristics of and interaction between the composition and role of both Management and the Board of Directors. Lack of either effective training or sufficient independence of the members of the Boards that govern our institutions may be the result of misguided emphasis, but the errors inherent in these omissions may be shown with recent events.

The U.S. Housing Bubble in 2007, the financial crisis among the US financial institutions in 2008, and the subsequent recession of 2009 are all interconnected and relevant to the future financial challenges facing our MNE. The economic interdependence of world markets and among individual national markets makes the events in the U.S., as the world's largest economy and major trading partner, a major influence on the health of the global environment [See Exhibit 1].

The Bureau of Economic Analysis provides an advance estimate of the annual value of the US GDP (Gross Domestic Product) of US$14.5 trillion[12] for 2010. Using the CIA World Fact Book, which provides 2009 GDP estimates for most of the world's nations, a comparison of the US GDP at $14.25 trillion to the European Union (EU GDP) at $14.5 trillion places the USA economy as second in the world; but the EU[13] is comprised of 27 member nations.[14] As a single nation, the US is the largest economy with China as the next largest economy at $8.8 trillion.[15] The Chinese economy, although much smaller than the U.S. economy, had grown during this recent period of crisis while the U.S. economy had shrunk; and the Chinese economy had been growing at a faster rate than most economies during the non-recessionary period [See Exhibit 2]. Therefore, the sheer size of the US economy (and eventually the Chinese economy) must have an impact on the economies of other nations; and events in the US market will affect other markets.

Exhibit 1: Top Five National Economies as measured by GDP

Rank	Country	GDP	Year
1	European Union	$14,520,000,000,000	2009 est.
2	United States	$14,250,000,000,000	2009 est.
3	China	$8,767,000,000,000	2009 est.
4	Japan	$4,141,000,000,000	2009 est.
5	India	$3,548,000,000,000	2009 est.

World Fact Book

---

[12] http://www.bea.gov/national/index.htm#gdp

[13] http://europa.eu/

[14] CIA (Central Intelligence Agency), *World Fact Book*: https://www.cia.gov/library/publications/the-world-factbook/rankorder/2001rank.html

[15] The size of the Chinese economy is projected to pass the U.S. economy by 2040. Goldman Sachs, *BRICs Monthly*, Issue 09/05, May 29, 2009: http://www2.goldmansachs.com/ideas/brics/lead-global-recovery-doc-2.pdf.

Exhibit 2: Comparative Accumulated GDP Growth

GDP accumulated growth, in percent, constant prices

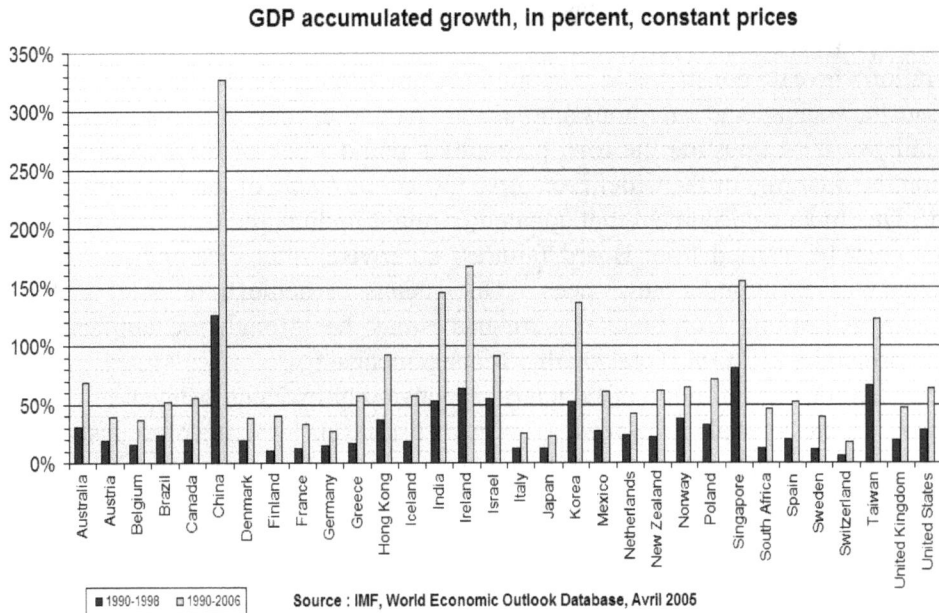

1990-1998 ☐ 1990-2006   Source : IMF, World Economic Outlook Database, Avril 2005

http://www.imf.org/external/pubs/ft/weo/2005/01/data/dbginim.cfm

In 2005, AIG (American Insurance Group)[16] became the target of a fraud investigation. Maurice Greenberg, Chairman and CEO of AIG, was forced to resign. But the questioning of the solvency of the institution came to a head in 2008 with the U.S. government's involvement with the salvaging of the failing AIG as an institution deemed TBTF (Too Big To Fail). The bursting of the Housing Bubble in 2007 resulted from the correction in asset prices begun in 2006 after housing prices peaked in 2005. This was coupled in 2007 with the collapse of the Sub-Prime Asset market, which extended far beyond mortgages to include Collateralized Debt Obligations, Structured Debt Instruments, and other innovative instruments which all proved to be too complex for accurate risk-pricing and to provide true transparency for investor evaluation. The wider nature of the financial crisis among U.S. institutions did not become obvious until after the collapse of Lehman Brothers[17] in 2008. When the depth of the problem was realized, the US government encouraged JP Morgan-Chase to purchase Bear Sterns[18] to prevent a widespread panic among the markets and institutions. Regardless of the efforts of the U.S. and many foreign governments, a recession was unavoidable. The recession in 2009 has led to an unemployment rate in the U.S. that peaked at just over 10% in January 2010 according to the U.S. Bureau of Labor Statistics.[19]

---

[16] In 2008, AIG was the largest insurance underwriter of commercial and industrial insurance in the USA employing 110,000 people worldwide with reported revenue of over $110 billion in 2008.

[17] Lehman Brothers ($639 billion in assets) is the largest investment banker to fail since Drexel Burnham Lambert failed in 1990 due to the collapse of the junk bond market; and surpasses WorldCom (2002) as the largest U.S. bankruptcy to date.

[18] Bear Sterns was a major financial institutional leader estimated to be the seventh largest firm in the investment services industry employing over 13,000 people.

[19] http://www.bls.gov/news.release/pdf/empsit.pdf

53

But the recent crisis is not isolated or so unique as not to be related to previous crisis periods. There may be lessons concerning governance that were ignored from the collapse of Enron (2001),[20] which may have been repeated in the failure of Lehman Brothers (2008).[21] This inaction has brought the plight of many firms to the doorstep of their Boards where a sign "out to lunch" seems to have been hung. As corporation after corporation reveal questionable accounting practices, executives are indicted for questionable trading, and enormous amounts are paid to executives whose companies then soon fail; we must question the role, preparation and actions of the Board members and question the dual role of the Chief Executive Officer as *Chair* of the firm and Chair of the Board. Due to an environment that apparently might include the lack of Board diligence, lessons must be learned from Board failures; otherwise, after cleaning house, the same problems will exist under new faces. One means to achieve reliable, viable Board leadership and strong Corporate Governance[22] may be through the application of the guiding principles of TQM, Total Quality Management.

Adapting the definition of fiduciary responsibility by Dennis Payette from his work published in the journal, *Corporate Governance* (2001),[23] we have an insight into the structure of the Board of Directors that could ensure a quality institution while enabling its members to perform as ideal role models.[24]

> "Fiduciary responsibility is the legally enforceable duty of **directors**, the **chief executive officer**, the **chief financial and operating** officers, and the **Comptroller** of the institution to fully abide by the institution's by-laws, ... federal and state laws, and regulations of **all appropriate** commissions, collective bargaining agreements, professional associations and organizations the institution has committed to uphold. The board is responsible for communicating these responsibilities to the **stockholders** and officers and the **directors** and officers are equally responsible for familiarizing themselves with **all** requirements and exercising common sense and due diligence in carrying out their responsibilities. Neglect of duty or indifference is no shield from liability in matters pertaining to fiduciary responsibility.... (Yet, a necessary expectation for directors and officers is) avoidance of conflict of interest by **directors** and officers resulting from the special position of trust placed on **directors** and officers of the institution."

The essence of the individual Board member's role lies in Rousseau's *Social Contract* concept wherein the role of a Director on the Board is one primarily as Agent. The Board receives the mandate of real authority to provide authoritative prescription of the ends desired for the institution. The Board, to function effectively, requires freedom of

---

[20] Enron employed about 22,000 people producing electricity, natural gas, communications, pulp and paper with revenues just over $100 billion in 2000.

[21] Lehman Brothers employed about 26,000 people as a global financial services firm involving investment banking, equity & fixed income sales, financial research & trading, investment management, private equity and banking, and was one of the limited number of US Treasury Primary Dealers with revenues just under $20 billion in 2008.

[22] For a tutorial on Corporate Governance provided by Professor Mike Peng at the University of Texas-Dallas: http://www.utdallas.edu/~sxl029100/BA4373_chapter%2011.ppt

[23] *Fiduciary Responsibility of Board Trustees and Officers in Universities and Colleges*, (2001) Dennis L. Payette, Corporate Governance, V. 1, N. 4, pp. 12-19.

[24] For the adaptation, the highlighted words have replaced the original words used by Dennis Payette.

justifiable means and a system-focused evaluation apparatus. Governance must be clear, flexible, fair, cooperative, and cohesive, within an environment of mutual respect, need and trust. As such, responsible governance requires the Board to demonstrate four professional characteristics: Leadership, Policy Orientation, Structured Decision Making, and Fact Based Management.[25] These encompass the fourteen points of TQM espoused by W. Edward Deming[26] concerning Quality and Excellence [See Exhibit 3].

Exhibit 3: Fourteen Principles of TQM (Total Quality Management)

1. create constancy of purpose
2. adopt the new philosophy
3. cease dependence on mass inspection targets
4. end practice of awarding price tag alone
5. improve constantly the system workmanship
6. institute training improvement for all
7. adopt and institute leadership transformation. (Deming, 1996)

8. drive out fear
9. break down barriers
10. eliminate slogans, exhortations,
11. eliminate numerical quotas
12. remove barriers that rob pride of
13. encourage education & self-
14. take action to accomplish

Carver (2001)[27] offers a solid theory of governance for Boards to perform their duties well with the following seven elements. The Board:

1-represents a specialized form of ownership, rather than management;

2-governs as a body, not as individual members;

3-provides management with a free choice of bounded means;

4-specifies the nature and cost of results;

5-monitors and evaluates ends and means systematically and rigorously;

6-involves itself in meetings to accomplish learning, debate, resolution;

7-has primarily a long-term view of all decisions concerning the institution.[28]

The following is then an expression of the ideals the Board should endeavor to achieve. The Board, with its members treated as professionals, provides guiding principles, discipline, and respectful leadership focused on the institutional mission and goals. The Board adopts a Policy Orientation that provides a process to guide, examine, select, and evaluate both actions and results. The Board enables a Structured Decision Making System that effectively analyses data, assesses goals, examines views, and

---

[25] *TQE Comes to the Board Room of Higher Education: lessons to be learned from corporate* boardrooms John Manley and Robert Manley, **Business Education and Training: a value laden process**, presented at Oxford University, July 2003, v. 8 , pp. 216-228.

[26] http://deming.org/.

[27] John Carver on Board Leadership, (2001) John Carver, foreword by Sir Adrian Cadbury, John Wiley & Sons, Inc., Jossey-Bass; a Wiley Imprint, San Francisco.

[28] Other resources from John Carver:

John Carver and Miriam Carver, *Basic Principles of Policy Governance*, The Carver Guide Series on Effective Board Governance, No. 1, San Francisco: Jossey-Bass, 1996; John Carver and Miriam Carver, Reinventing Your Board: a step-by-step guide to implementing Policy Governance, John Wiley & Sons, Inc., 1997; Basic *Principles of Policy Governance*, **PolicyGovernance.com**, A Theory of Corporate Governance, Finding a New Balance for Boards and their CEOs, http://www.carvergovernance.com/pg-corp.htm; Boards That Make A Difference: a new design for leadership in non-profit and public organizations, third edition, 2006.

provides efficient measures. The Board requires a Fact-based Management style to solicit data from broad sources, to demand appropriate Board committee assignments, to improve the expertise of its members, and to set parameters for ethical, appropriate behaviors.

Since the fall of Enron, various changes within the financial environment have been suggested but many have not yet been accomplished. A Fortune article (July 1, 2002) extols corporations to "Restore Confidence With Reforms." This remains true today in 2010 as it was in 2002. These reforms include:

1-trust and verification - state earnings and profits in a meaningful, simple, standard way subject to reliable audit & less subject to manipulation;

2-support the SEC – the enforcement staff is too small to watch over 17000 public companies, a multitude of mutual funds and brokerage firms, the exchanges, market manipulations, insider trading, accounting transgressions, all investigations of suspicious behavior, and a market covering roughly $12 trillion. This staff is paid 25%-40% less than the staff of the FDIC or the Office of the Controller, turnover is 30% versus the 15% at other U.S. Government positions; and the vacancy rate is twice that at other government agencies. Yet, the SEC has collected $2 billion in fees in a given year, five times its budget; but Congress uses the money elsewhere; the staff at the Library of Congress has expanded four times faster than at the SEC.

3-regulate Chair/CEO compensation. Consider the following examples of CEO earnings from the first half of the first decade of this current century for those leading their firms just prior to the firm declaring bankruptcy or the individual being charged with misappropriation of funds.

Person	Firm	Compensation	Event Year [Bankruptcy or Charges]
Jeff Skilling	Enron	$240 million	2001
Gary Winnick	Global Crossing	$735 million (3 years)	2002
Dennis Kozlowski	Tyco	$240 million	2004
Joe Nacchio	Quest	$232 million	2005

Although CEO compensation may now be more closely linked to firm performance, the amount of compensation is grossly out of sync with normal merit reward.[29] The Institute for Policy Studies has reported that the average productive worker in the U.S. would need to earn $120,500 annually or that the minimum wage should be $25.50 to match the increase in CEO compensation over 20 years and to maintain the ratio between worker salaries and CEO compensation.[30] In contrast, the current minimum wage in the US is $7.25 per hour, with Wal-Mart paying $8.23 on average per hour and $22.41 as the average per hour wage in the U.S. labor market overall.[31]

5-improve the Board – increase both the number and independence of the independent members, require education and training, and remove the CEO as Chair of the

---

[29] One suggestion is to require all annual compensation other than salary and benefits to be assessed only after a five-year firm-performance waiting period.

[30] CEO compensation in 1980 was 40 times the average employee salary; by 2000, CEO compensation was 600 times average worker salaries.

[31] http://www.bls.gov/eag/eag.us.htm.

Board.[32]   This latter issue is referred to as Duality, which is common in the US[33] but has been tightly restricted by Great Britain.[34]

7-involve Owners- empower the owners, the stockholders. Consider that the Board members are receiving special benefits as Directors, and the CEO and other top executives are receiving "perks" [access to private planes, apartments in New York City, special vacation packages, personal loans] such that Stockholder Value Maximization [a key concept for the true financial goal of management] is not the primary concern. Their individual compensation is a combination of stock value plus these perks (plus salary & compensation for the CEO and other senior management), as such they may be willing to receive these perks at the expense of other stockholders as rewards for their roles in the firm.

This is the essence of the Agency Problem discussed in all finance textbooks. In addition, consider that the largest portion of the stock value of the NYSE is held by institutional investors; these institutions then represent the individual rather than the individual investor him/herself being involved in the monitoring of the performance of the firms held in the portfolio.

If these Institutional Investors rely heavily on the management and boards of the firms in which the institutions have invested, then the institutional investor may very well feel a reduction in scrutiny is appropriate resulting in rubber-stamping the decisions of firm management. As such, the two primary keys of responsible governance are undermined: the scrutiny by the Board, especially the Executive Committee, and the involvement of significant independent stockholders (the Institutional Investors).

The Board, selected to review and monitor management, does not do either but rather benefits from the conflict of interest generated by this implied agency problem and the primary Investors, being the institutions, abdicate their responsibilities to monitor the performance of the firms in which they invest the funds of multiple individuals. Approximately seven (7%) percent of the institutional investors active in the market currently own forty-four (44%) percent of the stock market. How do they vote, when do they vote, do they vote, do their votes reflect the desires of the stockholders for whom they are the agent? If the institutions do not report how they vote and/or routinely vote with management, then stockholders are not exercising control.

Robert A.G. Monks, a shareholder activist, believes that CEOs have too much power, that the Boards of Directors are not minding the store, and that Corporate Democracy is a myth. He argues that large owners, especially institutional investors (pension funds, mutual funds, insurance companies) routinely vote with management, whereas, these institutions could otherwise have a significant impact. As examples, in 1942, the Gilbert Brothers used their position as investors to encourage the SEC to pass the first rules concerning shareholder proposals. In the 1960s, Ralph Nader and Saul Alinsky encouraged individual shareholders to pressure firms on social issues causing significant changes. In the 1980s, corporate raiders as significant shareholders changed poorly run firms either by taking control or forcing current investors to pay attention! In this same vein, Robert Monks has been working for 25 years to empower institutional owners. In 1985, he established Institutional Shareholder Services (ISS) to sell research

---

[32] http://www.directorship.com/separation-anxiety/.
[33] Several firms have taken the initiative to address these governance issues to provide greater financial accountability and performance: Disney has introduced separate audit and compensation committees, each with independent directors; outside directors now meet separate from insiders and management; outsider directors are also restricted on the number of other boards to which they are appointed and still serve on Disney's; and Disney will use different firms for audit and consulting.
[34] http://www.pace.edu/emplibrary/wp180.pdf

and advice concerning Proxy votes. It is often suggested that ISS's support for the Hewlett-Packarad/Compaq merger led to its completion. He also established LENS, a mutual fund that targeted lackluster firms, and then agitated for change and improvement. The fund's performance is reported to have outperformed the S&P 500 Index throughout the life of the fund.

> "The watchdog portfolio stewards at Lens Investment Management were never daunted or demurred...the firm has taken on close to two dozen under-motivated over-satisfied CEOs of companies whose solid underlying business were not being put to full use or harnessed for full value."   Michael Santoli, Barron's, *July 24, 2000*

Such market agents as the NYSE-EURONEXT, the NASDAQ, and the Toronto Exchange have taken these recommendations seriously. With the approval of the SEC, all firms to be listed on the **NYSE** must comply with the following:
    1-shareholders will vote on stock option grants;
    2-shareholders will vote on director performance evaluations;
    3-every Board will publish a code of ethics;
    4-every Board will define who is an Independent Director.

With SEC approval, **NASDAQ**'s new rules to strengthen Corporate Governance include:
    1-shareholder approval of any stock option plan that includes senior management;
    2-re-define Independent Director;
    3-limit receipt of payment to individuals for service on the Board;
    4-expansion of Conflict of Interest review for all Board members;
    5-reiterate that firms face delisting for intentional misrepresentation of information, omission of necessary information;
    6-provide more flexibility in releasing information due to technology.

The **Toronto Stock Exchange** sent its rule changes to the Ontario Securities Commission. These include:
    1-stipulate that the Board of Directors supervisory function is monitoring;
    2-Board must approve management's strategic plan;
    3-The audit committee should be comprised of independent directors.

These changes highlight several remaining problem areas: 1. the practice of allowing the CEO to select Board composition, 2. that there may be no true dialog among the Board membership due to privacy issues such as, independent members not meet in closed session, or between the membership and the firm management (such as, financial performance being reported with minimum explanation, dialog or discussion), and 3. the Board routinely rubber-stamps the presentations made by management. These issues may contribute heavily to fraudulent accounting practices and poor management decisions periodically resulting in scandal and collapse. On the other hand, these problems have led some companies to independently incorporate several changes: outsiders or independent directors should not be ex-employees, family members, or anyone whose livelihood derives some monetary benefit from the direct operation of the firm; and these independent directors should meet without management.

In addition, further attempts should be made to address Governance issues related to under-qualified directors, increasing awareness of Social investing,[35] concentrating on sustainability issues, removing lax standards for audits and for Board membership, furthering the Independence of Outside directors,[36] increasing the role of Institutional Investors in active management surveillance, addressing the inequities inherent in current CEO compensation, recognizing and dealing with emerging markets issues,[37] and the use of super majority voting (80%) instead of majority voting (51%).

The Investor Responsibility Research Center reports that in 1990, two-thirds (2/3 or 67%) of shareholder resolutions passed when stockholders voted, but in 2000 only 17% passed due to the restrictive nature of supermajority voting. In 2004, the California Public Employees' Retirement System, CalPers,[38] provides these examples of Governance lapses on their web page:

Gateway – requires no independent audit.

Quest Communication International – allows for a conflict of interest in dealings with the Anschutz Corp, since the Quest chair and founder is Phillip Anschutz who is also a director of the Anschutz Corp.

NTL – approved a re-capitalization using a Debt for Equity Swap that, in their estimation, will negatively impact on stockholders, such as themselves.

Lucent Technology – will not agree or act with the simple majority vote about the composition of the Board, requiring instead a super majority.

Cincinnati Financial – one half of the Board membership is insiders.

Three additional actions are suggested to provide better Corporate Board supervision and oversight. First, working to reduce U.S. opposition to adopting IAS (International Accounting Standards) instead of GAAP (Generally Accepted Accounting Principles) may bring about a convergence between the two sets of rules. Paul Volcker, former Chair of the U.S. Federal Reserve, has spearheaded the effort to increase communication between the SEC & IASC in London. In February 2006, FASB and IASB had issued a Memorandum of Understanding including a program of topics on which the two bodies were to seek to achieve convergence by 2008. In August 2008, the SEC announced a timetable that would allow some companies to report under IFRS as soon as 2010 and require it of all companies by 2014.[39] DeLoitte & Touche[40] provides periodic comparisons of the remaining differences among accounting standards. In their report, *Accounting Standards Compared* of 2002, they reiterated their support for worldwide

---

[35] A progressive company is one that respects the community, treats workers fairly and acts to conserve the environment.

[36] As early as November 1992, the *Fortune 1000 Survey* indicates that 93% of those executives surveyed believed the majority membership of a Board should be independents.

[37] Shareholder rights, legal systems and regulatory environments are different nation to nation; therefore different levels of protection exist.

[38] "The California Public Employees' Retirement System (CalPERS), an organization that provides numerous benefits to its more than 1.6 million members, including health insurance, long-term care insurance, death benefits, mortgage program, and distribution of pension and retirement-related financial benefits. CalPERS Investments is the nation's largest public pension fund and, given its size, it is able to exercise significant pressure to make desired changes within the companies in which it invests." Provided by *INVESTOPEDIA:* http://www.investopedia.com/terms/c/calpers.asp, accessed Feb. 2010.

[39] BusinessWeek: 28 August 2008.
http://www.businessweek.com/bwdaily/dnflash/content/aug2008/db20080827_422492.htm.

[40] One of the largest organizations in the field of insurance, tax consulting, business consulting, and legal services with 6,000 employees and 90 offices in the Netherlands alone, and 95,000 employees in 140 countries.

harmonization of accounting standards, while indicating the remaining significant differences among the US-GAAP, IAS and NL-GAAP Netherlands standards.

Second, a major step towards good governance may be achieved through more universal adherence to the *Comply or Explain* doctrine concerning issues such as independent directors, the audit committee, and the compensation committee. This approach allows the firm to determine freely if it believes it is appropriate to comply with a particular rule for standard behavior or reporting, but also requires the firm to explain fully its reasons for not complying while reporting clearly the means by which it is reporting the financial item in question.[41] On their website, KPMG provide an excellent discussion of the issue in a 2010 article by Andrew Rosenbaum, *Can Europeans comply or explain?*

http://www.kpmg.com/Global/en/IssuesAndInsights/ArticlesPublications/Pages/Can-Europeans-comply-or-explain.aspx.

Third, encouragement of the development of metrics to evaluate corporate governance practices is a necessary element to ensure good governance. A principle of TQM requires that one must be able to measure a goal to be able to know if it (can be) has been achieved. And, as indicated before, increasing stockholder activity[42] in the expectation of good management creates the environment needed to more readily ensure compliance to expectations and will lead to the encouragement, if not the requirement, that appropriate metrics be developed, established, and implemented. John G. Smale, Chair & CEO of Proctor Gamble in the 1980s, identifies several problems with current corporate governance: weak management disclosure of true performance to the BOD, weak auditor advice due to conflict of interest, and weak knowledge base for the members of the BOD.

He provided several suggestions: 1- the Chair should be from among the independents on the Board (as is done in the UK), 2- there should be stress placed on the role of the Board as the representative of shareholders as the overseer of management; 3- there should be a more rigorous oversight climate; 4-increase the cooperation between the Chair and CEO for agenda for the Board, once the issue of duality is addressed; 5- the Board should "own" its constituency (membership), governance guidelines, the charter of the committees, independent of management; 6-outside auditors should report to the Board; the client should be the BOD's Audit Committee, not management.

Fiduciary responsibility refers to what directors should be doing (and may not be). Ultimate responsibility of the governing board may not be delegated to protect the integrity and financial health of the firm. The Board must have the right to question, challenge and override decisions it deems inconsistent with the mission, integrity, or financial health of the firm.

Challenge Area Two: MNE Global Involvement

Deregulation of financial institutions, expansionary monetary policy, globalization, and innovation all conspired to produce the over-confidence of the first decade of the 21st

---

[41] *Implementation of the "Comply or Explain" Approach*: an application to charitable institutions, http://www.bschool.nus.edu/Research/CGFRC/download/events/NFP/2007/NFPConference2007_MYTSession1.pdf

[42] Proxy use by involved individual stockholders influenced Home Depot to stop selling timber harvested from old growth forests and Coca Cola to increase the recycled content of plastic bottles.

Century. Prolonged decreases in the level of interest rates since the 1980s which provided for a major run-up in asset prices, liberalization due to deregulation of the financial markets which provided even greater incentives for innovation, as well as easy access and relaxed lending standards each contributed to a major increase in debt as a percent of GDP or personal wealth. Add to these influences, an increased reliance on various market measures without consideration of how measures must change with time, as with the interbank TED spread[43] which remained subdued indicating (in error) no change in risk. The mispricing of risk associated with complex, opaque and/or rapidly changing instruments. The decrease in rates, increase in debt, and reduction in savings all conspired to produce a significant consumer-driven economy. The reaction to ten years of exuberance has been a major move towards protecting capital and liquidity, increasing savings with a decrease in consumption, and a tightening of the entire credit market.

All this translates to the financial challenges facing the MNE. These include greater competition that has accompanied the growth and expansion of MNE, greater scrutiny to justify strategies to investors and regulators due to the multiple scandals and management errors that have emerged, and the changing dynamics of both domestic and international financial markets due to re-assessment within the credit markets.

Market wide challenges include: 1. questioning the moral hazard that accompanies TBTF (too big to fail) that requires government bailout (and at times participation in ownership), 2. the shift in world growth to markets other than those dominant in the 20th Century with the emergence of the importance of the BRIC[44] markets, and 3. the changing political as well as economic landscape through the growth of the G7 into the G20 that has emerged as a forum for international policy coordination.[45] MNE must consider their own strategies concerning governments that are increasingly addressing the role and importance of the MNE. Governments espousing "free markets" have taken on an ownership posture, have reoriented economic policy (both monetary and fiscal policy) towards guaranteeing appropriate liquidity, adequate lending, and controlled spending, while using regulatory policy to bring increasing scrutiny to M&A (mergers and acquisitions), capital adequacy, funds sources, and the volatility inherent in the market. Government has involved itself in supporting major players with guarantees and underwriting to reduce risk, while now holding various positions in the issued debt or equity of an increasing number of firms.

Other crisis periods have led the way: the 1980s U.S.A. S&L crisis,[46] the 1990s Sweden Currency and Real Estate crisis,[47] and the 1990s Asian Crisis.[48] The Brookings

---

[43] The TED spread is the difference between the interest rate on the three-month U.S. Treasuries futures and the three-month Eurodollar futures contracts expiring in the same months. Since the U.S. Treasury issue is considered (default) risk-free and the Eurodollar futures is based on the three-month LIBOR [London Interbank Offer Rate] associated with demand by corporate borrowing, then the increase in the differential is considered an indication of an increase in market or corporate risk.

[44] BRIC: Brazil, Russia, India and China; sometimes referred to as BRICK, when including the Republic of Korea (South Korea).

[45] An informal association of nations to attempt coordination in response to a crisis; G7: Canada, France, Germany, Italy, Japan, United Kingdom and United States of America. The G7 became the G8 in 1997 upon adding Russia to the invitation list. The G20 is a combination of representatives (finance ministers or central bank governors) from 19 countries, the EU, the IMF, and the World Bank. [G20: Argentina, Australia, Brazil, Canada, China, France, Germany, India, Indonesia, Italy, Japan, Mexico, Russia, Saudi Arabia, South Africa, Republic of Korea, Turkey, United Kingdom, and the United States of America.]

[46] The Savings and Loan Crisis in the US began with the stagflation period of the 1970s and led to the first major deregulation legislature in the US: the Depository Institutions Deregulation and Monetary Control act of 1980 (DIDMCA). By the time of passage, about 70% of the Thrift Institutions in the US were said to be insolvent and the FSLIC [Federal Savings and Loan Insurance Corporation], which guaranteed deposits, itself was reported as insolvent due to the number of failures. The crisis was faced and resolved after

Institute provides funding for various research projects. One of these efforts, by the Brookings Global Economy and Development committee, is the ***Top 10 Global Economic Challenges facing America's 44th President***. This report provides a discussion of these ten challenges: restoring financial stability, setting the right green agenda, exercising smart power, re-imaging global trade, navigating China's rise, deciphering *Russia Inc.*, engaging an emerging India, revitalizing ties to Latin America, supporting Africa's growth turnaround, and pursuing a positive agenda for the Middle East.

Each of these challenges is an area of concern for the management of an MNE. Financial stability requires managing capital flows among and between nations with the changing landscape of unilateral or multilateral agreements and restrictions; managing price determination, transfer prices, and profit/fund repatriation with flexible exchange rate management; and improved transparency across divergent markets within the global firm. Establishing a Green agenda requires increased awareness, understanding and training concerning climate change, facility location choice, harbor/port facilities, alternates to carbon based energy, and supply chain issues. Simultaneously companies face the political & social pressure to reduce greenhouse gases, to reduce the firm's carbon footprint, to increase the firm's adaptability and adoptability of new processes, and to maximize market value while maintaining cost control. MNE must evaluate the use of a *cap-and-trade program*,[49] and a shift to alternative energies that may have unanticipated costs. Shifts to biofuels have already seen a rise in food costs as the dual demand now competes with each other in a new environment. MNE must consider the growing opportunities for financial support from governments and domestic/international agencies and/or attracting the growing number of social investors whose demand for the firm's bonds or stocks will reduce the cost of financing to the firm. The MNE must also identify opportunities for investment in technology or science associated with the firm's focus activity[50], project and anticipate government action. The use of Smart power involves the MNE creating innovative and effective means to invest in education, training, innovation that utilizes native workers, promoting and developing the host country labor force.

Redefining the rules and processes involving Global Trade requires reassessment of the MNE's ability to compete, its insurance needs required for both the anticipated and

---

passage in the 1980s with the establishment of the RTC {Resolution Trust Corporation], a redesigned and refunded insurance program, and the tight monetary policy of the FED under Chairman Paul Volker.

[47] Sound familiar: Leading up to the 1990s, Sweden enjoyed strong speculative markets, booming consumer debt, loosening of lending restrictions, devaluation of the currency (Krona), and increased foreign funds borrowing. But in 1990, German unification led to domestic inflation that was exported to the closely tied Swedish market. Credit dried up, the real estate bubble burst, and the Krona was floated diminishing steeply in value. Banks, firms and individuals defaulted on obligations to foreign markets.

[48] The 1997-98 period is often referred to as Asian Contagion Crisis since events in one nation impacted markets in others within the region. After enjoying 6% to 9% growth in GDP per year for a decade, within about six months the stock markets and currencies within the region lost 70% of their value. Strong Export growth had led to domestic wealth increases that were heavily invested (spent) driving up all asset values (inflation). Government policy had encouraged debt financing, mostly denominated in U.S. dollars. The markets eventually achieved extreme excess capacity, a slow down in exports, and a significant decrease in asset prices; the fall in the value of the local currencies made default on US$ denominated loans inevitable.

[49] "Cap and trade is an environmental policy tool that delivers results with a mandatory cap on emissions while providing sources flexibility in how they comply. Successful cap and trade programs reward innovation, efficiency, and early action and provide strict environmental accountability without inhibiting economic growth." U.S. Environmental Protection Agency: http://www.epa.gov/captrade/.

[50] In Finance, *focus* has a specific meaning and generally criticizes firm aspirations towards diversification as an inefficient use of resources. Corporate Focus may refer to either restricting geographic diversification or limiting operating and productive diversification, concentrating instead on the core industries that the firm has proven skill in achieving significant management goals.

unanticipated[51], changing environment of trade rules, changes in its accounting norms, and the MNE's involvement in guarantees for sustainable support for unemployment, health, pension, and security. The MNE face increasing challenges in Social Action by locating investment /expansionary opportunities that will aid in the reduction of poverty, and by identifying nations with markets that are identified as capable and accountable in advancing human development and security. Investing in areas with limited security, humanitarian or transnational threats, or other conflicts with social accountability will cause MNE to disappoint and disown risk-adverse investors who are becoming increasingly social investors as well. Within the social responsible firm, there is an effort to develop greater volunteer programs, to involve the firm through its workers in the health and wellness of the society, and to become an intricate player in the human and environmental sustainability of the area. MNE are entering into an even more integrated and interrelated realm wherein developing connections with other MNE, philanthropists, high profile advocates, grassroots/faith-based networks to encourage multi-stakeholder collaboration and development are required to achieve sustainability and strong corporate performance for both the short and long term survival and growth of the firm and community.

Re-imagining Global Trade must be accomplished with the awareness of the increasing concerns regarding the strong possibilities of a food crisis, water crisis and the impact of global warming. How will MNE respond? In what ways will MNE play a role in the liberalization of trade in agriculture, in the lowering of tariffs and subsidies, in the transfer of necessary resources for human survival? Governments may limit exports in response to a food crisis, introduce green tariffs in response to climate change [green tariffs: trade agreements that contain enforceable standards for worker rights and environment protection], and implement global changes to the "rules of operations" in answer to the impact of global warming.[52] On the national front, MNE will be impacted by efforts requiring social security net and universal health care. These domestic changes impacting the cost structure of and valuation of potential investment gain by the MNE, will be driven by cultural value sets that may be very different from Management's own corporate culture requiring an ever increasing awareness of and sensitivity to the dramatic cultural differences amongst and across the global community.

MNE will continue to expand, to grow and to spread throughout the next decade. Every MNE must analyze the opportunities associated with the benefits and costs of entry into another nation, referred to as geographic diversification. As such, the Brookings Institute report provides insights into the risks and gains associated with several key nations or areas in the global community. These observations on <u>Geographic Entities</u> provide insights for the challenges and opportunities the management of MNE will face in the next decade.

---

[51] This is a major aspect of Risk Management (disaster risk management, business continuity risk management etc.) and the focus of such recent books as <u>Blink</u> [http://www.gladwell.com/blink/] or <u>Black Swan</u> [http://www.amazon.com/Black-Swan-Impact-Highly-Improbable/dp/1400063515].

[52] Lands that are sinking beneath the sea due to the rising sea level: (in the Pacific Ocean area) Cataret Island of Papua-New Guinea with 1,500 people, Takuu with 2,500 people, the nation of Kiribati with 100,000 people on 33 coral atolls, the nation of Tuvalu with 12,000 people, Marshall Islands, Tonga, (in the Indian Ocean area) Maldives, (in Europe) Holland, the Netherlands, and (in the USA) Florida.

Exhibit 4: 20 Largest Nations By Estimated Population

RANK	COUNTRY OR AREA	POPULATION
1	China	1,323,591,583
2	India	1,156,897,766
3	United States	307,212,123
4	Indonesia	240,271,522
5	Brazil	198,739,269
6	Pakistan	174,578,558
7	Bangladesh	156,050,883
8	Nigeria	149,229,090
9	Russia	140,041,247
10	Japan	127,078,679
11	Mexico	111,211,789
12	Philippines	97,976,603
13	Vietnam	88,576,758
14	Ethiopia	85,237,338
15	Germany	82,329,758
16	Egypt	78,866,635
17	Turkey	76,805,524
18	Congo (Kinshasa)	68,692,542
19	Iran	66,429,284
20	Thailand	65,998,436

U.S. Census Bureau: http://www.census.gov/cgi-bin/broker

China provides strong opportunities for MNE due to the sheer size of its potential market [See Exhibit 4]. Currently, China's economy has been export-led, yet the government now recognizes the need to build a domestic consumer market to compliment the large role its export market plays in determining China's GDP. The government has begun a shift from an agriculture-based to manufacturing-based economy, wherein both are labor-intensive effectively utilizing its large and increasingly educated labor market. Until recently, China has placed its emphasis on production enclaves, excellent for controlling and encouraging exports but not effective in allowing the benefits of its growth in GDP to permeate the demographic distribution of its people. China's "Smile Diplomacy" has been effective in softening the perception of its posture and portrayal within the Asian region; this has led the government to be willing to settle territorial disputes and to support regional cooperation, having established several political agreements with Japan, South Korea, as well as ASEAN. These changes provide MNE with challenges to rethink opportunities. MNE must prepare to be able to manage possible appreciation of China's currency, the renminbi, while anticipating continuing demand from China and/or India for import commodities driving prices on the World market higher. How shall managers of MNE plan and control for, how flexible will they be with, shifts in production goals for China, India, and the EU? There are 1.2 billion low wage earners in China and India impacting costs and production decisions elsewhere. How will MNE protect their intellectual property rights within this global community with vast variants on legal recourse? Seventy percent (70%) of products seized in the USA for intellectual property rights infringements are reported by the US Dept of Homeland Security to originate in China. Managers must be prepared to anticipate, so as to handle appropriately, any changes in tax laws/rebates, subsidies, or shifts in policy towards trade imbalances.

Russia has emerged into a free market with a recent crisis of its own. The Russian Federation faced a currency crisis in 1998. The Government announced a devaluation schedule for the ruble (amounting to a 34% reduction in value versus the US$ over time), a moratorium on repayment of loans to foreign investors, and a rescheduling of US$40 billion of the Russian government's treasury issue. This announcement affirmed a growing fear of a mighty correction to the previous significant growth in the Russian economy. Value of its stock market plummeted, the ruble quickly lost 300% of its value against the US$, and bond or debt issuance ceased. Many factors had contributed to this Russian "correction": the global recession [those nations dependent upon the export of raw materials are always severely hit by global recessions] negatively impacted the Russian export market wherein oil/gas/metals/timber represent about 80% of exports. A crippling of the Government's ability to manage its cash flow was precipitated by the failure of the energy and manufacturing industries to pay taxes. Coupled with declining productivity, the crisis was further impacted by the overvalued fixed exchange rate, an increasingly large fiscal deficit in part caused by the war in and rebuilding of Chechnya, and the impact of the 1997-98 Asian crisis furthering its contagion. How do MNE prepare for these eventual corrections that occur in various nations, both emerging and developed? The ability to survive in an increasingly competitive and interconnected world depends upon management's ability to anticipate and weather these storms.

The challenge involves being able to see opportunities provided by the oil/gas/natural resource riches in the Russian Federation. Yet, MNE must recognize the soviet imprint still present within the Russian environment, indicated in part by the type and size of factories and the physical location of cities, each of which is inconsistent with normal market forces. As Russia responds more efficiently and effectively, these factors provide both challenges and opportunities for investment and development for MNE. The U.S. share of foreign direct investment (FDI) in Russia is small, but apparent corruption, over-regulation and government interference usually provide deterrents for investment. Yet, U.S. official policy may change towards encouragement of investment, albeit this may take the form of more indirect encouragement given the remains of the cold war on the attitudes of U.S. voters. Regardless, there are massive new energy investment opportunities within the Russian Federation, although at a high cost resource.

India has a large pool of educated labor, a young workforce, a booming service sector, a growing manufacturing sector; yet, India also has the largest portion of its immense population [See Exhibit 4] involved in agriculture, not manufacturing. In addition, according to the World Bank, India has among the World's most restrictive labor market regulations, a growth rate in job creation below the growth rate associated with its population.[53] The Climate Change policy of India appears to be oriented towards a quest for a technological solution, with an unwillingness currently to cooperate with emissions reductions or carbon trading; this issue provides specific challenges for appropriate

---

[53] The World Bank provides growth rates on both job creation and populations for most nations: http://www.worldbank.org.in/WBSITE/EXTERNAL/COUNTRIES/SOUTHASIAEXT/INDIAEXTN/0,,con tentMDK:20195738~menuPK:295591~pagePK:141137~piPK:141127~theSitePK:295584,00.html.

responses from MNE.[54] It is expected that India will develop a Free Trade Association with Australia, the EU and/or the USA.[55] If this be so, then MNE should be poised adequately to appropriate benefits from these opportunities. In addition, opportunities for MNE investment abound with India's willingness to continue its liberalization of the financial sector and the development of its stock market into a very wide (large number of players) and deep (able to handle very large value trades quickly) market place, although still measured as small relative to India's GDP. There remain important difficulties that liberalization has to address. The Debt-Bond market is generally weak with the Treasury Bond and Corporate Bond markets small and not indicating any strong growth in the foreseeable future, and the bank loan market having the lowest lending ratio [loans / GDP] among emerging markets according to the World Bank. Yet, MNE have a distinct advantage in that, when the local host market has limited or restrictive sources for funds, the MNE can create their own internal funds market by borrowing in other markets with the intention of using the funds in the more restrictive market.

Exhibit 5: Euro-Disney Bond- from Mickey's European Theme Park

Latin America & Caribbean, including 33 nations, provide opportunities for MNE as their economies have only recently show significant growth potential with the political and social changes emerging. Democracy has strengthened throughout the region, with strong

---

[54] "This document primarily offers a list of eight technological efforts, the pride of place being given to research and development of solar energy. But the report does not set any numerical goals for emission reductions or for energy intensity." Commentary on India, Parliament of Australia, Parliamentary Library, Background Note, *Climate Change Policy: Brazil, China, India, and Russia*, Leslie Nielsen, Economics Section; accessed on line 25 February 2009: http://www.aph.gov.au/Library/pubs/bn/2008-09/ClimateChange.htm#_Toc222285926.

[55] Australia and India began a joint feasibility study in August 2007: http://www.dfat.gov.au/geo/india/fta-study/index.html. Japan and India held their tenth round on negotiations on a FTA in October 2008: http://fta.icrindia.org/index.html. The EU and India have been discussing a FTA since 2007: http://www.business-standard.com/india/news/social-environmental-issues-may-delay-india-eu-trade-pact/371221/. Although negotiations have been on going, the US has expressed a lack of interest currently: http://www.expressindia.com/latest-news/No-FTA-with-India-for-now-says-US/275510/.

fiscal and monetary policy being used in a consistent fashion providing necessary discipline for the markets. This translates to a reduction in uncertainty for the MNE encouraging consideration of the benefits for FDI. Yet feeble growth rates for the GDPs or in job creation still plague the region with issues of poverty, violence, and inequality.

Exhibit 6: World map showing the CIA estimate of GDP growth rates for 2009.

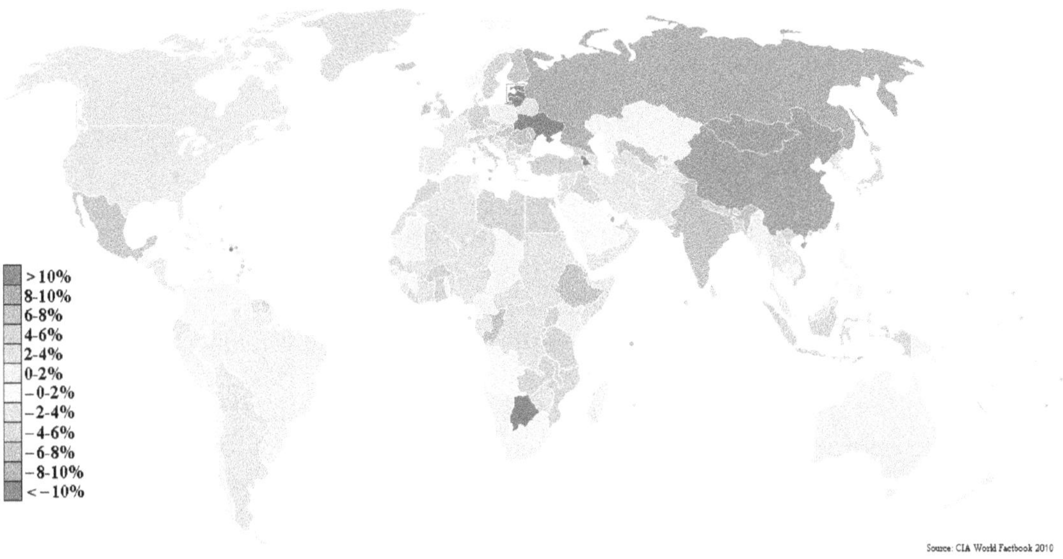

Source: CIA World Factbook 2010

This is a file from the <u>Wikimedia Commons</u>. Commons is a freely licensed media file repository.

Opportunities and challenges for the MNE may be affected by the perception by the region's citizens that only 14% consider current U.S. policy with the region is of good or excellent quality, while 27% believe China (30% believe the U.S.) will be an important driver for the future well being of the region. This opens the way for MNE to pursue both traditional and non-traditional key interests in the region. More traditional issues would include MNE efforts to make strides in foreign direct investments, innovation and development in the areas of counter-narcotics, investment opportunities, trade promotion, and combating criminal networks. Non-traditional opportunities are emerging for MNE to expand energy cooperation and integration, to manage worker migration, to introduce appropriate water management, to aid in the development of incentive-based financial regulation, and to strengthen the regions efforts towards environmental protection. Energy particularly offers strong opportunities and challenges for a region with about 9% of the world's population [See Exhibit 5]. Areas of potential growth in energy include ethanol, power grids, nuclear, and renewable sources; but the emphasis, especially possible through the efforts of MNE, should be multinational or even hemispheric rather than bilateral agreements.

Exhibit 7: The Population of Regions

region	population est. 2008-07-01	population est. 2009-07-01	% of World Population
Asia	4,053,868,076	4,102,169,683	60.4%
Africa	972,752,377	996,457,117	14.6%
Northern America	337,168,480	340,831,819	5.0%
Latin America and the Caribbean	579,285,804	587,540,404	8.6%
Europe	731,682,934	727,867,583	10.7%
Oceania	34,375,093	34,846,412	0.5%
World	6,706,993,152	6,790,062,216	

source: "The World Factbook 2008 and of 2009", CIA.

Africa provides MNE with the opportunity to tap into the enormous future commodities market through resource-rich exports from these nations. These nations challenge MNE through their need for a reduction in excess regulation, an increase in means to combat corruption, FDI to increase the available infrastructure, and development of appropriate trade/exchange policies. The good news, as reported by the IMF, is that the banking industry in many areas of Africa, such as CEMAC[56], has been little affected by the global recession and previous elements of the current crisis period.[57] The bad news is that the reason for this is the disconnect between the area banks and the rest of the world, providing a very limited and slow growth funding opportunity within the region. A major portion of African states need investment in secondary and higher education and development of trained, reliable, and responsible government agents. MNE have the opportunity to engage with many international and government agents in their attempts to address the needs of African continent, such as the U.S. Overseas Private Investment Corporation, the Millennium Challenge Corporation, the Group of Eight Gleneagles, and the China-Africa Development Fund. Opportunities and challenges exist in the ability to finance operations and development within the region. The intent of all of these agents is to address poverty, violence, terrorism, trafficking, and disease. The result will be a growing market with 15% of the world's population ready and able to participate in trade, development, and sustainability.

Mid-East is a unique environment with two (2) working age people (ages 15-64) for every one non-working person (ages ≤ 14 & ≥ 65), but unemployment is twice the world average. There have been significant changes in the customary values exercised throughout the area with many states providing an accommodating environment for a market economy, expansion of education, and increased civic participation. MNE have the opportunity to aid in the development of programs that target the youth of the area, to focus on education and training, and to provide the necessary skills to address the chronic unemployment. Within the USA, our own MNE may address (lobby) Congress to advocate for changes to the Foreign Assistance Act to enhance investment in youth development in areas where

---

[56] CEMAC: Central African Economic and Monetary Community, including Cameroon, Central African Republic, Chad, the Republic of Congo, Equatorial Guinea, and Gabon.
[57] IMF Staff Position Note, July 22, 2009, *The International Financial Crisis & Global Recession: Impact on the CEMAC Region & Policy Considerations*, John Wakeman-Linn, Rafael Portillo, Plamen Iossifov, and Dimitre Milkov; accessed Feb. 2010:http://www.imf.org/external/pubs/ft/spn/2009/spn0920.pdf.

youth unemployment is chronic, such as the Mid-East. The benefits of engaging those who are disenfranchised, regardless of where or why, have often been significant whenever programs have been established to address the isolating forces. The development throughout a region influenced by Islamic principles requires the MNE to become knowledgeable concerning the conditions under which business may flourish. This may be seen in the enormous growth of the Islamic Banking Industry.[58] The challenge for the MNE is the understanding of the principles associated with this system. This is a banking system based on the principles of Islamic law (also known Shariah) and guided by Islamic economics. Two basic principles behind Islamic banking are the sharing of profit and loss and, significantly, the prohibition of the collection and payment of interest, such practices make financial transactions within Islamic banking a culturally distinct form of ethical investing. Following the practices of social investing mutual funds elsewhere in the world which choose to avoid investments that violate specified social goals, Islamic Banks are prohibited to make investments involving alcohol, gambling, or pork. The Dubai Islamic Bank has the distinction of being the world's first full-fledged Islamic bank, formed in 1975.[59] MNE should consider that there are estimated to be over 1.5 billion Muslims in the world population, whereas from 2000 to 2005, Islamic Banks have grown at a 15 to 20% rate. This has resulted in US$270 billion in assets managed by 300 Islamic banks in 25 countries. Using per capita income with the level of population, Scott Schmith of the U.S. International Trade Administration has estimated the largest markets for expansion to be Turkey, Indonesia, Saudi Arabia, United States, and France; whereas the currently fastest growing markets have been Malaysia, Bahrain, United Arab Emirates, Indonesia, and Pakistan. MNE will find that the Islamic financial instruments are more expensive to implement and manage, while not being responsive to innovation. These growth opportunities and challenges for the MNE have great potential, with US$905 billion in total assets in the Middle Eastern countries alone.

Conclusion

MNE come from many nations of the world; yet using the Fortune 500 listing for 2008, there are only nineteen (19) nations on the list, and five that dominate the list.[60]

Exhibit 8: Home Nation for the Fortune 500 MNE

Country alphabetical	# MNE	Country frequency	# MNE
Belgium	2	USA	**31**
Brazil	1	Germany	**13**
Britain	9	France	**10**
China	3	Britain	**9**
Finland	1	Japan	**8**

---

[58] Chapter 4: Islamic Banking, Interest-Free Commercial Banking, by A.L.M. Abdul Gafoor , 1995; available on the web at: http://www.islamicbanking.nl/chap4.html.

[59] *Islamic Banks Experience Rapid Growth*, Scott Schmith, International Trade Specialist, International Trade Administration, U.S. Department of Commerce, December, 2005: http://www.ita.doc.gov/mas/pdf/Islamic_Banking.pdf.

[60] http://money.cnn.com/magazines/fortune/global500/2008/snapshots/10893.html.

France	10	Italy	4
Germany	13	South Korea	4
Italy	4	China	3
Japan	8	Spain	3
Luxembourg	1	Switzerland	3
Malaysia	1	Belgium	2
Mexico	1	Netherlands	2
Netherlands	2	Russia	2
Norway	1	Brazil	1
Russia	2	Finland	1
South Korea	4	Luxembourg	1
Spain	3	Malaysia	1
Switzerland	3	Mexico	1
USA	31	Norway	1

Questions for Discussion Board

1. In the section dealing with *governance*, there are many issues mentioned that might either provide for strong, ethical management or lead to disappointing or scandalous outcomes. Describe for us one issue from among these that is prevalent in discussions, news items or classroom lessons within your nation that is reflective of the cultural/political influences within your financial environment.

2. In the second section dealing with *MNE challenges*, choose one of the ten areas of challenges and opportunities identified by the Brookings Institute. If you choose one of the first four issues listed by the Brookings study, how would you relate that issue to your own awareness of business opportunities or challenges in your nation? Choose one of the geographic areas to discuss (China, Russia, India, Latin America, Africa, or the Middle East), then how would you apply the first four concerns (restoring financial stability, setting the right green agenda, exercising smart power, re-imaging global trade) expressed by the Brookings Institute report to that geographic area?

Chapter Eight
Sustainability in an
Interdependent Global Economy
-John L. Cusack

Chapter Concepts

- Definitions of Sustainability
- Definitions of a Sustainable Enterprise & Society
- Key Concepts of Sustainability
- Core Principles of Sustainability
- Sustainability & Globalization
- A Big Globalization Problem- Outsourcing of Carbon Emissions
- The Sustainable Development Challenge
- Major Sustainability/Globalization Issues
- Sample Sustainability Risk: Climate Change
- Good News: Sustainability as Opportunity
- Solutions To A Real World Sustainability/Globalization Issue
- Sustainability & Interdependence
- The Business Case for Sustainability
- Sustainability Metrics
- Sustainability Leadership
- Summary- How We Can Materially Improve both Businesses' and
  Society's Bottom Line by Being Sustainable

Definition Of Sustainability

Sustainability is a difficult concept to define, due to its complexity and inter-disciplinary nature, as it means many different things to different people. The first major application of the term came about in the 1970's and 1980's, in partnership with the term "Sustainable Development," and at the first Earth Summit in 1972 in Stockholm. The United Nations appointed a Commission in the mid-1980's to look at sustainable development in the context of multinationals and global development banks investing in emerging markets. The UN appointed Mrs. Gro Brundtland, at the time the Environment Minister of Norway, to lead this Commission. [She later became the first Environment Minister to become a major country Prime Minister.]

That Commission defined 'Sustainable Development' as "meeting the needs of the present generation without compromising the ability of future generations to meet their own needs." Later, Dr. John Ehrenfeld, then Professor and Director of the Technology, Business and Environment Program at MIT, coined the definition of 'Sustainability' as "The possibility that human and other forms of life on earth will flourish forever."

One of my favorite definitions for 'Sustainable Development' was given by an African delegate at the 2002 Johannesburg Earth Summit (a decade after the first Earth Summit in Rio), when he simply defined it as "Enough- for all- forever".

In the business world, the concepts of sustainability started to merge with the interests of some investors for responsible investment, leading to the term "Corporate Social Responsibility (CSR)." CSR was defined by a business organization formed in the 1990's of over 150 multinational firms called the World Business Council for Sustainable Development (WBCSD) as "The commitment of business to contribute to sustainable economic development – working with employees, their families, the local community and society at large to improve their quality of life."

However, my personal favorite definition of Sustainability is one that I have assembled from a variety of sources, and I define it as "Integrating environmental, social and economic issues into *ALL* decisions of an organization, to achieve a balance of protecting the environment, creating economic development, increasing stakeholder value, and providing meaningful jobs, as part of creating a safe, just and equitable society."

This places the emphasis on the three key parts of sustainability; environmental sustainability, social sustainability, and economic sustainability. This chapter deals with those components of sustainability and how they relate to the globalization of the world's economy. Globalization itself is the increased integration and interdependence of national economies over the past 50 years and we will discuss how these issues of sustainability and globalization interact.

Definitions Of Sustainable Enterprise And Society

As business has started to recognize the impact of sustainability issues on their bottom line, both business researchers and practitioners started to try to define what a Sustainable Enterprise would look like. One of the leading proponents of the concept is a not-for-profit organization called "the Natural Step (TNS)," founded by Dr. Karl-Henrik Robèrt, a Swedish doctor that aimed to build consensus among governments, business people and environmentalists as to what must be at least agreed to as needed to safeguard a prosperous life. Following preparation of this consensus document, Dr. Robèrt worked out a first version of system conditions for sustainability and a planning method that later evolved into and became known as The Natural Step Framework (or the Framework for Strategic Sustainable Development). Dr. Robèrt published these results in 1992 in a book called "The Necessary Step." He also employed a team who began building the non-for-profit organization, The Natural Step, with the purpose of facilitating the further development and application of the TNS Framework.

The Natural Step Framework has taken people beyond the arguments of what is and is not possible and what is politically left or right wing. Instead, the Framework builds on a basic understanding of what makes life possible and how our biosphere functions and how we are part of the earth's natural systems. Rather than get lost in abstract definitions and causes, it builds on a platform of basic science designed to allow true interdisciplinary, cross sector cooperation for concrete and measurable change towards sustainability. After all, if you want to achieve 'success', you have to first understand what this means in real terms before you can then take strategic steps to achieve it.

The Natural Step has helped thousands of leaders, corporations and communities, educational facilities and governments to develop blueprints toward sustainability and it now has offices in 11 countries around the world. In typical Natural Step training courses, they define a "sustainable enterprise" as an organization that does **not** contribute to increasing:

- concentrations of substances extracted from the Earth's crust (by mining, or oil/gas extraction),
- concentrations of substances produced by society (new chemicals, materials),
- degradation of nature by physical means (air, water, solid waste pollution),
  and does not contribute to conditions that systematically undermine people's capacity to meet their needs.

They went further and defined a "Sustainable Society" as a society where nature is **not** subject to increasing systematically:

- concentrations of substances extracted from the Earth's crust,
- concentrations of substances produced by society,
- degradation of nature by physical means,
- and, in that society, people are not subject to conditions that systematically undermine their capacity to meet their needs.

In this sustainable society as defined by the Natural Step Framework, **people's** needs are met worldwide for clean air, water, food, shelter, and quality of life. At the time of its start in the 1980's this approach was considered radical, but it has been adopted by increasing larger companies and organizations, including the home furnishings firm Ikea, Nike, Boeing, Jones Lang Lasalle, and the Portland Trail Blazers basketball team.

Key Concepts Of Sustainability

All of these definitions have several key concepts in common. They include:

- *Futures Thinking* and a responsibility for future generations,
- *Eco-Systems Thinking* regarding measuring the capacity of the planet to absorb waste and support life,
- *Social Justice* and a belief in the need for equity, dignity, basic services, human rights and stakeholder voices,
- *Economic, Environmental and Social Responsibilities* (i.e., sustainability).

These concepts have begun to be accepted by leading business people and leading investors, as well as politicians of both liberal and conservative leanings, albeit for different reasons.

Core Principles Of Sustainability

Certain basic assumptions form the core principles behind the drive to sustainability by businesses and other organizations. They include:

- The World Has Finite Resources
- Survival Will Depend on Interdependence
- Inequalities in Quality of Life & Social and Economic Well-Being Will Need to Be Minimized

- Respect for Different Cultures Needed
- We Will Need to Take Responsibility for Leaving a Legacy for Future Generations

As a result, sustainability leaders initially supported Globalization in the 1970's and 1980's as a solution to increase the interdependence of various nations and societies, so as to minimize waste of valuable finite resources, improve equality in the quality of life and economic well-being, and respect our differences while celebrating our similarities. Alan ATkisson (not a misspelling!), the founder of the Seattle Sustainability Initiative in 1990, started consulting on sustainability to governments and companies, and identified seven "Principles of Sustainability" in his latest book *("The ISIS Agreement: How Sustainability Can Improve Organizational Performance and Transform the World," Earthscan, Sept 2008)*.

They include:

– Think long-term	- Understand systems
– Recognize limits	- Protect nature
– Transform business-as-usual	- Practice fairness
– Embrace creativity	

Geographically, this application of sustainability to business started in Scandinavia, but moved rapidly through Europe and into the Northeast USA, specifically Oregon and Washington State. It has been adopted by large cities such as New York City (where Mayor Bloomberg established a City Sustainability Office), London and Rio de Janeiro, to state governments in the United States and Germany, and to large firms such as General Electric, Wal-Mart and HSBC Bank.

Sustainability And Globalization

Globalization is a term that Dr. Theodore Levitt popularized in his famous 1983 essay in the *Harvard Business Review* entitled, "In the Globalization of Markets," where he proclaimed that new technologies had "proletarianized" communications, transport and travel, creating a new commercial reality- the emergence of global markets for standardized consumer products at lower prices. However, others, such as Stephen Green, Chairman of HSBC, say globalization is a natural evolution of the human spirit, rather than a concept or ideology.

Early adopters of Sustainability believed that increased globalization and interdependence of the world's economies would automatically raise the economic well-being of all people in the world. Many began to have second thoughts after seeing the dislocations caused by free trade agreements, outsourcing of production to developing countries, and the lack of environmental and social standards setting up a world of lowest-denominator social, environmental and labor standards, rather than a world of ever-increasing standards.

Thus, Globalization may be a two-edged sword. It can help poor people increase their living standards and improve quality of life by providing jobs and, in the rush to industrialize and develop, if too many short-cuts are tried, it can lead to environmental degradation, health problems and social disintegration. Ironically, many of the trials and tribulations that developed countries went through during their rapid development stage seemed to repeat themselves in the developing world, only on a larger scale. For example, think of the air pollution in London and Pittsburgh in the early/mid-1900, when the UK and USA were developing countries. Compare that to the air pollution in China that was so bad that it led to the closing temporarily of all factories in Beijing so that athletes could breathe at the 2008 Olympics.

A Big Globalization Problem- Outsourcing Of Carbon Emissions

One of the major sustainability problems associated with globalization is the "outsourcing" of carbon emissions to other countries. Over a third of carbon dioxide emissions associated with consumption of goods and services in many developed countries are emitted outside their borders. Some countries, such as Switzerland, "outsource" over half of their carbon dioxide emissions, primarily to developing countries. A recent study by Steven Davis of the Carnegie Institution of Science finds that, per person, about 2.5 tons of carbon dioxide are consumed in the U.S. but produced somewhere else. Most of these emissions are outsourced to developing countries, especially China.

In effect, western, developed countries are attempting to clean their air and water by outsourcing dirty industries to foreign, developing countries, most of which have little or very poor enforcement of environmental regulations. This works for localized pollution, like contaminated drinking water, but not for global pollution, such as carbon emissions that cause climate change. Thus, the USA and Europe are saying they are getting "cleaner", but in reality they are just moving risks around, and often to countries that can least afford those long-term risks, while only receiving short-term benefits. One can see why the Chinese and Indian governments want help in reducing their carbon emissions from developed countries, since much of their carbon emissions are caused by our outsourcing of production and carbon emissions to their countries.

China "exports" goods to the USA with a carbon emissions footprint of over 295 million megatons of carbon emissions per year!

Source: Steven Davis- Carnegie Institution of Science, March 2010

The Sustainability Challenge

The key is preventing history from repeating itself is to develop emerging economies in a more sustainable fashion, without re-creating the problems of past development and industrialization. It was not easy when the population of the USA went from 100m people with more than 50% living on farms to 300M with less than 3% on farms. China, India, Mexico, Indonesia and Brazil are dealing with similar problems as technology allows their farmers to grow crops more efficiently and massive numbers of people are moving to the 10m+ populations of mega-cities like Mumbai, Calcutta, Beijing, Shanghai, Mexico City, Sao Paulo and Jakarta. To succeed will require creativity and going against the status quo to move rapidly towards a more efficient and sustainable society, as certain sustainability problems such as climate change and water quality/quantity are occurring now, not decades in the future.

For example, according to the noted UK economist Sir Nicolas Stern's Economic Impact of Climate Report issued in 2006, if we address the climate change management problem in a timely and rapid concerted approach, we could increase global Gross Domestic Product (GDP) by 5% or more (over $2.5 trillion) in the next half-century. New clean, well-paying jobs would become available to lift the 2-3 billion people presently in poverty to above a minimum standard of living. If we do it wrong, and if we fail to take action quickly in a continued unsustainable manner, and continue to export dirty production of goods to poorer countries we ensure disastrous results. Poor countries that can least afford the needed mitigation measures for remediation of environmental, health and social effects of climate change could plunge the world into another Great Depression with a reduction in global GDP of 5-20% by 2050. Thus, key sustainability issues like climate change and clean, available water, are not just environmental and social problems, but also major economic problems that threaten global stability, peace and business activity.

The noted S.C. Johnson Professor of Sustainability at Cornell University's Business School, Dr. Stuart Hart said in 2007, "The major challenge -and opportunity - of our time is to create a form of commerce that uplifts the entire human community of 6.5 billion and does so in a way that respects both natural and cultural diversity. Indeed, that is the only realistic and viable pathway to a sustainable world, and business can - and must - lead the way." This is the kind of sustainability **leadership** needed by business if the world is to become a better world for all human beings.

I had the honor of working for another noted business leader, Bjorn Stigson, President of ABB Flakt, in early 1990's when I worked for Asea Brown Boveri (ABB). Mr. Stigsom later that decade became President of the World Business Council for Sustainable Development, and in 2008, he said: "Business cannot succeed in societies that fail. There is no future for successful business if the societies that surround it are not working. Governments and business must create partnerships to deliver essential societal services like energy, water, health care and infrastructure." Collaboration again is the type of leadership needed from senior business leaders if we are to address the important issues of sustainability for our world.

Twelve Sustainability/Globalization Issues

Climate change is not the only major sustainability issue affected by globalization. Here is a list, courtesy of Bob Willard, a noted Canadian sustainability consultant, of 12 major sustainability issues that interact with Globalization issues in both negative and positive fashion:

1) *Climate crisis*: Carbon caps / taxes; big impact on economy

2) *Energy crisis*: High energy prices; GHG risks; new clean / storage technologies; clean-tech investment wave

3) *Water wars*: Rising sea levels; shortage of potable water; mass migrations; China, India, Australia, EU, western NA;

4) *Food crisis*: Caused by droughts, speculation, "peak soil," population explosion, climate change, new demand for meat and milk, crop diversion to biofuels, "natural" disasters

5) *Pollution and disease*: Pandemics; HIV / AIDS; new disease vectors; nutrition concerns; air, water, soil pollution risks; bacterial resistance to antibiotics

6) *War on poverty*: Globalization backlash; risk of civil disorder; closing the chasm between rich and poor

7) *Racial tensions*: Immigration waves; racial / religious tensions in developed countries; eco-refugees

8) *Investor activism*: Climate risk review demanded by mainstream investors, insurance regulators & new SEC guidance document

9) *National security*: Terrorism phobias; walled countries

10) *Re-legitimization of role of government*: big vs. small govt., national/federal

11) *Rise of "social enterprises" because of erosion of trust*; demand for risk transparency, disclosure, reporting; stakeholder capitalism vs. shareholder capitalism; revisiting the purpose of the corporation and capitalism

12) *"Blessed Unrest:"* Rise of millions of environmental, social justice, indigenous people's Non Government Organizations (NGOs); an organic movement of movements-perhaps, or do we revert to warfare?

The Insurance International Institute indicated that the value of insured costal property at risk from a Category 3 hurricane was nearly $2 trillion dollars in both Florida and New York states. Coastal property at risk exceeded $400 billion in four other states, Texas, Massachusetts, New Jersey and Connecticut, as indicated in the chart below.

Insured property losses are typically only one-third of the property losses from such weather events, so the total damage to the economy of these states would be 2-3 times the amount of insured losses. Since there are over 900 colleges and universities in these six states, even higher education has a major economic sustainability risk from increasingly severe weather events caused by climate change related to increased carbon emissions. Nearly 700 US colleges and university presidents have committed to make their campuses "climate-neutral" by 2050 (i.e., reduce their net carbon emissions to zero).

Unfortunately, the average citizen often does not understand these issues. A Pew Global Attitudes Survey conducted in 25 countries in August 2009 shows that the people surveyed in the United States gave a lower priority to protecting the environment than Canadian or Chinese citizens, and only 41% of Americans think people should pay higher prices to deal with climate change. In that same survey, only 30% of Chinese respondents and 44% of U.S. respondents thought climate change was a serious problem vs. 90% in Brazil, 67% in India and 65% in Mexico.

We have a major educational process needed to make people across the globe aware of the real sustainability risks and opportunities facing the globe that will negatively affect their economic, social and environmental condition if not managed and mitigated properly.

The Good News- Sustainability As Opportunity

As mentioned in Sir Nicholas Stern's Report on the Economic Impacts of Climate Change, there are many opportunities for business, governments and society to benefit from better management of sustainability risks such as climate change, and many of these advantages apply to the list of a dozen major sustainability and globalization risks mentioned earlier in this lecture. These opportunities include using a number of business and public policy strategies that have short-term and medium-term economic paybacks while significantly reducing risks and creating new job and wealth-creation opportunities. These strategies include:

- Reducing energy use/increase energy efficiency (which cuts GHG emissions and save money by reducing energy expenses)
- Using sustainable building design & land use planning
- Considering sustainability issues in risk management/insurance practices
- Encouraging efficient transportation system options
- Purchasing renewable energy and/or invest in renewable energy projects
- Evaluating sustainability-related financial risks in investments
- Increasing research spending on new/improved sustainable technologies
- Implementing purchasing practices that reduce sustainability footprint
- Make internal & external education about sustainability part of business and

society's mission to create a just, equitable, and long-term sustainable society, lifting people out of poverty and improving their quality of life
– Think globally, act locally, make a fair return, do good & minimize harm

In the next section, we will discuss a specific real world sustainability issue, and potential solutions for this issue.

Solutions For A Real World Sustainability & Globalization Issue

One of the side effects of the tremendous economic growth in the BRIC (Brazil, Russia, India China) economies related to developed countries outsourcing production of goods to BRIC countries, has been a staggering increase in ocean shipping of raw materials (coal, minerals, oil, etc.). BRICs finish goods (toys, electronics, clothing, etc.) in addition, ship to the developed world.

Container ship trade grew eight-fold between 1985 and 2007, as larger and faster container ships were built to serve this market. The efficiencies of larger ships are counter-acted by the need for higher speeds of those ships to serve the perceived "just-in-time" needs of the marketplace. However, this growth in ocean shipping has had major air quality, water quality and heath impacts, and has increased the energy costs of shipping to over 50% of total costs, with an 800% increase in energy used by the shipping industry over 25 years. Global shipping traffic represents about 2-5% of all global CO_2 emissions, about 7% of global SO_2 emissions, and 11-12% of global NOx emissions. All of these emissions have major direct and indirect health and climate impacts.

This has led to a major public relations problem for the shipping lines, as studies published by the American Chemical Society in 2007 indicated that 60,000 premature deaths could be attributed to increased ocean shipping, and that this death toll would increase by 40% by 2012. The U.S. Senate passed the Marine Vessel Emissions Reduction Act of 2008 in response, requiring any ocean-going vessel using US ports to burn fuel with reduced sulfur content, taking effect in 2010 (implemented by regulation in Dec. '09).

There has also been bad publicity about how climate change will affect shipping on the Great Lakes, dropping water levels and increasing evaporation rates of lakes that contain 20% of all of the surface fresh water on the planet. While climate change may raise sea levels by a meter over the next 100 years, it may also drop the levels of the Great Lakes by a meter, thus impact shipping costs and the costs of infrastructure (such as harbor dredging and pier heights) for all ports and shipping lines involved.

So, what are the potential mitigation/management measures that the shipping industry might adopt to mitigate their climate change risks, as well as those of the entire planet? Well there are high-tech/old tech and low-tech solutions for the energy costs and related emission problems of the shipping lines.

One company has come up with a potential high-tech/old-tech combination solution, the SkySails System, using computer-controlled sails to reduce container ship energy use by 10-35% annually, and up to 50% under optimal wind conditions. Another potential solution is very low-tech, but so obvious that it was ignored for several years, namely, just **slowing down** the container ships' cruising speed down from 30 knots to 6-12 knots.

In a 17 February 2010 article in the NY Times, "Slow Trip Across the Sea Aids Profit and the Environment" the Maersk shipping line described how its container ships now take 4 weeks instead of 3 weeks to go from China to Germany. This slow-down reduces fuel costs by 30% and cuts GHG and other emissions by a similar amount. The cost savings allows Maersk to cut prices, allowing them to be more competitive, even in a market where oil is $80/barrel versus the $10/barrel of a few years ago. A Maersk executive was quoted saying about climate change risks/costs, "This is not going away, and those of us who are starting now are ahead of the regulators." Maersk offers a great example of business leadership in sustainability that increases business competitiveness.

Ironically, similar studies done for the airline industry, where adding 5-6 minutes to a cross-Atlantic trip and optimizing the cruising altitude, can cut aircraft emissions by 10% on such a flight, according to Peter Jensen of the European Environment Agency. Studied by the International Energy Agency have shown that cutting automobile speeds from 65 to 55 miles per hour can reduce carbon emissions by 20%.

Finally, the most obvious solution to the globalized shipping problem has been presented by Dr. David Bonilla of the Oxford University Transportation Studies Unit, when he stated, "What you may have to do is to shift the location of industrial plants in international supply chains to shorten the distance between production and consumption." These ideas point out that many solutions to the climate change, sustainability and globalization problem are not "rocket science" technology such as hydrogen or electric cars or carbon sequestration, but rather simple changes in behavior and business decision-making processes.

Business leaders must set the sustainability values and vision that guide the "why" of a company, and let the integration of sustainability issues into the business decision-making process allow the "hows" of sustainability solutions by lower-level managers and staff.

Sustainability & Interdependence

The key business issues for businesses to address will include rethinking their approach to competition and cooperation, and building more partnerships with governments, academia, and yes, even prime competitors. For example, Pepsi and Coca-Cola are cooperating recently on getting government policies on water quality and availability around the world to be sustainable, because they both realize they could go out of business otherwise.

To reiterate Bjorn Stigson's comments, "Businesses cannot succeed in societies that fail." Living in a carbon-constrained economy will require more interdependent decision-making by governments, business and society on sustainability and globalization issues. We need better mitigation and management solutions, and some solutions and approaches will be new or improved technology, and some will be encouraging people and managers to change their behavior to become more sustainable in every day decision-making, either through the right incentives or through better education, including business school education.

The Business Case For Sustainability

Andrew Savitz, a former Pricewaterhouse Coopers (PWC) partner, stated in a 2005 article in the Financial Times that part of the leadership changes required in the business sector include realizing that there is a business case for being sustainable, and without such, is just philanthropy. He added that companies also have to measure their sustainability performance and report it to shareholders, otherwise it is just public relations and whimsy and not part of the vision and culture of a company. He went on to say that

"Today's best-run companies – and smartest investors – are seeing sustainability for what it truly is: a **strategic business driver** that will separate the winners from the losers in the next decade."

A key part of the success of implementing sustainability in business organizations is that one must chose the right sustainability metrics to measure and report your progress to employees, clients, the press, government, investors, and the public. Over the past 15 years, over 70 methodologies have been developed to evaluate the sustainability performance of publicly-traded companies, and these methodologies are starting to be acquired by, an improved upon, by major business data providers such as Thomson Reuters, Bloomberg, MSCI, Risk Metrics, Dow Jones and NASDAQ OMX. There are even methodologies to evaluate the sustainability performance of cities, governments and higher education institutions. Saying we do not know how to measure business sustainability performance is no longer an excuse.

Sustainability Leadership

Business cannot wait for politicians and society to lead, but must take the leadership itself in implementing sustainability. One sees this when major industrial companies join organizations lobbying for a "cap-and-trade" carbon emissions trading system in the U.S. Congress, because they know they cannot afford to wait for several decades for regulations especially when they face major investment decisions now.

A key part of leading this change is changing the culture of business and our decision-making processes. Lou Mobley was the founder of the IBM Executive Training Institute at Sand's Point Long Island, a member of the 15 person task force that developed IBM's first computer, and the developer of the Management Scorecard and Management Dashboard concepts. He said that the key to a successful business was that "Executives don't manage people, they manage culture."

Therefore, we must train future business executives, and re-train present business executives, to understand sustainability issues and create a vision and values for their organization that includes sustainability principles and policies. A good example of how this could work has been the subject of research by a noted business executive, entrepreneur and scholar, Augie Turek. In a recent article in Forbes Magazine (and a soon-to-be-published book), Mr. Turek explains the business secrets of the Trappist Monks, who have followed a successful business model for over 1,200 years.

Mr. Turek summarized the Business Leadership Model of the Trappist Monks as revolving around seven key factors for executives to implement that were applicable to any business. In a conversation I had with him on 12 March 2010, he noted particularly that businesses should want to be sustainable for the long run; and the Trappist business model offered 1,200 years of long-term success. He identified seven factors in the Trappist sustainability model:

1) - Have a High Overarching Mission (only do worthy work, products & services)
2) - Selflessness (focus on the organization's goals, not the me)
3) - Commitment to Excellence (only do it right)
4) - Ruthless Dedication to Highest Ethical Standards (set values, ethics will follow)
5) - Faith (not religious faith, but trust that good business will take care of itself)
6) - Trust Each Other (the most valuable commodity of leadership)
7) - Living the Life (practice what you preach, no $100+m bonuses)

I believe that applying these principles to sustainable business management would be an excellent step forward in moving towards a sustainable economy and society.

Summary

Sustainable business leadership can materially affect the bottom line of business and society in a positive fashion. Sustainability issues do have direct <u>material</u> financial impact, and stakeholders are using such indicators of good business management as product quality/innovation, talent recruitment and future performance of organizations.

However, we need to look at improving potential **business models, structures and solutions** in terms of *globalization, interdependence and sustainability*, and better understand more fully a comprehensive range of inter-disciplinary issues involved. As present or future business leaders and educators, <u>together,</u> we are responsible for the leadership to make change happen globally and locally.

An Afterthought

After finishing writing this chapter, an afterthought came to me from a quotation from Stephen Green, Chairman of the international bank, HSBC, and who is the only major bank chairperson who is an ordained minister of the Church of England. He said in his recent 2010 book, *Good Value,* that "…Globalization is about something far deeper than economics, commerce and politics. It is an evolution of the human spirit. And, on this view, the end of globalization remains radically open precisely because of the ambiguities that seem intrinsic to the human spirit as it evolves."

Your answers to the questions below and comments you share with peers about sustainability in social and business enterprises may be equally ambiguous, but they will never be without meaning for each of us.

Discussion Questions

Are a global economy and a sustainable economy incompatible? Please explain your response.
What can an individual do to help raise living standards for all of the world's population while minimizing sustainability risks?

References

Our Common Future, also known as the *Brundtland Report*, from the United Nations World Commission on Environment and Development (WCED), 1987

Sustainability by Design, John Ehrenfeld, Yale University Press, 2008

Presentation to the WEF in Davos, Bjorn Stigson, President WBCSD, 2007

Training Materials, The Natural Step, 2001 (courtesy of Bob Willard)

Stern Review on the Economics of Climate Change, Sir Nicholas Stern, UK Treasury Department, October 2006

The Globalization of Markets, Dr. Theodore Levitt, Harvard Business Review, 1983

Good Value, Stephen Green, Atlantic Monthly Press, 2010

Carbon Emissions 'Outsourced' to Developing Countries, Steven Davis & Ken Caldeira, Proceedings of the National Academy of Sciences, March 8, 2010

Capitalism at the Crossroads, Second Edition, Stuart L. Hart, Wharton School Publishing Division of Pearson Education Inc., 2007

12 Sustainability/Globalization Issues, Bob Willard, personal communication, with modifications by John Cusack, 2008

Climate Change Policy Briefing- Harvard Medical School, Andrew Logan, CERES, 2005 [Insurance Information Institute/AIR Worldwide Slide]

Pew Global Attitudes Study, the Pew Trust, August 2009

Mortality from Ship Emissions: a Global Assessment, Dr. James Corbett & Dr. James Winebrake, et al, Environmental Science & Technology, Journal of the American Chemical Society,pp. 8512-8518, 5 November 2007

S. 1499: Marine Vessel Emissions Act, passed Senate Committee, law never passed- EPA did announce stricter final emission standards for ocean-going vessels effective 18 December 2009, www.epa.gov/otaq/oceanvessels.htm

Great Lakes Lower Water Levels Propel a Cascade of Hardships, Ken Lydersen, Washington Post, 27 January 2008

Great Lakes Restoration and the Threat of Global Warming, Healing Our Waters- Great Lakes Coalition, May 2008

SKY Sails Information, www.skysails.info

Slow Trip Across the Sea Aids Profit and Environment", Elisabeth Rosenthal, New York Times, 17 February 2010

Presentation to UN Environment Program-Finantial Initiative, - Bjorn Stigson, President, the World Business Council for Sustainable Development, 2008

The Business Case for Sustainability, Andrew Savitz, the Financial Times, 25 October 2005

Business Secrets of the Trappists, August Turak, 4-part series available at: www.forbes.com/2009/04/14/trappist-business-lessons-leadership-management-mepkin1.html , April 14-17, 2009

Chapter Nine
Leadership Challenges
in Human Resource Management
-Richard J. Walter

Introduction

Organizations exist to carry out essential functions for human society that individuals or family units cannot accomplish. Organizations by their very nature comprise groups of human beings who have come together in some way to accomplish collective goals. In essence, organizations cannot exist without individuals serving within them. Leadership of the human resource function in businesses and schools is a complex task that attempts to balance the goals of the organization with the needs of the members who make up the organization.

In all organizations, conflict will inevitably arise as individual or collective needs begin to impact organizational objectives. As organizations have evolved, the human resource function has become an integral process embedded in the interactions of the members.

Rebore (2007) describes the following dimensions of the human resource function in school systems:

1. Human resources planning. Establishing a master plan of long- and short-range human resources requirements is a necessary ingredient in the school district's curricular and fiscal planning processes.
2. Recruitment. Quality personnel, of course, are essential for the delivery of effective educational services to children, youth, and adults.
3. Selection. The long and short-range human resources requirements are implemented through selection techniques and processes.
4. Placement and induction. Through appropriate planning, new personnel and the school district accommodate each other's goals.
5. Staff development. Development programs help personnel meet school district objectives and also provide individuals with the opportunity for personal and professional growth.
6. Performance evaluation. Processes and techniques for evaluation help the individual grow professionally and help the school district attain its objectives.
7. Compensation. Establishing programs that compensate quality performance helps to motivate personnel.

8. Collective negotiations. The negotiating process gives personnel an opportunity to participate in matters that affect their professional and personal welfare. (pp. 11-13)

Rebore cautions these dimensions "are not discrete, isolated entities, but rather, integral aspects of the same function." Each of the dimensions overlap and impact some or all of the others. Adding to the complexity of the human resource function is that these eight dimensions are enacted by many members of the school district through daily interactions and that many of these interactions are beyond the formal control of the human resource department.

For example, a building principal who fails to perform the necessary classroom observations for select teachers can subvert a well-planned school district performance evaluation system. In another instance, a single case of nepotism or "who you know" can damage workers' confidence in the impartiality and fairness of the school district's hiring policies.

Challenge: Workforce Security in an Economic Downturn

Each of the eight dimensions may strengthen the social contract between the individual and the organization or cause dysfunction in the workplace. "The investment in human capital or human resources is the most important one made within any organization. The focus is on creating an organization that serves its own goals while meeting the personal needs of the school system's employees" (Cunningham & Cordiero, 2006, p. 276).

The theory of the social contract in organizations holds that workers enter into a relationship with their organization that goes beyond mere wages and benefits to include the quality of life in the organization and the intrinsic nature of the work itself. "The implicit social contract that governed work for many years---the norm that hard work, loyalty, and good performance will be rewarded with fair and increasing wages, dignity, and security---has broken down and been replaced by a norm in which employers give primacy to stock price and short-term gains often at the expense of America's workers" (Kochan & Shulman, 2007, p. 1).

In the 2008-2012 economic downturn human resource leaders are faced with serious dilemmas. School districts in the United States are coping with the prospect of severe budget cuts as funding from state and federal sources declined. "The human resource function has an impact on the continual staffing of positions, which in turn directly affects the quality of educational programs, but it also has a significant effect on the budget. Approximately 80 percent of all school district expenditures are for salaries and benefits" (Rebore, 2007).

The challenges of human resource management are reflected in the motto found on the website of The American Association of School Personnel Administrators (www.aaspa.org): "Keeping the Human in Human Resources." This international organization, which "provides leadership in promoting effective human resources practices within education through professional development activities and a broad-based resource network," affiliated with many similar state organizations. The New York State Association of School Personnel Administrators (www.nysaspa.org) focused its 2009 annual conference on teacher termination and layoff, legal issues, and collective bargaining trends in an economic downturn.

Many human resource professionals are struggling to find the balance between organizational needs in light of severe budget constraints and the needs of the workforce.

They want to find humane ways to restructure and make necessary cuts, while remaining sensitive to the needs of their employees.

In the United States, the Economic Recovery and Reinvestment Act of 2009 provided needed funding to preserve jobs in many school districts. Human resource administrators in 2012 face challenges to preserve and retain jobs without the benefit of the stimulus money.

"But as helpful as many state and local officials have found the one-time stimulus aid in coping with current and anticipated revenue shortfalls, it creates some awfully big holes to fill when the money begins to run out late next year in what's widely known as the 'funding cliff'" (Robelen, 2009).

In its analysis of the use of stimulus money, The American Association of School Administrators' report, "One Year Later: How the Economic Downturn Continues to Impact School Districts" (AASA, 2009) , stated that a sample of 875 school district administrators across the United States revealed that, "two-thirds (66 percent) of respondents reported having to eliminate positions for the 2009-10 school year. An overwhelming 83 percent anticipate having to eliminate further positions in 2010-11" (p.8).

Human resource administrators have to provide for a sense of belonging for members of the school district who are fearful of losing their jobs. They may also have to discuss contractual givebacks with labor leaders in an effort to save jobs. The manner in which these actions take place can have a great impact on the morale of the workforce and employee perception of the school district's commitment to and vision of the social contract.

The social contract between individuals and organizations varies based on the political, economic, and social environment in which the organization exists. Acceptable practices change as customer and employee interpretation and viewpoints respond to societal norms and urgent economic realities. In their paper, "The Acceptability of Layoffs and Pay Cuts: Comparing North America with Germany," Gerlach, Levine, Stephan & Struck (2005) queried respondents as to "the fairness of layoffs and pay cuts in different scenarios" (p. 11). The researchers found that all respondents had negative reactions to layoff and pay cut scenarios, but that their negative responses were moderated by specifics within the scenarios. For example, all employee respondents regarded layoffs "as more fair when the CEO refused to accept a bonus for successful cost-cutting" (p.14).

Comparing workers in the United States, Canada, and Germany, the researchers found "dismissals are perceived as less fair in the vast majority of scenarios in Germany than in the United States and Canada" (p.15). They concluded that "These differences can be traced to fundamental and differing social perceptions concerning the acceptability of the market and market outcomes and go hand in hand with differences in institutional labour market arrangements that affect the evolution of social norms and psychological contracts within countries" (p.16).

In an exploratory study of compensation practices in ten countries, Lowe, Milliman, DeCieri, & Dowling (2002) stated: "In these turbulent times and increasingly global competitive markets, no function is under greater scrutiny than the human resource function" (p. 45). Compensation practices in the study used variables of employee performance, employee job satisfaction, and organizational effectiveness. Employees ranked the compensation items on their current state and desired future state.

The authors described how "Compensation items in survey order questioned the extent to which: (1) pay incentives are important to compensation strategy; (2) benefits are an important part of total pay; (3) pay is contingent on group or organizational performance; (4) long-term performance is emphasized over short term; (5) seniority influences pay decisions; (6) pay incentives are a significant amount of total earnings; (7) benefits are generous; (8) pay system has a future orientation; (9) pay raises are determined by job performance" (p. 48). They examined these variables in Australia, Canada, China, Indonesia, Japan, Korea, Latin America, Mexico, Taiwan, and the United States. They noted cultural and societal differences which led to their conclusion that, "adopting a lens focused on what employees in a given culture want from a compensation system rather than replicating current cultural norms may help motivate employees to engage in high performance behaviors" (p. 62).

When employees feel supported in their work by both the tangible resources (pay, benefits, workplace environment, etc) and intangible resources (organizational culture, sense of organizational fairness, supervisor relationships) of the organization, they report strong positive emotions associated with the performance of their jobs. Conversely, as they see the organizational resources withdrawn, their emotions related to their work are negatively affected.

In their study, "Flow at Work: Evidence for an Upward Spiral of Personal and Organizational Resources," the researchers surveyed 258 secondary teachers in 34 schools in Spain. "Flow" at work is defined as "a short-term peak experience at work that is characterized by absorption, work enjoyment and intrinsic work motivation" (Salanova, Bakker, & Llorens, 2006). Workers who experience flow are happy in their workplace and highly involved in their tasks, "endorsing a very positive judgment about the quality of the working life" (p.15).

The researchers found that teachers' sense of personal efficacy was reinforced by the experience of flow, increasing their perception of support by and for their school and its leaders. The importance of intangible organizational resources that contribute to this sense of involvement and well-being by the teachers was noted:

> Organizational resources - a combination of different types of organizational climate orientation indicators such as social support (e.g., people help each other mutually, there are [sic] a good relationship between the co-workers), innovation (e.g., teachers can give suggestions to improve the quality of work, and they can put forward new ideas to improve the work), rules (e.g., the work that the teacher must do is plenty [sic] of norms and the decisions about the work process is made by the supervisors and goals, e.g., objectives are clearly defined) - had a positive influence on the occurrence of flow among teachers over the time. (p.16)

Organizational resources and their fair distribution contribute to the human experience of flow at work. The human resource leader has to take into account the impact of the actual and perceived withdrawal of organizational resources on the remaining members of the workforce. A significant challenge is the responsibility to set clearly defined goals for the organization despite the budgetary challenges and to maintain program quality despite morale issues.

Sensitivity to the needs of laid-off workers who will typically work until the end of the school year, can help both those who will be leaving and those who will remain. All workers facing layoffs are concerned about health care in countries where universal health care is not available. Any effort by human resource managers to extend health care makes a difference in the attitude of those who depart an organization. Since many institutions pay quarterly premiums for health care, employee coverage can be extended through one quarter of the year in many cases. Support for transitions to new opportunities give evidence that an enterprise and its leaders do care about what happens to employees.

As leaders of the human resource function, the challenge is to establish norms of behavior among all organizational members that transcend the short-term effects of layoffs and budget cuts. "Leaders, whether at the district or building level, must always be mindful of the internal and external forces placing demands upon their system. Internally, the forces within a leader's organization that encourage sustainable change or inertia are the employees and the organizational culture. External politics, policies, fiscal realities, and community values affect an organization. Strong leaders, combined with willing and knowledgeable followers working in a collaborative and creative enterprise, can mitigate many of these forces and achieve laudable goals" (Manley & Hawkins, 2010).

Challenge: Implementing Best Practices and Theoretical Models in Reframing Organizations,

Bolman and Deal point out those human resource managers often ignore theoretical models that could enhance the commitment of members of the workforce to the organization. They also fail to implement best practices within their businesses. "Why do managers persist in pursuing less effective strategies when better ones are at hand? One reason is that Theory X managers fear losing control or indulging workers. A second is that investing in people requires time and persistence to yield a payoff. Faced with relentless pressure for immediate results, managers often conclude that slashing costs, changing strategy, or reorganizing is more likely to produce a quick hit" (Bolman & Deal, 2008).

The Human Perspective

Human resource managers can learn much by looking at their organizations through the "human resource frame." In this frame, the leaders of the organization adhere to the following values:
1) Human resource leaders communicate their strong belief in people.
2) Human resource leaders are visible and accessible.
3) Effective human resource leaders empower others (Bolman & Deal, 2008).

This human resource framework is effective in numerous corporations and schools, and has one critical aspect, a caring attitude towards employees who are the most valuable asset a company has. Yet, many managers still react to their workforce in an adversarial manner. A growing body of research shows the need for caring management is even greater during times of difficulty or crisis; yet many managers revert to other less effective and authoritarian models.

An example of this adversarial tendency appears in the article, "The Very Separate Worlds of Academic and Practitioner Periodicals in Human Resource Management: Implications for Evidence-Based Management." In this study, the authors discuss the growing research interest in evidence-based management as a way to bridge the gap between researchers and practitioners in human resource management. In fact, many human resource managers in business lack a bachelor's degree in business administration or a related field. Frequently, they earn a promotion to Director of Human Resources after working in a variety of managerial levels within a particular business enterprise and have greater expertise in sales, finance or accounting than they do in human resource management.

The researchers reviewed the most widely read periodical aimed at practitioners, "HR Magazine," published by the Society for Human Resource Management, as well as "Human Resource Management" magazine and the "Harvard Business Review" to "examine the extent to which three important HR-related research findings are being 'translated' and 'transferred' to practitioners via these three widely read periodicals" (Rynes, Giluk & Brown, 2007).

The content analysis of these periodicals centered on three important research areas within evidence-based management: intelligence as related to job performance; goal setting and feedback for performance; and personality as a predictor of performance. For each of these areas the authors analyzed the three periodicals to determine: "1. How much coverage did each of these three topics receive in major practitioner and bridge periodicals between 2000 and 2005; 2) To what extent is the content of coverage…consistent or inconsistent with peer-reviewed research findings? 3) What sources of evidence does each periodical present? (Rynes, Giluk & Brown, 2007, pp. 989-990)

The content analysis of Rynes, et al., revealed, "practitioner journals have barely covered topics that HR researchers believe to be among their most important findings. In other words, their results suggested a very significant failure of academic research to transfer new knowledge to important practitioner sources of information" (p.999).

The results are consistent with other fields, including teaching, where many practitioners fail to read in their field or to be aware of current research beyond a superficial awareness of a "theory" or findings heard about in a staff development meeting.

> Take the case of new information influencing teaching and learning. Over the last ten years, the knowledge we have gained about how the brain works and how learning occurs has opened new vistas for educational practice. Yet, on a practical level, much of this new information has not reached the classroom. Little research-based information about how the brain learns has influenced pedagogical practices. (Manley & Hawkins, 2010, p. 33)

The human resource leader in a school system should ensure that he or she is aware of current research in the field and that teachers in the school system are learning about current research that could improve student learning. In all organizations, human resource managers should have continuous education and development so that their skills and creative insights reflect the latest evidence based research about human motivation for productive enterprises.

Certainly, human resource managers must be acutely aware of the cultural, demographic, political and financial issues that impact their organization internally and externally. If they are to participate effectively in the executive leadership team, they must comprehend deeply the current research in their field of human resource management and development. As executives charged with the development and motivation of the workforce, they must first provide for their own development and motivation before they attempt to care for others.

Discussion Questions

What are the critical human motivational factors within your preferred industry and country?
How would you manage these human motivational issues to create new opportunities in your enterprise?

References

Bolman, L. G., Deal, T. E. (2008). *Reframing Organizations: Artistry, Choice, and Leadership.* San Francisco: Wiley & Sons.

Cunningham, W. G., Cordeiro, P. A. (2006) *Educational Leadership: A Problem-Based Approach.* New York: Pearson Education, Inc.

Gerlach, K., Levine, D. I., Stephan, G., Struck, O. (2005) The acceptability of layoffs and pay cuts: Comparing North America with Germany. UC Berkeley: Institute for Research on Labor and Employment. Retrieved from http://www.escholarship.org/uc/item/1k21dOrg.

Kuchan, T., Shulman, B. (2007) A new social contract: Restoring dignity and balance to the economy. Economic Policy Institute. Retrieved from http://www.eri.org.

Lowe, K. B., Milliman, J., DeCieri, H., Dowling, P. J. (2002) International compensation practices: A ten-country comparative analysis. *Human Resource Management,* 41(1), 45-66.

Manley, R. J., Hawkins, R. J. (2010) *Designing School Systems for All Students.* Lanham, MD: Rowman & Littlefield Education.

Rebore, R.W. (2007) *Human Resources Administration in Education.* New York: Pearson Education, Inc.

Robelen, E.W. (2009) "Funding cliff" fueling worry among states. *Education Week.* Retrieved from http://www.edweek.org/ew/articles/2009/10/30.

Rynes, S. L., Giluk, T. L., Brown, K. G. (2007) The very separate worlds of academic and practitioner periodicals in human resource management: Implications for evidence-based management. *Academy of Management Journal,* 50, (5), 987-1008.

Salanova, M., Bakker, A.B., Llorens, S. (2006) Flow at work: Evidence for the upward spiral of personal and organizational resources. *Journal of Happiness Studies,* 7, 1-22.

Chapter Ten
Do Chief Finance Officers for School Districts Receive the Proper Training?
-Michael Shane Higuera
-Robert J. Manley

Introduction

Since 2000, the United States has experienced corporate and municipal unethical practices and criminal activities in finance at the highest levels of executive responsibility. One of the more notorious corporate examples involved both a company (Enron) and its auditors (Arthur Anderson and Co.). According to Patsuris (2002), Enron's scandal became public knowledge in October 2001. It involved hidden, off-balance sheet, debt in excess of one billion dollars, manipulation of the Texas and California power markets, and bribery of foreign governments to win contracts abroad. Arthur Anderson and Co., shredded documents relating to the audit of Enron after learning that the Securities and Exchange Commission had launched an inquiry into Enron. Neither company survived the criminal and unethical behavior of its leaders.

At the municipal level, and specifically in New York State, malfeasance has been nearly parallel, though on a much smaller scale. One of the more notorious municipal scandals involved the Roslyn Union Free School District. The scandal became public in 2002 and according to the State of New York Office of the State Comptroller's Office (2005), involved theft and misappropriation of funds by the Superintendent, Assistant Superintendent for Business, and others in excess of 11 million dollars. The school district's external auditor pleaded guilty in a court of law to altering district financial records after he learned a forensic investigation would be conducted. While the school district survived, many of its leaders lost jobs and two were incarcerated. The auditing firm disbanded and its principal partner was sent to jail.

In response to the Enron scandal, and others such as those affecting Tyco International, Adelphia, Peregrine Systems, and WorldCom, the Sarbanes-Oxley Act of 2002 became law in the United States under President George W. Bush (Donaldson, 2005). This law contained 11 sections that established new standards for boards, managers, and accounting firms of all publicly traded U.S. companies (Oxley, 2002).

The response by the New York State Governor, George E. Pataki, to the Roslyn School District scandal, and others, was to propose the School District Accountability Act of 2005 (State of New York Office of the State Comptroller, 2005a). This legislation addressed school district accountability by amending various sections of the Education Law.

The legislation addressed seven key areas including:

- Requirements for training of school board members,
- Establishment of an internal audit function,
- Clarifications related to the position of claims auditor,
- Enhancements related to audits,
- Establishment of an audit committee,
- The requirement to use a request for proposal (RFP) for the procurement of the annual audit of financial statements, and
- Audits of school districts and BOCES by the Office of the State Comptroller. (New York State Education Department, 2005)

The requirement for school board training listed above consisted of six hours of training in fiscal oversight that new school board members must receive during the first year of service on the board. This training requirement need only be satisfied once in the lifetime of each board member. Those board members who were already serving when the legislation went into effect were not required to receive the training until they were re-elected to that or any other school district's board of education.

These two nearly parallel laws resulted in higher levels of reporting, government and public scrutiny, and personal accountability for chief financial officers of publicly traded corporations and school business administrators. Throughout this chapter, the terms school business administrator, school district business leader, and school chief financial officer are used interchangeably.

Chief Financial Officer (CFO) and School District Business Leader (SDBL)

Chief Financial Officers

The role of the corporate chief financial officer has evolved significantly in the Twenty-first Century. Glitman, Murphy, and Setton (2002) interviewed chief financial officers at the eighth Annual Forbes CFO Conference almost one year after public disclosure of the Enron scandal. Glitman et al. reported that, "Smart, pro-active companies reacted by moving the head corporate bean counter, the chief financial officer, front and center to a new position of power shoulder-to-shoulder with the CEO" (¶ 1).

The pace at which the chief financial officer's role was evolving and or expanding seemed to quicken just a few years after the implementation of the Sarbanes-Oxley legislation. Couto, Heinz, and Moran (2005) stated,

> Few business roles have changed as dramatically during the last generation as that of the chief financial officer. The classic model – the CFO as chief accountant and technical expert focused narrowly on the firm's financial statements and capital structure – has been passé for a decade or more. The CFO has long since operated as more of a business partner with the CEO, closely involved in designing and overseeing strategy, operations, and performance.

Elizabeth Acton, Executive Vice President and Chief Financial Officer of Commercial Incorporated, writing for the Detroit Regional Chamber in 2007 offered the opinion that, "it is no longer good enough to simply be the smartest number cruncher in the world. The CFO, today, has to be accountable for more than just accounting" (¶ 1). Acton emphasized the need for the chief financial officer to be a partner with the chief executive officer and the various unit managers in shaping corporate strategy. She acknowledged that it was important to know the financial tools of the trade. She emphasized the importance of communicating in a credible and clear manner to all the internal and external stakeholders. She observed that the chief financial officer must measure risks and manage them.

Desai (2008), writing about the finance function within global corporations, observed that a competent finance department reconciled the financial, managerial and institutional priorities across multiple business units.

School District Business Leaders

School district business leaders in New York State serve as the Chief Financial Officers of their respective school districts and report directly to the Superintendent of Schools who is the Chief Executive Officer of the school district and to the Board of Education whose members serve as a community elected Board of Trustees (Directors).

In New York State, there are school business administrators in the 685 school districts who managed the receipt and expenditure of more than $48 billion dollars not including construction projects during the 2006-2007 fiscal year (New York State Education Department, 2008). School Finance Officers manage revenue, expenditures, resident voter referenda for annual budget approvals, personnel negotiations and community relations in cooperation with the District Superintendent and School Board (Sielke, 1995). "The school business administrator is, in fact, the school district's chief operating and financial officer, the person responsible for all the tasks involved in keeping the district running smoothly" (DiBella, 1999, p. 7).

Financial Skills of School District Business Leaders

It is important that school business administrators (SDBL) be highly competent in the technical skills of financial management. School business administrators must also maintain the highest professional ethics, interact well with people, and be skilled leaders. Superintendent of Schools recommend to the Board of Education a school business administrator who has acquired the complex skills and dispositions required for the chief financial officer role. In New York State, the Board of Education may employ *only* a School District Business Leader who has the recommendation of the Superintendent of Schools.

Financial management skills include the administration of school budgets, the ability to work with the residents of the community who vote on the budget, and a political acumen that enables the school district CFO to balance the needs and desires of the community with available resources within the school district. Financial management also consists of the acquisition of goods and services at the best price for the required quality, the review of budget modifications and treasurer's reports on a regular basis, and the preparation of timely, accurate and anticipatory reports (Grucci, 2003; Eisenberg, 2004; Burak, 2006; Chen, 2007).

These financial management skills range from the clerical bookkeeping tasks of maintaining accounts to the analytical processes of data analysis and in the end, to systems design and evaluation. It is management's role to develop the profound knowledge required to perform its most important work; that of system design, evaluation, and improvement (Deming, 1982).

Financial management skills include planning skills that include the development of multi-year budget plans that consider the long-term projection of expenditures and revenues to sustain programs and provide for the personnel and facility needs of the district (Grucci, 2003; Eisenberg, 2004; Burak, 2006; Chen, 2007). Financial planning requires estimating skills, a thorough understanding of the condition of the school district's physical plant, instructional programs, and the community's financial capacity to support the school district's vision, mission, and goals.

Interpersonal Dispositions and Skills

The moral environment of a group, organization, or society is the obligation and responsibility of the leader (Greenleaf, 1997). Kouzes and Posner (1993) avowed that a leader's credibility depends on his or her moral purpose, the trust of his or her followers, and the hope that trust creates. Ciulla & Burns (1998) identified ethics as the core of leadership and concluded that a culture's ethical values defined its leadership.

The New York Office of the State Comptroller (2003) reported that standards of business ethics required continuous commitment, enforcement, and modeling by leaders in organizations. The Comptroller referred to this commitment, enforcement, and modeling of ethical behavior by top management as the tone at the top.

Leaders, managers, and supervisors may find themselves in the position of dealing with conflict within and across departments and with external customers and residents. The conflict may be petty or important, personal or professional, and real or imagined. The school business administrator must be able to successfully identify and mediate conflict, promote harmony, minimize distraction from the daily work of the office and actively listen to internal and external respondents.

Poor relationships with supervisors or staff may result in job dissatisfaction (Gibson et al, 2003). Job dissatisfaction may lead to negative employee behaviors such as theft of time or assets, psychological withdrawal, absenteeism, and resignation. Such behaviors result in lower employee productivity and higher school district costs (Gibson et al, 2003; Mancini, 2007).

Ethical beliefs and interpersonal skills are important attributes that a School District Business Leader or a Chief Financial Officer must cultivate. Basic leadership skills and a disposition of care and concern for others engrained into a high sense of personal integrity often characterize the most effective leaders (Kouzes and Posner, 1993; Ciulla & Burns, 1998). Several researchers have documented that leader behaviors associated with stewardship, transactional and transformational efforts influence followers to achieve high reaching goals (Burns, 1978; Ciulla & Burns, 1998; Bredeson, 2004; and Bass & Riggio, 2006).

In this chapter, with its focus on the leadership skills of school business administrators, we examine ethical and interpersonal behavior, stewardship, transactional leadership, and transformational leadership.

Stewardship is a leader's "commitment to core democratic values and principles and making them a lived reality within schools and the communities they serve" (Bredeson, 2004, p. 710).

Transactional leaders hold a clear vision and communicate clearly the responsibilities of and their expectations for followers. They establish the benefits and rewards for compliance and the sanctions for failure to comply with these responsibilities and expectations (Bass & Riggio, 2006). The relationship between the leader and followers revolves around the exchange of services and rewards, expectations and duties (Mancini, 2007).

Transformational leadership is the relationship between the leader and followers in which the leader motivates the followers to be creative and encourages the followers to extend their best effort. The transformational leader, in adhering to high ethical standards, raises the ethical behavior of the followers (Burns, 1978). Mancini (2007) reported that the relationship between the transformational leader and the followers relied upon the leader's commitment to the individual growth of the followers. She found that job satisfaction among employees in the five for profit enterprises she investigated related to their leaders' capacity to inspire them.

Job Satisfaction

Job satisfaction, according to Herzberg's (1966) two-factor theory, is comprised of content and context factors. The content factors include an employee's feeling of accomplishment, the sense that the employee's work is meaningful, recognition of the employee's work, and increased responsibility based on merit. Content factors reflect the internal dispositions of the employee that relate to how the employee feels about his or her work. The context factors reflect externally focused dispositions that the employee holds regarding compensation, status, personal relationships, and management policies.

Content factors tend to be satisfiers because their presence leads to strong levels of motivation and job satisfaction, while their absence does not lead to dissatisfaction. Context factors tend to be dissatisfiers because their absence leads to job dissatisfaction, while their presence above the level necessary to avoid dissatisfaction does not lead to increased motivation or job satisfaction. Job satisfaction is the disposition that individuals hold towards their job (Mancini, 2007).

The attitude that employees have towards a job, whether positive, neutral, or negative, is based on their attitudes towards their surrounding work environment, which includes the leadership, opportunities for growth, policies, procedures, working conditions, co-worker and supervisor relationships and fringe benefits. Job satisfaction levels below neutral may lead to negative employee behaviors such as theft of time or assets, psychological withdrawal, absenteeism, and resignation. Such behaviors result in lower employee productivity and higher school district costs (Gibson et al., 2003).

In summary, this chapter examines the relationships among job preparedness in financial management and financial planning skills, dispositions of ethics and interpersonal relations, leadership skills in the dimensions of stewardship, transaction, and transformation, and job satisfaction for school business administrators working in school districts within the suburban metropolitan region of New York State.

Survey Research And Validity Of Content

Originally, we intended to investigate school business administrators' attitudes towards ethics, interpersonal relations, transactional and transformational leadership endeavors, financial management and planning skills and their relationship to the job satisfaction that these chief financial officers expressed.

Survey research requires researchers to establish the validity of the survey items that they use to measure the constructs within their survey instrument. We used a jury of experts to examine the content validity of the items in our scale. Then, we employed a factor analysis of the responses from our 87 respondents. We learned that the constructs and the items in our survey required us to reduce some of the items in the survey to increase the construct validity of the survey and its subscales. We discuss the factor analysis in this section and demonstrate how our survey and its subscales changed as a result of factor analysis. Finally, we subjected each subscale to a Cronbach analysis of internal consistency to establish its reliability.

After a factor analysis of the responses from 87 school district business leaders, three research questions addressed in this chapter were refined and the original seven variables set forth in the study were changed to those listed in the following questions.

1. When a purposeful sample of New York State certified school business administrators from several regions of the state is administered to volunteer respondents, how do they differ in their attitudes towards their actual preparation and the importance of the preparation requirements for school business administrators in the dimensions of stewardship, leadership skills, interpersonal relations, financial planning, financial management, public fund accounting, and forecasting?

2. What relationships exist among school district budget size, student enrollment, gender, race, and age of the school business administrator, and length of the school business administrators' time in the role and in the district; school business administrators' perceptions of their actual preparation and its importance in leadership disposition of stewardship, leadership skills, interpersonal relations, financial planning, financial management, public fund accounting, and forecasting? Gender issues were examined through a t-test comparison of independent mean scores for each of the financial practices and leadership variables identified in question two.

3. How do school district budget size, student enrollment inside a school district; age of the school business administrator; length of the school business administrators' time in the role and in the district; school business administrators' perceptions of their actual preparation and its importance in leadership disposition of stewardship, leadership skills, interpersonal relations, financial planning, financial management, public fund accounting, and forecasting predict the job satisfaction of practicing New York State certified school business administrators?

Validity

Whenever a new survey instrument is under construction, a variety of procedures should be undertaken to establish that the items within the survey measure what they purport to measure.

Content Validity

We chose two methods to verify the validity of our survey instrument. First, we employed a jury of five experts in school finance to examine each of the items and identify any item that was unclear. After hearing from the jury members, we adjusted the content of several items to improve the content validity of the survey. Secondly, we employed a factor analysis with 87 respondents to develop the construct validity of each scale.

Construct Validity

A factor analysis established the construct validity of the instrument. The 66 items on part two of the survey were subjected to a factor analysis using the data from the 87 surveys that were completed and returned. Table 1 lists these items grouped by the original seven dimensions thought to define them and the range of scores for each of the original dimensions.

Table 1

66 Items, Original Seven Dimensions, Associated Items, and the Range of Scores

Factor	Items	Range of Scores
Financial Management	11, 13, 15, 17, 19, 21, 23, 25, 27, 29, 31, 33, 35, 37, 39, 41, 43, 49, 51	21 – 105
Financial Planning	22, 34, 46, 53, 55, 57, 59, 61, 63, 65, 67, 69, 71, 73, 75	15 – 75
Ethics	12, 24, 36, 50, 54, 68	6 – 30
Interpersonal Relations	14, 26, 38, 56, 64, 70	6 – 30
Stewardship	16, 28, 40, 58, 72	5 – 25
Transactional Leadership	18, 30, 42, 48, 60, 66, 74	7 – 35
Transformational Leadership	20, 32, 44, 52, 62, 76	6 – 30

A Principal Components extraction method with an Equamax rotation procedure revealed that there were seven factors with eigenvalues ranging from 1.71 through 23.43, explaining 64.1 percent of the variance in the responses. Three factors were renamed using the content of the highest loading factors and two were new factors that appeared as items moved into new relationships based on the participant responses.

Table 2

Resulting Seven Factors after the Factor Analysis, with Items, Range of Scores, and Cronbach Alpha Coefficients

Factor	Items	Range of Scores	Cronbach Alpha
Leadership Disposition of Stewardship	28, 32, 40, 44, 52	5 – 30	Importance = .865 Received = .905
Leadership Skills	13, 30, 48, 49, 54, 60, 62, 66, 74, 76	10 – 50	Importance = .896 Received = .876
Interpersonal Relations	12, 14, 16, 18, 24, 36, 42	7 – 35	Importance = .882 Received = .892
Financial Planning	19, 22, 25, 27, 29, 33, 35, 55	8 – 40	Importance = .901 Received = .906
Financial Management	63, 67, 69, 71, 73	5 – 25	Importance = .852 Received = .907
Public Fund Accounting	37, 39, 41, 43, 75	5 – 25	Importance = .866 Received = .859
Forecasting	11, 17, 21, 23, 31, 34, 57, 59	8 – 40	Importance = .878 Received = .867

Reliability Of Survey Scales

Each of the 66 items on part two of the survey had two parts. One part reported the importance to the successful performance of his or her professional responsibilities that the School Business Administrator assigned to the item. The other part reported the degree to which the School Business Administrator reported having received preparation regarding the item as part of his or her certification process. The factor analysis used the items regarding importance. Cronbach Alpha Coefficients were calculated for the items in each dimension. See Table 2.

Dimensions Of Survey After Factor Analysis

Leadership Disposition of Stewardship – The leadership disposition of stewardship factor consists of five items with loading factors ranging between .578 and .728. The Eigenvalue is 23.43 and the percent of variance explained by the factor is 35.50. Two of the five items (28 and 40) were originally assigned to the factor of stewardship and three of the five items (32, 44, and 52) were originally assigned to the factor of transformational leadership. Our respondents in this study emphasized that their disposition of stewardship was reflected in their commitment to serving the community, students, and staff above themselves, their motivation of staff to apply their best efforts to performing their roles and their efforts to provide all staff with meaningful work and a model of ethical behavior. Table 3 shows the loading factors, item numbers, and items for the leadership disposition of stewardship factor.

Table 3

Factor Loading, Leadership Disposition of Stewardship

Factor Loading	Item Number	Item	h^2
.728	28	Training in the importance of placing commitment to the organization ahead of personal gain is important.	.657
.698	40	Training in the importance of serving others, including community members, students, and staff first, is important.	.674
.649	32	Training in the ability to motivate staff members to apply their best efforts to the performance of their roles is important.	.751
.578	52	Training in the importance of motivating staff members through providing challenges and meaningful work is important.	.686
.573	44	Training in the importance of motivating staff members through the ethical belief system of the leader(s) is important.	.543

Leadership skills – Eighty-seven (87) school business administrators identified 10 items with loading factors ranging between .368 and .662 for the factor of general leadership skills. The Eigenvalue is 7.86 and the percent of variance explained by the factor is 11.91. Two of the 10 items (13 and 49) were originally assigned to the factor of financial management, one item (54) was originally assigned to the factor of ethics, five items (30, 48, 60, 66, and 74) were originally assigned to the factor of transactional leadership, and two items (62 and 76) were originally assigned to the factor of transformational leadership.

Our school business administrators report that as leaders they should design reward systems for staff, provide a vision for the district's critical goals, monitor staff performance, coach staff to meet expectations, act ethically, work with an information management system and interpret monthly financial reports.

Table 4

Factor Loading, Leadership Skills

Factor Loading	Item Number	Item	h^2
.662	48	Training in the ability to design effective rewards for compliance and sanctions for non-compliance with expectations for staff performance is important.	.632
.589	30	Training in the ability to translate staff responsibilities into step-by-step tasks is important.	.586
.571	66	Training in the ability to coach staff members that fall short of expectations is important.	.736
.561	62	Training in the importance of motivating staff through provision of the intellectual stimulation of problem solving is important.	.708
.556	76	Training in the importance of developing a vision for the transformation of the organization is important.	.540
.548	74	Training in the ability to document staff performance in relation to expectations is important.	.655
.517	60	Training in the ability to design systems to monitor staff performance is important.	.613
.483	54	Training in the implications of acting based on political expedience rather than on ethical grounds is important.	.449
.476	49	Training in the fundamentals of management information system development is important.	.545
.368	13	Training in the interpretation of monthly financial reports is important.	.361

The respondents in this study did not separate behaviors that the literature associated with transactional and transformational leadership. Instead, their responses indicated that they held a distinct belief that stewardship was a selfless and ethical approach to leadership and they believed that general leadership entailed transactional, transformational, ethical and financial skills.

The ability to develop a vision for the transformation of the organization, to coach staff, to design systems to monitor staff performance and to act on political and ethical grounds, and the ability to design systems and to gather and interpret information comprised the general leadership skills that our respondents stated were important. Table 4 shows the loading factors, item numbers, and items for the leadership skills factor.

Interpersonal Relations – The interpersonal relations factor consists of seven items with loading factors ranging between .602 and .786. The eigenvalue is 3.27 and the percent of variance explained by the factor is 4.96. One of the seven items (14) remained assigned to the factor. Three of the seven items (12, 24, and 36) were originally assigned to the factor of ethics, one item (16) was originally assigned to the factor of stewardship, and two items (18 and 42) were originally assigned to the factor of transactional leadership. Our respondents indicated that effective interpersonal behaviors were characterized by integrity, ethics, clear communications, knowing right from wrong, and communicating clear expectations for staff responsibilities.

Table 5 shows the loading factors, item numbers, and items for the interpersonal relations factor.

Table 5

Factor Loading, Interpersonal Relations

Factor Loading	Item Number	Item	h^2
.786	16	Training in the power of integrity in interpersonal relations is important.	.688
.715	24	Training in the fundamentals of ethics is important.	.654
.690	14	Training in the fundamentals of interpersonal communications is important.	.743
.662	12	Training in the importance of right and wrong as a foundation for all action is important.	.559
.621	18	Training in the ability to clearly communicate responsibilities to staff members is important.	.658
.613	36	Training in the application of ethics to my work is important.	.737
.602	42	Training in the ability to clarify expectations for staff performance is important.	.769

Financial Planning – The financial planning factor consists of eight items with loading factors ranging between .385 and .699. The eigenvalue is 2.34 and the percent of variance explained by the factor is 3.54. Table 6 presents items for the financial planning factor.

Table 6

Factor Loading, Financial Planning

Factor Loading	Item Number	Item	h^2
.699	29	Training in the strategic considerations for investing school district funds is important.	.725
.655	22	Training in the preparation of revenue projections is important.	.727
.648	27	Training in the regulatory parameters for investing school district funds is important.	.729
.617	25	Training in the strategic considerations for borrowing money is important.	.590
.560	33	Training in the maximization of current year revenues is important.	.585
.532	55	Training in the preparation of a technology plan for the acquisition and/or replacement of equipment and infrastructure in the future is important.	.729
.508	35	Training in the analysis of program costs is important.	.497
.385	19	Training in the fundamentals of purchasing is important.	.530

Financial Management – The factor of financial management consists of five items with loading factors ranging between .551 and .787. The eigenvalue is 1.92 and the percent of variance explained by the factor is 2.91. All five items were originally assigned to the financial planning factor. Our respondents believe that these behaviors are more basic financial management practices that ensure clear communications to constituents or investors about the budget, refinancing efforts, bond proposals and debt service. Table 7 shows the loading factors, item numbers, and items for the financial management factor.

Table 7

Factor Loading, Financial Management

Factor Loading	Item Number	Item	h2
.787	67	Training in the fundamentals of communicating with the community regarding the proposed budget is important.	.762
.692	63	Training in the fundamentals of proposed budget development is important.	.611
.619	69	Training in the projection of debt service expenditures is important.	.647
.592	73	Training in the strategic considerations for bond referendums, sales, and refinancing is important.	.637
.551	71	Training in the operational requirements for bond referendums, sales, and refinancing is important.	.747

Public Fund Accounting – The public fund accounting factor consists of five items with loading factors ranging between .570 and .765. The eigenvalue is 1.78 and the percent of variance explained by the factor is 2.69. Four of the five items (37, 39, 41, and 43) originally were assigned to the factor of financial management and one item (75) was originally assigned to the factor of financial planning. Our respondents noted for us a separate category that was important to their role as Chief Finance Officers (CFO) and that role was Public Fund Accounting. They noted that auditing financial statements, preparing financial statements, basic public fund accounting skills, internal auditing practices and the preparation of multi-year budgets were vital skills for the CFO.

Table 8 shows the loading factors, item numbers, and items for the public fund accounting factor.

Table 8

Factor Loading, Public Fund Accounting

Factor Loading	Item Number	Item	h2
.765	41	Training in the fundamentals of auditing the annual financial statements is important.	.720
.726	39	Training in the fundamentals of preparing the annual financial statements is important.	.792
.639	43	Training in the fundamentals of the internal audit function is important.	.646
.600	75	Training in the preparation of multi-year budgets is important.	.577
.570	37	Training in the fundamentals of public fund accounting is important.	.676

Financial Forecasting – The factor of financial forecasting consists of eight items with loading factors ranging between .517 and .823. The eigenvalue is 1.71 and the percent of variance explained by the factor is 2.60. Five of the items (11, 17, 21, 23, and 31) originally were assigned to the factor of financial management and three items (34, 57, and 59) were originally assigned the factor of financial planning. Our respondents demonstrated a belief that the public forecasting of financial obligations on a monthly basis was important. They prized very highly an ability to verify state aid calculations, the ability to execute a fair budget vote and trustee election, to manage payroll changes accurately, to monitor cash flow issues, to assess assets, borrow money, and anticipate changes in customer needs or student enrollments.

Table 9 shows the loading factors, item numbers, and items for the forecasting factor.

Table 9

Factor Loading, Financial Forecasting

Factor Loading	Item Number	Item	h2
.823	17	Training in the verification of aid calculations prepared by the State is important.	.739
.618	59	Training in the operational requirements for the annual meeting (budget vote and board election) is important.	.629
.555	11	Training in the preparation of monthly financial reports is important.	.562
.545	31	Training in the fundamentals of payroll administration is important.	.619
.535	21	Training in the preparation of cash flow reports is important.	.624
.519	23	Training in the regulatory parameters for borrowing money is important.	.547
.518	34	Training in the projection of district assessed valuation levels is important.	.562
.517	57	Training in the projection of student enrollment is important.	.673

Job Satisfaction – The 12 items within the job satisfaction factor on part three of the survey were subjected to a factor analysis using the data from the 87 surveys that were completed and returned. A Principal Components extraction method with an Equamax rotation procedure revealed that twelve items measured the job satisfaction of the respondents. The loading factors range between .523 and .740. The eigenvalue is 5.49, and the percent of variance explained by factor is 45.77. Our respondents revealed that their sense of job satisfaction related to relationships with peers and their supervisors, the members of the Board of Trustees, and the scope of their job. They noted that relationships with members of the community or the public at large were important, as were relationships with other administrators and the people whom they supervised. In studies by Mancini (2007) with private enterprise supervisors and Markowitz (2008) with newly hired nurses in a hospital system, relationships with peers and supervisors were highly related to the job satisfaction of employees. Table 10 shows the loading factors, item numbers, and items for the job satisfaction factor.

Table 10

Factor Loading, Job Satisfaction

Factor Loading	Item Number	Item	h2
.740	79	Overall, I am satisfied with my relationships with the other central office administrators.	.548
.737	88	Overall, I am satisfied with my job.	.543
.731	77	Overall, I am satisfied with the scope of my job.	.538
.726	78	Overall, I am satisfied with my relationship with my supervisor.	.527
.713	83	Overall, I am satisfied with my relationships with the members of the board of education.	.508
.702	84	Overall, I am satisfied with my relationships with the members of the community.	.492
.668	86	Overall, I am satisfied with the recognition I receive from my supervisor for my contributions to the success of the school district.	.446
.664	81	Overall, I am satisfied with my relationships with building administrators.	.441
.655	80	Overall, I am satisfied with my relationships with those whom I supervise.	.428
.630	82	Overall, I am satisfied with my relationships with program department administrators.	.397
.596	87	Overall, I am satisfied with the intellectual stimulation I receive from my job responsibilities.	.355
.523	85	Overall, I am satisfied with my compensation.	.273

Eliminated Items – As a result of the factor analysis, we renamed four of the seven factors and we gained insight into the working world of Chief Financial Officers in public schools. Several items from our original survey moved into different factors, and other items were eliminated from the scales of the study. Table 11 shows the items eliminated from the scales of the study because they had multiple factor loadings above .35 on more than two factors or they demonstrated that the items measured very closely more than one factor. The items that remained in the scales for this study did not reduce the scale reliability. Table 11 presents the items moved from the original scales.

Table 11

Items Eliminated from the Scales of the Study

Original Factor	Item #	Items
Financial Management	15	The preparation of State aid submissions
	45	The claims audit process
	47	The monitoring of current year revenues and expenses
	51	The evaluation of internal controls of financial activities
Financial Planning	46	The projection of program and staffing costs
	53	The preparation of a facilities plan for future necessary capital projects
	61	The preparation of a contingency budget
	65	The fundamentals of proposed budget presentation
Ethics	50	The recognizing and resolving ethical dilemmas
	68	The difference between ethics and personal values
Interpersonal Relations	26	The fundamentals of active listening
	38	The importance of establishing appropriate interpersonal boundaries
	56	The importance of empathy skills in interpersonal relations
	64	The power of being kind in interpersonal relations
Stewardship	70	The role of the leader as steward of the community's values and traditions
	58	The importance of committing to the development and achievement of a shared mission
	72	The identification of a community's core values
Transformational Leadership	20	The ability to motivate staff members to be creative and imaginative in the performance of their roles

Future researchers should revise the items that we eliminated from the scales in this study so that they could add to the analysis of Chief Financial Officers' work.

Reliability

After the factor analysis, the factors in this study were subjected to a reliability test to determine the internal consistency of each subscale. Cronbach Alpha Coefficients of internal consistency were calculated for each subscale using the data gathered from the respondents. These alpha coefficients ranged from .852 to .901 for the part of the items regarding importance and from .859 to .907 for the part of the items regarding the training that respondents received in their preparation programs for the role of Chief Financial Officer at various universities. These values appear in Table 2.

Description of the Subjects

The participants in this study were New York State certified school business administrators working as the chief school business administrator in public school districts within the suburban metropolitan region of New York. This region is comprised of all school districts within Suffolk, Nassau, Westchester, Rockland, and Putnam Counties. Surveys were mailed to 179 school districts in November 2008. Surveys were accepted for this study for approximately four weeks. Eighty-seven surveys were received and used in this study. These 87 responses yielded a response rate of 48.6 percent based on the full potential respondent population of 179 school districts. The entire school district population for New York State is 700.

Demographics of the Respondents

Of the 87 respondents, 22 (25.3 percent) reported possessing New York State certification as a school business administrator (SBA), 25 (28.7 percent) reported possessing certification as a school district administrator (SDA), 37 (42.5 percent) reported possessing both an SBA and an SDA, and 3 (3.4 percent) reported possessing certification as a school district business leader (SDBL). The New York State Education Department began issuing SDBL certification on or around September 2, 2007. These data are presented in Table 12.

Table 12

Demographics – Certification

		Frequency	Percent	Valid Percent	Cumulative Percent
Valid	SBA	22	25.3	25.3	25.3
	SDBL	3	3.4	3.4	28.7
	SDA	25	28.7	28.7	57.5
	SBA & SDA	37	42.5	42.5	100.0
	Total	87	100.0	100.0	

Respondents reported receiving their state certification as a school business administrator from 1974 to 2008. Of the 85 responses, 23 (27.1 percent) received their certification within the last 5 years, 46 (54.1) percent received their certification within the last 10 years, and 16 (18.8 percent) received their certification within the last 15 years. Two respondents did not report the year in which they received certification.

Forty-nine (56.3 percent) of the 87 respondents reported their gender as male, and 38 (43.7 percent) reported their gender as female. These data are presented in Table 13.

Table 13

Demographics – Gender

		Frequency	Percent	Valid Percent	Cumulative Percent
Valid	Male	49	56.3	56.3	56.3
	Female	38	43.7	43.7	100.0
	Total	87	100.0	100.0	

Of 86 responses, 2 (2.3 percent) reported their most closely related race / ethnic group as Asian or Native, 4 (4.6 percent) reported as Black or African American, 1 (1.1 percent) as Hispanic or Latino, and 79 (90.8 percent) as White. One respondent did not answer this question. These data are presented in Table 14.

The 85 responses regarding age ranged from 32 to 66 years old. Thirty (35.3 percent) of the respondents reported their age as 55 or older, while 24 (28.2 percent) reported being less than 45 years old. The mean age was 49.8 with a standard deviation of 7.9. Two respondents did not answer this question.

Table 14

Demographics – Race / Ethnic Group

		Frequency	Percent	Valid Percent	Cumulative Percent
Valid	Asian or Native	2	2.3	2.3	2.3
	Black or African American	4	4.6	4.7	7.0
	Hispanic or Latino	1	1.1	1.2	8.1
	White	79	90.8	91.9	100.0
	Total	86	98.9	100.0	
Missing	System	1	1.1		
Total		87	100.0		

The 87 responses regarding the number of years the respondents had served as a chief school business administrator ranged from 1 month to 34 years. Thirty-seven (42.5 percent) respondents reported serving as a chief school business administrator for 5 years or less, 55 (63.2 percent) reported serving for 10 years or less, and 68 (78.2 percent) reported serving for 15 years or less. The mean years of service as a chief school business administrator was 9.8 with a standard deviation of 8.0. The number of years the respondents had served as the chief school business administrator in their current school district ranged from 1 month to 23 years. Thirty-eight (43.7 percent) of the respondents reported serving in their school districts for two years or less, 53 (60.9 percent) reported serving for three years or less, and 69 (74.7 percent) reported serving for five years or less. The mean number of years served as a chief school business administrator with their current district was 4.5 with a standard deviation of 4.7. The 86 useable responses regarding the amount of the annual budget of the districts in which the respondents worked ranged from 5.8 million dollars to 294.5 million dollars. The mean annual budget amount was 85.8 million with a standard deviation of 55.3 million.

Table 15

Demographics – Total Budget for Fiscal Year 2008-2009 in Millions of Dollars

Millions		Frequency	Percent	Valid Percent	Cumulative Percent
Valid	< 5	1	1.1	1.1	1.1
	5 – 9.9	3	3.4	3.4	4.6
	15 – 19.9	1	1.1	1.1	5.7
	20 – 24.9	1	1.1	1.1	6.9
	25 – 29.9	2	2.3	2.3	9.2
	30 – 34.9	5	5.7	5.7	14.9
	35 – 39.9	1	1.1	1.1	16.1
	40 – 44.9	8	9.2	9.2	25.3
	45 – 49.9	3	3.4	3.4	28.7
	50 – 54.9	6	6.9	6.9	35.6
	55 – 59.9	4	4.6	4.6	40.2
	60 – 64.9	2	2.3	2.3	42.5
	65 – 69.9	6	6.9	6.9	49.4
	70 – 74.9	5	5.7	5.7	55.2
	75 – 79.9	5	5.7	5.7	60.9
	90 – 94.9	3	3.4	3.4	64.4
	95 – 99.9	3	3.4	3.4	67.8
	100 – 109.9	3	3.4	3.4	71.3
	110 – 119.9	2	2.3	2.3	73.6
	120 – 129.9	4	4.6	4.6	78.2
	130 – 139.9	3	3.4	3.4	81.6
	140 – 149.9	3	3.4	3.4	85.1
	150 – 159.9	3	3.4	3.4	88.5
	160 – 169.9	1	1.1	1.1	89.7
	170 – 179.9	3	3.4	3.4	93.1
	180 – 189.9	1	1.1	1.1	94.3
	190 – 199.9	4	4.6	4.6	98.9
	290 – 299.9	1	1.1	1.1	100.0
	Total	87	100.0	100.0	

How does a purposeful sample of New York State certified school business administrators differ in their perceptions of their actual preparation and the importance of the preparation as school business administrators in the dimensions of stewardship, leadership skills, interpersonal relations, financial planning, financial management, public fund accounting, and forecasting? A paired sample t-test of related means analysis was utilized to assess if school business administrators differed significantly between their perceptions of the importance of their preparation and their actual preparation in the factors of stewardship, leadership skills, interpersonal relations, financial planning, financial management, public fund accounting, and forecasting.

Table 16 shows the results for each of the seven factors of stewardship, leadership skills, interpersonal relations, financial planning, financial management, public fund accounting, and forecasting. The letter 'i' designates the part of the item measuring the importance for success in the respondents' professional roles and the letter 'r' designates the part of the item measuring the actual training reported as having been received by the respondents. In addition to the raw mean scores, arithmetic or average mean scores (*AM*) and arithmetic mean score differences (*AMD*) are reported for each factor to enable comparison between factors. In each of the seven factors, the difference between the importance of the preparation and the preparation actually received was significant at the *p* < .01 level. The respondents both somewhat agreed or agreed that training in each of these factors was important for success in their professional roles and they disagreed to somewhat agreed that they received training in these areas in preparation for their certification. The difference in the mean scores for importance of the training and actual training received for each factor, ranged from 1.21 response categories on the 5-point Likert scale for the factor of leadership disposition of stewardship to a difference of 1.98 response categories for the factor of public fund accounting. Sadly, these CFOs felt they were not prepared by their professional schools for the job they had to do.

Table 16

Paired Sample t-Test Comparing the Importance of Preparation with the Actual Preparation Received

Factor	Item Part	N	*M*	*AM*	*AMD*	*SD*	*t*	*Df*	*p*
Leadership Disposition of Stewardship	i	83	19.94	3.99	1.21	3.75	10.86	82	.000
	r	83	13.89	2.78		5.26			
Leadership Skills	i	84	39.08	3.91	1.49	6.60	15.12	83	.000
	r	84	24.21	2.42		8.21			
Interpersonal Relations	i	83	31.63	4.52	1.25	3.56	12.88	82	.000
	r	83	22.87	3.27		6.43			
Financial Planning	i	82	33.39	4.17	1.82	4.67	15.56	81	.000
	r	82	18.82	2.35		7.51			
Financial Management	i	86	21.53	4.31	1.82	2.96	14.51	85	.000
	r	86	12.44	2.49		5.14			
Public Fund Accounting	i	84	20.65	4.13	1.98	3.66	15.29	83	.000
	r	84	10.77	2.15		5.03			
Forecasting	i	82	31.91	3.99	1.84	5.15	15.82	81	.000
	r	82	17.20	2.15		7.05			

Correlation Analysis

The items within the factors of leadership disposition of stewardship, leadership skills, interpersonal relations, financial planning, financial management, public fund accounting, and forecasting consisted of two parts. One part measured the degree to which respondents felt training in the factors listed above is important to success in their professional roles. The part of the items related to importance is designated with the suffix 'i'. The other part measured the degree to which respondents felt they received actual training in the factors listed above. The part of the items related to actual training received the suffix 'r'.

The legend for the abbreviations of the eight factors on Tables 17 through 35 appears below.
- JS – Job Satisfaction
- LDS – Leadership Disposition of Stewardship
- LS – Leadership Skills
- IR – Interpersonal Relations
- FP – Financial Planning
- FM – Financial Management
- PFA – Public Fund Accounting
- F – Forecasting

The legend for the questions on Tables 4.183 through 4.201 appears below.
- Q9 – What is your district's total budget for the 2008-09 fiscal year?
- Q10 – What is your district's total BEDS enrollment for the 2008-09 fiscal year?
- Q6 – What is your age?
- Q7 – How many years have you been a chief school business administrator?
- Q8 – How many years have you served as chief school business administrator in your current district?

For this correlation analysis, effect size was considered small for r^2 between .05 and .20, effect size was considered moderate for r^2 between .20 and .40, and effect size was considered large for r^2 equal to or above .40. Items with r^2 of less than .05 were not considered important enough to report. Research question two was answered through a binary correlation analysis and a t-test for gender differences.

Relationships – Importance of Training

As Table 17 shows, of the seven major independent variables and the five demographic items measured, only two were correlated with the dependent variable of job satisfaction at a level worthy of reporting. Those two variables were the perception that training in the leadership disposition of stewardship ($r^2 = .06$) was important and the perception that training in interpersonal relations ($r^2 = .08$) was important.

Table 17

Correlation Matrix for Importance of Training

	JS	LDSi	LSi	IRi	FPi	FMi	PFAi	Fi	Q9	Q10	Q6	Q7	Q8
JS	1.00												
LDSi r	.25	1.00											
r^2	.06												
LSi r	.18	.72	1.00										
r^2	.03	.52											
IRi r	.29	.62	.59	1.00									
r^2	.08	.62	.35										
FPi r	.18	.48	.60	.37	1.00								
r^2	.03	.23	.36	.14									
FMi r	.12	.31	.47	.37	.68	1.00							
r^2	.01	.10	.22	.14	.46								
PFAi r	.14	.32	.51	.24	.68	.56	1.00						
r^2	.02	.10	.26	.06	.46	.31							
Fi r	.09	.43	.53	.29	.75	.62	.70	1.00					
r^2	.01	.18	.28	.08	.56	.38	.49						
Q9 r	.18	.10	-.07	-.14	-.10	-.17	-.25	-.18	1.00				
r^2	.03	.01	.00	.02	.01	.03	.06	.03					
Q10 r	.16	.09	-.00	.11	-.05	-.11	-.20	-.08	.96	1.00			
r^2	.03	.01	.00	.01	.00	.01	.04	.01	.92				
Q6 r	.10	.22	.16	.03	.13	.06	.02	.09	-.04	-.12	1.00		
r^2	.01	.05	.03	.00	.02	.00	.01	.01	.00	.01			
Q7 r	.12	.04	.08	-.03	-.01	.11	-.09	-.18	-.13	-.02	.58	1.00	
r^2													

.01	.00	.01	.00	.00	.01	.01	.03	.02	.00	.34	
Q8 r	r -	r -	r	r	r -	r	r -	r -	r -	r	1.00
.15	.03	.01	.01	.13	.01	.03	.10	.10	.11	.21	.53
r^2	r^2	r^2	r^2	r^2	r^2	r^2	r^2	r^2	r^2	r^2	r^2
.02	.00	.00	.00	.02	.00	.00	.01	.01	.01	.04	.28

The data presented in Tables 17 indicate that a sense of importance assigned to training in the factors of leadership disposition of stewardship, leadership skills, and interpersonal relations was related to job satisfaction. As shown in Table 17, the perception that training in the leadership disposition of stewardship was important was positively correlated with job satisfaction ($r^2 = .06$), leadership skills ($r^2 = .52$), interpersonal relations ($r^2 = .39$), financial planning ($r^2 = .23$), public fund accounting ($r^2 = .10$), and forecasting ($r^2 = .18$). Item Q6 (respondents' age) was also positively correlated ($r^2 = .05$).

As shown in Table 18, there was a weak negative correlation ($r^2 = .06$) between the size of district budgets and the perceived importance of training in public fund accounting. There was a weak positive correlation ($r^2 = .05$) between the respondents' ages and the perceived importance of training in leadership disposition of stewardship.

Table 18

Correlation Matrix for Importance of Training and Selected Demographic Items

	JS	LDSi	LSi	IRi	FPi	FMi	PFAi	Fi	Q9	Q10	Q6	Q7	Q8
Q9	r	r -	r -	r -	r -	r -	r -	r -	1.00				
	.18	.10	.07	.14	.10	.18	.25	.18					
	r^2	r^2	r^2	r^2	r^2	r^2	r^2	r^2					
	.03	.01	.00	.02	.01	.03	.06	.03					
Q10	r	r -	r	r	r -	r -	r -	r -	r	1.00			
	.16	.09	.00	.11	.05	.11	.20	.08	.96				
	r^2	r^2	r^2	r^2	r^2	r^2	r^2	r^2	r^2				
	.03	.01	.00	.01	.00	.01	.04	.01	.92				
Q6	r	r	r	r	r	r	r	r -	r -	r -	1.00		
	.10	.22	.16	.03	.13	.06	.02	.09	.04	.12			
	r^2	r^2	r^2	r^2	r^2	r^2	r^2	r^2	r^2	r^2			
	.01	.05	.03	.00	.02	.00	.01	.01	.00	.01			
Q7	r	r	r -	r -	r	r -	r -	r -	r	r	r	1.00	
	.12	.04	.08	.03	.01	.11	.09	.18	.13	.02	.58		
	r^2	r^2	r^2	r^2	r^2	r^2	r^2	r^2	r^2	r^2	r^2		
	.01	.00	.01	.00	.00	.01	.01	.03	.02	.00	.34		
Q8	r	r -	r -	r	r	r -	r	r -	r -	r -	r	r	1.00
	.15	.03	.01	.01	.13	.01	.03	.10	.10	.11	.21	.53	
	r^2	r^2	r^2	r^2	r^2	r^2	r^2	r^2	r^2	r^2	r^2	r^2	
	.02	.00	.00	.00	.02	.00	.00	.01	.01	.01	.04	.28	

As shown in Table 19, training in leadership skills and stewardship actually were positively correlated ($r^2 = .06$ and .04 respectively) with job satisfaction.

114

Table 19

Correlation Matrix for Actual Training Received

	JS	LDSr	LSr	IRr	FPr	FMr	PFAr	Fr	Q9	Q10	Q6	Q7	Q8
JS	1.00												
LDSr	r	1.00											
	.20												
	r²												
	.04												
LSr	r	r	1.00										
	.24	.78											
	r²	r²											
	.06	.61											
IRr	r	r	r	1.00									
	.07	.80	.72										
	r²	r²	r²										
	.00	.64	.52										
FPr	r -	r	r	r	1.00								
	.04	.39	.52	.40									
	r²	r²	r²	r²									
	.00	.15	.27	.16									
FMr	r	r	r	r	r	1.00							
	.11	.29	.46	.35	.81								
	r²	r²	r²	r²	r²								
	.01	.08	.21	.12	.66								
PFAr	r	r	r	r	r	r	1.00						
	.11	.26	.49	.21	.80	.76							
	r²	r²	r²	r²	r²	r²							
	.01	.07	.24	.04	.64	.58							
Fr	r	r	r	r	r	r	r	1.00					
	.06	.36	.53	.44	.91	.82	.75						
	r²	r²	r²	r²	r²	r²	r²						
	.00	.13	.28	.19	.83	.67	.56						
Q9	r	r -	r -	r -	r -	r -	r -	r -	1.00				
	.18	.19	.18	.27	.07	.06	.07	.04					
	r²	r²	r²	r²	r²	r²	r²	r²					
	.03	.04	.03	.07	.00	.00	.00	.00					
Q10	r	r -	r -	r -	r -	r -	r -	r	r	1.00			
	.16	.20	.18	.24	.07	.04	.01	.14	.96				
	r²	r²	r²	r²	r²	r²	r²	r²	r²				
	.03	.04	.03	.06	.00	.00	.00	.00	.92				
Q6	r	r	r	r -	r -	r -	r -	r -	r -	r -	1.00		
	.10	.04	.03	.04	.15	.14	.07	.17	.04	.12			
	r²	r²	r²	r²	r²	r²	r²	r²	r²	r²			
	.01	.00	.00	.00	.02	.02	.00	.03	.00	.01			
Q7	r	r -	r -	r -	r	r	r	r -	r	r	r	1.00	

.12	.09	.08	.16	.02	.03	.12	.04	.13	.02	.58			
r^2	r^2	r^2	r^2	r^2	r^2	r^2	r^2	r^2	r^2	r^2			
.01	.01	.01	.03	.00	.00	.01	.00	.02	.00	.34			
Q8 r	r	$-r$	$-r$	$-r$	r	r	r	r	$-r$	$-r$	r	1.00	
.15	.13	.06	.21	.11	.11	.25	.01	.10	.11	.21	.53		
r^2	r^2	r^2	r^2	r^2	r^2	r^2	r^2	r^2	r^2	r^2	r^2		
.02	.02	.00	.04	.01	.01	.06	.00	.01	.01	.04	.28		

As shown in Table 20, training in the leadership disposition of stewardship received was positively correlated with leadership skills ($r^2 = .61$), interpersonal relations ($r^2 = .64$), financial planning ($r^2 = .15$), financial management ($r^2 = .08$), public fund accounting ($r^2 = .07$), and forecasting ($r^2 = .13$). Stewardship is a vital foundation for effective financial leaders.

Table 20

Correlation Matrix for Actual Training Received in Leadership Dimension of Stewardship

	JS	LDSr	LSr	IRr	FPr	FMr	PFAr	Fr	Q9	Q10	Q6	Q7	Q8
LDSr r		1.00	r	r	r	r	r	r	r $-$	r $-$	r	r $-$	r $-$
	.20		.78	.80	.39	.29	.26	.36	.19	.20	.04	.09	.13
r^2	r^2		r^2	r^2	r^2	r^2	r^2	r^2	r^2	r^2	r^2	r^2	r^2
	.04		.61	.64	.15	.08	.07	.13	.04	.04	.00	.01	.02

In Table 21, training in leadership skills received was positively correlated with job satisfaction ($r^2 = .06$), leadership disposition of stewardship ($r^2 = .61$), interpersonal relations ($r^2 = .52$), financial planning ($r^2 = .27$), financial management ($r^2 = .21$), public fund accounting ($r^2 = .24$), and forecasting ($r^2 = .28$).

Table 21

Correlation Matrix for Actual Training Received in Leadership Skills

	JS	LDSr	LSr	IRr	FPr	FMr	PFAr	Fr	Q9	Q10	Q6	Q7	Q8
LSr r	r	r	1.00	r	r	r	r	r	r $-$	r $-$	r	r $-$	r $-$
	.24	.78		.72	.52	.46	.49	.53	.18	.18	.03	.08	.06
r^2	r^2	r^2		r^2	r^2	r^2	r^2	r^2	r^2 $-$	r^2	r^2	r^2	r^2
	.06	.61		.52	.27	.21	.24	.28	.03	.03	.00	.01	.00

As shown in Table 22, the perception that training in interpersonal relations was received was positively correlated with the leadership disposition of stewardship ($r^2 = .64$), leadership skills ($r^2 = .52$), financial planning ($r^2 = .16$), financial management ($r^2 = .12$), and forecasting ($r^2 = .19$). The perception that training in interpersonal relations was received just missed being positively correlated public fund accounting ($r^2 = .04$. The perception that training in interpersonal relations was received was negatively correlated with the size of district budgets ($r^2 = .07$) and amount of student enrollment ($r^2 = .06$).

Table 22

Correlation Matrix for Actual Training Received in Interpersonal Relations

	JS	LDSr	LSr	IRr	FPr	FMr	PFAr	Fr	Q9	Q10	Q6	Q7	Q8
IRr r	.07	.80	.72	1.00	.40	.35	.21	.44	.27	.24	.04	.16	-.21
r^2	.00	.64	.52		.16	.12	.04	.19	.07	.06	.00	.03	.04

As shown in Table 23, the perception that training in financial planning was received was positively correlated with the leadership disposition of stewardship ($r^2 = .15$), leadership skills ($r^2 = .27$), interpersonal relations ($r^2 = .16$), financial management ($r^2 = .66$), public fund accounting ($r^2 = .64$), and forecasting ($r^2 = .83$).

Table 23

Correlation Matrix for Actual Training Received in Financial Planning

	JS	LDSr	LSr	IRr	FPr	FMr	PFAr	Fr	Q9	Q10	Q6	Q7	Q8
FPr r	-.04	.39	.52	.40	1.00	.81	.80	.91	-.07	-.07	-.15	.02	.11
r^2	.00	.15	.27	.16		.66	.64	.83	.00	.00	.02	.00	.01

As shown in Table 24, the perception that training in financial management was received was positively correlated with the leadership disposition of stewardship ($r^2 = .08$), leadership skills ($r^2 = .21$), interpersonal relations ($r^2 = .12$), financial planning ($r^2 = .66$), public fund accounting ($r^2 = .58$), and forecasting ($r^2 = .67$).

Table 24

Correlation Matrix for Actual Training Received in Financial Management

	JS	LDSr	LSr	IRr	FPr	FMr	PFAr	Fr	Q9	Q10	Q6	Q7	Q8
FMr r	.11	.29	.46	.35	.81	1.00	.76	.82	-.06	-.04	-.14	.03	.11
r^2	.01	.08	.21	.12	.66		.58	.67	.00	.00	.02	.00	.01

As shown in Table 25, the perception that training in public fund accounting was received was positively correlated with the leadership disposition of stewardship ($r^2 = .07$), leadership skills ($r^2 = .24$), financial planning ($r^2 = .64$), financial management ($r^2 = .58$), and forecasting ($r^2 = .56$). The perception that training in public fund accounting was received just missed being positively correlated with interpersonal relations ($r^2 = .04$). The perception that training in public fund accounting was received was positively correlated with the number of years respondents had served as chief school business administrator within their current districts ($r^2 = .06$).

Table 25

Correlation Matrix for Actual Training Received in Public Fund Accounting

	JS	LDSr	LSr	IRr	FPr	FMr	PFAr	Fr	Q9	Q10	Q6	Q7	Q8
PFAr	r	r	r	r	r	r	1.00	r	r	$-r$	$-r$	$-r$	r
	.11	.26	.49	.21	.80	.76		.75	.07	.01	.07	.12	.25
	r^2	r^2	r^2	r^2	r^2	r^2		r^2	r^2	r^2	r^2	r^2	r^2
	.01	.07	.24	.04	.64	.58		.56	.00	.00	.00	.01	.06

As shown in table 26, the perception that training in forecasting was received was positively correlated with the leadership disposition of stewardship ($r^2 = .13$), leadership skills ($r^2 = .28$), interpersonal relations ($r^2 = .19$), financial planning ($r^2 = .83$), financial management ($r^2 = .67$), and public fund accounting ($r^2 = .56$).

Table 26

Correlation Matrix for Actual Training Received in Forecasting

	JS	LDSr	LSr	IRr	FPr	FMr	PFAr	Fr	Q9	Q10	Q6	Q7	Q8
Fr	r	r	r	r	r	r	r	1.00	r	$-r$	r	$-r$	$-r$
	.06	.36	.53	.44	.91	.82	.75		.04	.14	.17	.04	.01
	r^2	r^2	r^2	r^2	r^2	r^2	r^2		r^2	r^2	r^2	r^2	r^2
	.00	.13	.28	.19	.83	.67	.56		.00	.00	.03	.00	.00

Gender Analysis

An independent sample t-test was conducted to determine if there was any significant difference between the male and female reports that training within the factors of leadership disposition of stewardship, leadership skills, interpersonal relations, financial planning, financial management, public fund accounting, forecasting was important, and job satisfaction based on gender. The test was significant, $t(85) = 2.07$, $p = .04$ for the factor of financial management. The test indicates that males ($M = 20.94$, $SD = 3.11$) on average reported that training in the factor of financial management was important less often than did females ($M = 22.24$, $SD = 2.59$). Table 27 presents these results. Two interesting demographic observations should be noted here.

One, the female population of School District Chief Financial Officers rose from less than two percent to 44 percent in the last twenty years and two, 90 percent of the CFOs are white. Diversity among CFOs remains an issue in New York State in 2008.

Table 27

Independent Sample t-Test for Gender, Importance of Training, and Job Satisfaction

Factor	t	df	Sig. (2-tailed)	Mean Difference
Leadership Disposition of Stewardship	-.57	83	.573	-.47
Leadership Skills	-.66	85	.514	-.94
Interpersonal Relations	-1.33	83	.186	-1.03
Financial Planning	-1.64	81	.106	-1.67
Financial Management	-2.07	85	.041	-1.30
Public Fund Accounting	-1.79	84	.077	-1.39
Forecasting	-1.36	82	.177	-1.55
Job Satisfaction	-.16	83	.877	-.21

Regression Analysis

Research question three asked: How do school districts budget size, student enrollment inside a school district; age of the school business administrator; length of the school business administrators' time in the role and in the district; school business administrators' perceptions of their actual preparation and its importance in leadership disposition of stewardship, leadership skills, interpersonal relations, financial planning, financial management, public fund accounting, and forecasting predict the job satisfaction of practicing New York State certified school business administrators?

Regression analysis evaluated how well these independent variables predicted the dependent variable of Job Satisfaction. The items within the factors of leadership disposition of stewardship, leadership skills, interpersonal relations, financial planning, financial management, public fund accounting, and forecasting consisted of two parts. One part measured the degree to which respondents felt training in the factors listed above is important to success in their professional roles. The part of the items related to importance is designated with the suffix 'i'. The other part measured the degree to which respondents felt they received actual training in the factors listed above. The part of the items related to the reception of actual training is designated with the suffix 'r'.

Table 28

Regression Analysis of Perceived Importance of Major Variables as Predictors of Job Satisfaction

Model Summary

Model	R	R Square	Adjusted R Square	Std. Error of The Estimate	R Square Change	F Change	df1	df2	Sig. F Change
					Change Statistics				
1	.254[a]	.065	.053	5.95017	.065	5.449	1	79	.022

Predictors: (Constant), LDSi

ANOVA[b]

Model		Sum of Squares	df	Mean Square	F	Sig.
1	Regression	192.921	1	192.921	5.449	.022[a]
	Residual	2796.956	79	35.405		
	Total	2989.877	80			

Predictors: (Constant), LDSi
Dependent Variable: JS

Coefficients[a]

Model		Unstandardized Coefficients		Standardized Coefficients		
		B	Std. Error	Beta	T	Sig.
1	(Constant)	41.353	3.581		11.549	.000
	LDSi	.409	.175	.254	2.334	.022

Dependent Variable: JS

Table 28 indicates that the respondents' perception that training in the factor of the leadership disposition of stewardship was important for success in their professional roles, accounted for 6.5 percent of the variance in their sense of job satisfaction. This relationship is significant at the $p = .02$ level (F5.449, $p = .022$).

Table 29 indicates that the respondents' perception of receiving actual training in the factor of leadership skills accounted for 5.1 percent of the variance in their sense of job satisfaction. This relationship was significant at the $p = .05$ level (F4.161, $p = .045$).

Table 29

Regression Analysis of Actual Receipt of Training in Major Variables as Predictors of Job Satisfaction

Model Summary

Model	R	R Square	Adjusted R Square	Std. Error of The Estimate	Change Statistics				
					R Square Change	F Change	df1	df2	Sig. F Change
1	.226[a]	.051	.039	6.08146	.051	4.161	1	77	.045

Predictors: (Constant), LSr

ANOVA[b]

Model		Sum of Squares	df	Mean Square	F	Sig.
1	Regression	153.887	1	153.887	4.161	.045[a]
	Residual	2847.784	77	36.984		
	Total	3001.671	78			

Predictors: (Constant), LSr
Dependent Variable: JS

Coefficients[a]

Model		Unstandardized Coefficients		Standardized Coefficients		
		B	Std. Error	Beta	T	Sig.
1	(Constant)	45.463	2.109		21.560	.000
	LSr	.168	.082	.226	2.040	.045

Dependent Variable: JS

Conclusions

School Business Administrators who serve in the role of Chief Financial Officer for school districts in New York should possess the requisite technical finance and leadership skills, as well as the appropriate disposition of stewardship to perform their modern roles. Their ethical foundation and interpersonal relationship skills need to develop if they are to establish a level of employee trust necessary for collaborative leadership (Kouzes and Posner, 1993; Rebore, 2001). School district CFOs in our study expressed a strong disposition towards stewardship where a spirit of generosity, selflessness, and a general purpose to serve others informed all of their actions.

In this study, our respondents combined transactional and transformational leader behaviors into a construct that we termed as general leader behaviors. These leader behaviors were associated with constructs that were in the best interest of all affected stakeholders and the mission of the enterprise (Burns, 1978).

As the complexity of the expectations and responsibilities that school business administrators face continue to grow they will need to be prepared with extensive financial skills, ethical dispositions, and interpersonal, communication, and leadership skills. Our respondents separated their financial responsibilities into four categories: financial management, financial planning, financial fund accounting and financial forecasting skills. They expressed a need for training in all four areas.

The related literature on leadership makes clear that leadership has to be practiced across a continuum of transactional, managerial, and transformational behaviors mixed with a high sense of personal integrity and ethics (Burns, 1978; Greenleaf, 1997). The literature also identified moral leadership as positively related to job satisfaction (Herzberg, 1966; and Greenleaf, 1997).

Job Satisfaction

School business administrators were less satisfied with compensation ($M = 3.62$, $SD = 1.00$) and most satisfied with relationships with other central office administrators ($M = 4.34$, $SD = .66$). This data supports Herzberg's (1966) hygiene theory of job satisfaction. Herzberg classified compensation as a dissatisfier, which has both a unidirectional and short-term effect on job satisfaction. Two conclusions result from this data. The first is that, while school business administrators on average failed to agree that they were satisfied with their compensation, they were compensated at levels that did not result in dissatisfaction with their jobs. The second is that the satisfiers – job content – were positive enough to cause the school business administrators to agree that they were satisfied with their jobs in spite of some level of dissatisfaction with their compensation.

Superintendents of school districts and school boards who want to keep their school business administrators satisfied with their jobs should continue to develop the leadership skills of their administrator and continue to involve the business administrator in the long-term development of the school district (Syptak, Marsland & Ulmer, 1999). In addition, superintendents and the Board of Education should provide a very positive work environment, assign their school business administrator challenging and meaningful work and recognize their contributions. Boards of trustees should note that no amount of money will determine positive job satisfaction for school business administrators if they are not satisfied with the nature of their work. On the other hand, too low compensation can become a source of dissatisfaction.

Gibson, Ivancevich, Donnelly, & Konopaske (2003) noted how job dissatisfaction leads to lower employee productivity. In the current financial decline in funds for education, school districts should pay more attention to assuring the job satisfaction of their school business administrators.

Herzberg (1966) identified job satisfaction as the moral responsibility of business leaders, and by extension, government leaders. In a practical sense, high levels of job satisfaction result in greater organizational efficiency and effectiveness (Gibson et al, 2003). The literature is clear that job satisfaction is an important part of the effectiveness and efficiency of employees (Syptak, Marsland & Ulmer, 1999).

In addition, school business administrators who understand the importance of training in leadership skills and stewardship are more likely to have staff members who are satisfied with their jobs, thereby resulting in increased success of those school business administrators. Chief Financial Officers require continuous development as leaders as do all executives.

Interpersonal Relations, Stewardship, and Leadership Training

School business administrators identified interpersonal relations as an important factor for success in their professional roles. Murphy (1997) identified interpersonal relations as the greatest challenge for school business administrators transitioning into their roles.

Glass et al. (1998) identified these technical financial skills as being of highest priority to school business administrators. The Glass study relied on school business administrators to prioritize their daily tasks. Those tasks resulted in 16 skill areas:

- Accounting
- Property Management
- Risk Management
- Purchasing
- Data Processing
- Auditing
- Salary Administration
- Finance
- Federal Programs
- Special Education
- Cash Management
- Budget Planning
- Facilities
- Auxiliary Services
- Collective Bargaining
- Strategic Planning

Only one of those areas, strategic planning, is a true leadership skill. The school business administrators who participated in our 2008 study agreed that training in the leadership disposition of stewardship, general leadership skills and interpersonal relations was important for success in their professional roles.

The gain in importance assigned to leadership skills found in our study supports DiBella's (1999) contention that chief finance officers and chief school business administrators operate in an environment in which they must be both financial leaders and financial technicians within their organizations.

Even though training in leadership skills was considered more important in our study than in the Glass 1998 study, school business administrators still considered training in technical financial skills to be more important than training in leadership skills.

The literature suggests that training in the leadership disposition of stewardship and general leadership skills that include transactional and transformational capacities would be necessary for current CFO's in school districts.

Burns (1978) described transactional leadership as necessary within a continuum of moral and transformational leadership. He believed that moral leadership was more about the care of others and the purpose of the institution than it was about the leader's desires. More recently, Greenleaf (1997) described the moral leader as servant to the needs of the followers and the institution's long-term goals.

A fresh critical look is being taken at the issues of power and authority, and people are beginning to learn, however haltingly, to relate to one another in less coercive and more creatively supporting ways. A new moral principle is emerging, which holds that the only authority deserving one's allegiance is that which is freely and knowingly granted by the led to the leader in response to, and in proportion to, the clearly evident servant stature of the leader. (Greenleaf, 1997, pp. 23-24)

If stewardship is a leader's commitment to core democratic values and principles (Bredeson, 2004, p. 710), we have much work to do in the preparation of chief financial officers for school districts.

College Curriculum and Internship Needs

All colleges and universities that prepare school business administrators for the role of Chief Financial Officer must evaluate their curriculum so that their graduates are prepared better for the challenges that they will meet in the public sector of school finance.

School district business administrators identified the technical skills of financial planning, financial management, public fund accounting, and forecasting as more important than the leadership disposition of stewardship and general leadership skills. Yet, the technical skills did not predict job satisfaction.

These findings are interesting because administrators report financial skills as most important for their success in their job, and they report stewardship and general leadership skills as predictors of their job satisfaction. This dichotomy between what school business administrators reported as being important for success and what predicted their job satisfaction is similar to Herzberg's (1966) two-factor motivation theory. The technical financial skills are hygiene factors that must be present in a chief finance officer or their weaknesses become dissatisfiers. A lack of technical skills may lead to the loss of a school business administrator's position. The technical skills are necessary for job success. One's job satisfaction is more dependent on content, or satisfiers, elements of leadership where one serves a desired vision, a clear mission, and purpose that come together among people bound together by positive interpersonal relations and trust.

Mancini (2007) found that individualized consideration, intellectual stimulation, and inspirational motivation accounted for the variance within job satisfaction in for-profit enterprises.

Motivating employees to perform at their best is one of management's most constant and elusive challenges. Nohria, Groysberg, and Lee (2008) reported, "It's hard to argue with the accepted wisdom – backed by empirical evidence – that a motivated workforce means better corporate performance" (p. 80).

In our study, school business administrators seemed unaware of the positive impact that job satisfaction would have on their departments' productivity and/or the positive impact that enhanced leadership skills and stewardship would have on the job satisfaction of their staff members. This suggests that one of the changes to the certification preparation curriculum should be that students be educated about the importance of leadership skills and stewardship for success in their professional roles.

The certification preparation and finance curriculum should focus on improving the internship experience for all candidates. Selecting cooperating administrators who are experienced, successful, chief school or executive finance officers will not ensure they are able to mentor new business administrators. Mentors have to be trained in the art of mentoring not just the knowledge of their job. The internship experience for each graduate student should be customized within a standardized framework to optimize the experience to fit with the student's existing background, dispositions, and skills. This customized internship experience should be negotiated with the cooperating administrator and then memorialized in writing between the school district, the student, and the institution of higher education.

Ideally, the internship should last for at least one full 12-month business cycle. Since the internship is the SDBL or MBA student's opportunity to apply in a real setting the abstract or theoretical knowledge acquired from the coursework, the internship should be the final or culminating activity in the program.

Schools of Higher Education and school districts should assure that their current school business administrators receive training in the seven factors identified as being important in this study:

- Leadership Disposition of Stewardship
- Leadership Skills
- Interpersonal Relations
- Financial Planning
- Financial Management
- Public Fund Accounting
- Forecasting

Institutions of higher education and other organizations that provide professional development to school business administrators should adjust their continuing education programs and offerings to include online supplemental materials to assist school business administrators with their continuing professional development.

School business administrators should use the findings in this study to self assess both their attitudes regarding what is important and any deficits in training they may have as they design and implement a professional development program specific to their needs. At a minimum, school business administrators should revisit their attitudes regarding the importance of leadership skills and dispositions with regard to the effect those attitudes may have on the job satisfaction, and the resulting effectiveness and efficiency of their staff members.

Discussion Questions

What preparation would you require for Chief Financial Officers in your preferred industry and country? Why?
What would you emphasize in the continual development of financial executives in your organization? Why?

References

Acton, E. S. (2007). Finance: The changing role of the CFO. *Detroit Regional Chamber.* Retrieved on August 5, 2008 from
http://www.detroitchamber.com/detroiter/articles.asp?cid=7&detcid=320

Argyris, C. (1957). *Personality and organization: The conflict between the system and the individual.* New York: Harper & Brothers Publishers.

Avolio, B., & Bass, B. M. (1994). *Improving organizational effectiveness through transformational leadership.* Thousand Oaks, CA: Sage Publications.

Barwise, P., & Meehan, S. (2008). So you think you're a good listener. *Harvard Business Review,* April, p. 22.

Bass, B. M., & Riggio, R. E. (2006). *Transformational leadership (2nd ed.).* Mahwah, NJ: Lawrence Erlbaum Associates Publishers.

Bredeson, P.V. (2004). Creating spaces for the development of democratic school leaders: A case of program redesign in the United States. *Journal of Educational Administration, 42(6), (708-723).*

Burak, M. (2006). *Governance practices, teamwork, effectiveness, and curriculum responsibilities in urban and suburban school board members in the northeast region of the United States.* Doctoral dissertation, Dowling College, Oakdale, New York.

Burns, J. M. (1978). *Leadership.* New York, NY: Harper & Row Publishers.

Calandro, J. & Flynn, R. (2007). On financial strategy. *Business Strategy Series, 8(6), (409-417).*

Carver, J. (2002). *On board leadership.* San Francisco, CA: Jossey-Bass Publishers.

Chen, J. A. (2007). *The role of school boards, their governance practices and sense of effectiveness in suburban, urban, and rural settings in the United States.* Doctoral dissertation, Dowling College, Oakdale, New York.

Ciulla, J. B., & Burns, J. M. (1998). *Ethics, the heart of leadership.* Westport, CT: Greenwood Publishing Group.

Collins, J. (2001). *Good to Great*. New York, NY: HarperCollins Publishers, Inc.

Couto, V., Heinz, I., & Moran, M. J. (2005). Not your father's CFO. *Strategy + Business, Spring*.

Deming, W. E. (1982). *Out of the crisis*. Massachusetts Institute of Technology, Cambridge, Massachusetts: The MIT Press.

Desai, M. A. (2008). The finance function in a global corporation. *Harvard Business Review*, July – August, pp.108-112.

DiBella, C. M. (1999). Leading people, managing processes: School business administrators in the 21st century. *School Business Affairs, 65(12), (6-11)*.

Donaldson, W. H. (2005). *Testimony before the House Committee on Financial Services: Concerning the impact of the Sarbanes-Oxley Act*. U.S. Securities and Exchange Commission. Retrieved on June 28, 2008 from
 http://www.sec.gov/news/testimony/ts042105whd.htm

Dowling College, School of Education, Department of Educational Administration, Leadership and Technology, (2005). *Style & publication manual for all proposals & dissertations* (6th rev.). Oakdale, NY: Dowling College

Eisenberg, C. (2004). *New York State school board members' attitudes towards school governance, finance practices, conflict, teamwork and board effectiveness*. Doctoral dissertation, Dowling College, Oakdale, New York.

Gibson, J. L., Ivancevich, J. M., Donnelly, J. H., & Konopaske, R. (2003). *Organization: Behavior structure processes*. New York, NY: McGraw-Hill Companies, Inc.

Glass, T. E., Everett, R. E., & Johnson, D. R. (1998). Survey results: Preparing school business administrators. *School Business Affairs, 64(9), (19-23)*.

Glitman, R., Murphy, T., & Setton, I (2002). The CFO's changing role. *Forbes.com*. Retrieved on August 5, 2008 from http://www.forbes.com/2002/10/03/1003cfo.html

Greenleaf, R. K. (1997). *Servant leadership: A journey into the nature of legitimate power and greatness*. New York, NY: Paulist Press.

Grucci, C. (2003). *Executive team stability and school board members' attitudes toward school finance and governance practices in selected Nassau County, Long Island, New York school districts*. Doctoral dissertation, Dowling College, Oakdale, New York.

Hack, W. G., Candoli, I. C., & Ray, J. R. (1995). *School business administration: A planning approach*. Needham Heights, MA: Allyn and Bacon Publishers.

Herzberg, F. (1996). *Work and the nature of man*. Cleveland, OH: World Publishing Co.

Johnson, D. R. (1999). Budgeting for early retirements. *School Business Affairs, 65(10), (30-34)*.

Knowledge@Wharton (2002, May 8). *The changing role of the CFO*. Retrieved on August 5, 2008 from http://knowledge.wharton.upenn.edu/article.cfm?articleid=556

Kouzes, J. M., & Posner, B. Z. (1993). *Credibility: How leaders gain and lose it, why people demand it.* San Francisco, CA: Jossey Bass Publishers.

Mancini, B. A. (2007). *The relationship of transformational and transactional leadership to job satisfaction and organizational commitment within for-profit organizations on Long Island, New York.* Unpublished doctoral dissertation, Dowling College, Oakdale, New York.

McCarthy, F. & Lussier, D. (1996). Reflections on my role: Thoughts of two school business administrators. *School Business Affairs, 62(6), (34-39)*.

Murphy, D. T. (1997). From the outside in: Noneducators take up the profession. *School Business Affairs, 63(9), (34-38)*.

New York State Department of State (2008). *New York Codes, Rules, and Regulations (NYCRR)*. St. Paul, MN: Thomson/West Publishers.

New York State Department of Civil Service (2008). *Summary of New York State Civil Service Law*. New York State Department of Civil Service.

New York State Education Department. (2005). *School district accountability pursuant to Chapter 263 of the Laws of 2005 (A6082-A/S5050-A)*. Retrieved on June 28, 2008 from http://www.emsc.nysed.gov/mgtserv/accountability_legislation05.htm

New York State Education Department. (2008). *Analysis of school finances in New York State school districts 2005-06*. Fiscal Analysis Research Unit.

Nohria, N., Groysberg, B., & Lee, L. (2008). Employee motivation: A powerful new model. *Harvard Business Review*. July – August 2008, pp. 78-84.

Oxley, M. G. (2002). *Sarbanes-Oxley Act of 2002: Conference report to accompany H.R. 3763*. Report 107-610. House of Representatives, 107th Congress, 2d Session.

Patsuris, P. (2002). *The Corporate Scandal Sheet*. Retrieved on June 28, 2008 from http://www.Forbes.com/2002/07/25/accountingtracker.html

Pick, K. (2008). Can you hear me know? *Harvard Business Review,* July – August, pp. 23-24.

Publication manual of the American Psychological Association (5th ed.). (2001). Washington, DC: American Psychological Association.

Rebore, R.W. (2001). *The Ethics of Educational Leadership.* Upper Saddle River, NJ: Prentice-Hall, Inc.

Schuster, K., & Laikin, E. (2006, October 11). Roslyn scandal superintendent sentenced. *Newsday, Nassau and Suffolk Ed.,* p. A7.

Sielke, C. C. (1995). More than a number cruncher: The business administrator's changing role. *School Business Affairs, 61(6), (33-37).*

State of New York Office of the State Comptroller. (2003). Local government management guide: *Internal controls.*

State of New York Office of the State Comptroller. (2005). *Roslyn Union Free School District: Anatomy of a scandal.* Report of Examination.

State of New York Office of the State Comptroller. (2005a). *Laws of New York, 2005 Chapter 263.* Retrieved on June 28, 2008 from
 http://www.osc.state.ny.us/localgov/schoolsfa/ch263.htm

State of New York Office of the State Comptroller. (2008). *Schools and BOCES audit reports.* Available at attp://www.osc.state.ny.us/localgov/audits/schools/index.htm.

Stevenson, K. R., & Warren, E. (1996). Weathering the future: The changing role of the school business official. *School Business Affairs, 62(4), (35-38).*

Syptak, M. J., Marsland, D.W., & Ulmer, D. (1999). *Job satisfaction: Putting theory into practice.* American Academy of Family Physicians. Retrieved on July 24, 2008 from http://www.aafp.org/fpm/991000fm/26.html

Strategic Direction, (2004). The evolving role of the CFO: Interview with Calvin Massmann, SVP, CFO, and Treasurer, Tractor Supply. *Strategic Direction 20(3), (26-28).*

Strategic Direction, (2004). The strategic CFO: Interview with Amin I. Khalifa, Executive Vice President and CFO, Apria Healthcare. *Strategic Direction 20(3), (20-22).*

Uebbing, S. J., & Kerwin, F. A. (1997). The impact of the SBO on the educational process. *School Business Affairs, 63(12), (4-6).*

VEDA Advantage (2005, December 21). *Decision making and the changing role of the CFO.* Retrieved on August 5, 2008
 http://www.vedaadvantage.com/vantage/credit_decisioning/
decision-making_role_of_cfo.aspx

Weeks, D. (1994). *The eight essential steps to conflict resolution.* New York, NY: Tarcher/Penguin.

Chapter Eleven
Women Leading in a Global Economy
-Ranjana Mishra
-Ceena Paul

Introduction

Women are now a power to be reckoned with at national or at international levels. In the 21st century as international trade has become a key source of economic prosperity, women have to play a very crucial role. The survey of National Foundation of Women Business Owners (NFWBO) has indicated that women in the Global Economy have a greater share. They are not only optimistic, but want to expand their domestic oriented economy to have the global sphere. The burgeoning power of women in all areas cannot be ignored by the policy makers and the global executers. Today's world is changing at an astonishing speed. There are radical transformations in political and economic areas right from the regional to the global sphere. These alterations have created immense economic opportunities for women. Anyone having aspirations to have one's own business or lead businesses has ample opportunities. It is believed now that women in developing countries are also keeping pace in economic contributions with women of opulent countries.

There are some mixed views on this issue. Some social scientists believe that this type of transformation can threaten gender inequality. They believe that these transformations may push women behind and they may get marginalized and subordinated. Under such circumstances women would be forced to adopt traditional norms and values that may relegate women to a secondary status.

After the Fifth Global Summit of Women it was reported that the number of women business entrepreneurs have swelled.[i] The inherent qualities of women have enabled them in excelling in business activities, economic empowerment, entrepreneurial development and innovative programme. Women unlike their male counterparts do not hesitate to seek the professional and personal support from business partners and business associations. This quality also helps them in breaking the glass ceiling created by male dominated society. Economic globalization has opened a new vista of female business ownership. This has been corroborated with the fact that women produce more than 80 percent of the food for Sub-Saharan Africa, 50-60 percent for Asia, 26 percent for the Caribbean, 34 percent for North Africa and the Middle East, and more than 30 percent for Latin America.[ii]

Methodology

This research monologue addresses three issues: first, that women are increasingly moving into senior positions in the corporation that has traditionally kept them away from positions of influence and authority; secondly, how these particular women have dealt with issues of career and family life; and lastly, the strategies that can help them to strike a balance between their professional and personal life. An effort has been made to understand the similarities and differences of women across the globe. The paper also examines how women entrepreneurs affect the global economy The lecture is based on various data collected from national and international periodicals, books and reports published from ILO, UN reports, NFWBO and studies from corporate sectors and NGO's.

The Present Scenario

Of late, women are excelling in the economic sphere. Now they are breaking the glass ceiling that has traditionally kept them away from power and positions of influence. With the advent of global economy, throughout the world, more and more women are joining the Labor market to the extent that the ILO speaks of the "world-wide feminization of the Labor force and employment." Never before have so many women been economically active. The women's share in the labor force has increased worldwide. By the year 2010, their share will be just over 41 % in comparison to just 38% in 1970. In some regions, the increase is more significant. By the year 2010, Latin America women are expected to account for almost 37% of the labor force compared with 24% in 1970. Over the same period, women's share of the job market has grown from 36% to 47%.[iii]

In July 2007, 100 of the most senior women in ten US based multi-national companies convened in Prague as part of a new research project being carried out by Catalyst, The Center for Work & Family at Boston College and the Families and Work Institute. The project team came together to develop a research model to assess the issues facing women managers in four key regions of the world: North America, Latin America, Europe-Middle East-Africa and Asia-Pacific.[iv] The major purpose of this project was to illuminate the issues related to women's leadership in the global business community.

The Participating companies included companies like Baxter International, Citigroup, Deloitte Touché Tohmatsu Dow Chemical Company, Eli Lilly and IBM, JP Morgan Chase, Marriott International, Merck & Co., Inc. Merrill Lynch & Company. The project addressed issues related to women as how there is upward mobility into senior women business positions and upward graph of their careers. But in most cases no question was raised as how women find it difficult to strike a balance between work and home and how they have to prove themselves much better than their counterparts to reach to that position. These types of data were missing more in developing countries. The data collected after interviews suggested that there were various positive factors that helped them to reach to the height and at the same time there were various impediments that hindered their achievements. According to the study the factors which hindered the successes of women executives' were lack of mentors or coaches, exclusion from the old boy network, managing work with home responsibilities, and limits based on stereotypes about women and isolation. The factors which acted as instruments of women success were-mentor/boss, spouse/partner, networking/professional relationships, leadership training/executive coaching and flexible schedules.

The different companies have different approaches and strategies for benchmarking the advancement of senior women. Generally there are three different ways of gauging women's success. First, women's ties to the CEO or the management committee; secondly, the respectable position they are holding in the company or corporation; and thirdly, on the basis of diverse initiative taken by them. A recent United Nations report concluded that the economic growth of a country is directly related with women's advancement. The economic growth of a country is steady if women are advanced and where they are backward the economic growth is stagnant.

According to a 1995 UN survey,[v] "two changes have occurred over the past 10 years in enabling environment for women in the economy. One is the establishment of legal equality for women. The other is granting women equal access to education and training. The report also avers that women are significantly affecting the global economy ownership and the facts are as follows. Women in advanced market economies own more than 25% of all businesses. In Japan 23% of private firms are established by women.[vi] In Russia women own 64% of firms.[vii] In China; women founded 25% of the businesses since 1978.[viii] In Germany, women have created one-third of the new businesses since 1990 representing more than one million jobs. In Europe and newly independent States where economies are in transition there are women controlling 25% of the business whereas in Hungary women started more than 40% of all businesses since 1990.[ix] In Poland, women own 38% of all businesses.[x] In Mexico, 32% of women-owned businesses were started less than 5 years ago. In France, women head one in four firms. In Switzerland, women account for about 70% of micro, small, and medium Enterprises.[xi] In USA, women own 38% of all businesses (8 million firms), employ 27.5 million people (or 1 in every 5 women workers), and conduct businesses that generate $3.6 trillion in annual sales.[xii] In Great Britain, women constitute one fourth in the self-employed sector.

In the EU one-third of new businesses are initiated by women.[xiii] It is believed even in developing countries that women are becoming the engine of global economy. There are now more women in paid services and for every 100 men there are now 83 women in services. The manufacturing work which used to have male dominance is now on the decline and now both the sex is on equal footing. In Asia, textile and clothing export industries success is dependent on the women workforce. Where 60 to 80 percent work is being taken care of by women. The women at a higher level work more efficiently and produce more output than fewer in number. It was felt that mixed teams of men and women are better than single-sex groups at solving problems and spotting external threats. It was also found that women have better communication skills and capacity to work in cohesion.

Challenges Faced By Women

There is no denying a fact that there are individual achievements of women but achievement in general is miniscule. It has been revealed by a national survey that women hold only 2 to 3% of the posts at higher level in the companies. In the US where women are equally qualified as men and constitute about 46% of the workforce, they were shown by a 1999 survey to hold only 5.1% of executive positions and form a mere 3.3% of top earners among the largest companies. [xiv]

In another study in the USA in the year 2002, women held only 10% of the 6,428 total line corporate officer positions. A 1999 survey of over 584 different companies in the UK indicated the percentage of women directors was 4.5%. A French government study of 5000 leading enterprise in France (1997) showed that women represented only 2% of the CEO of the companies. In India according to one of the sources, the study by Koshal, (2006), indicated that 2 women per 100 economically active men hold administrative and managerial positions. Very recently, Confederation of Indian Industry gave the report that very few women are holding higher posts of multinational companies and corporations.

These analyses reveal the fact that despite adequate representation in the work-force at large, very few women are holding respectable higher positions. This variance was labeled as a 'glass ceiling' by Morrison and Von Glinow (1990). This top side covering is considered as an obstruction faced by women who dream and aspire to hold high positions in corporations, government, education and nonprofit organizations. The grass root reason of this is the gender stereotyped thinking of the society. The discrimination does not end here. On the contrary, it goes up to the income level and the salaries of women in non-organized sectors are lesser than men. Countless studies and anecdotal reports have shown huge discrepancies in salary in favor of men, even for similar positions in similar organizations.

Another area of challenge is that very few women are exposed to opportunities to gain additional competencies. It is very challenging for them to acquire extra skills. What their male counterparts get on the platter, they have to strive hard to get it.

Another indicator of obstruction is the corporate culture which is inadvertently in favor of men. For example, corporate policies and practices favor male needs. In most of the case the Boards of Directors, which are mostly comprised of men, sometimes perpetuate the status quo by selecting CEOs who look like them. Other gender-based hurdles include behavioral and communication styles that differ vastly from the company's norms. Generally women lack opportunity to gain general management/line experience.

The work and the life style of women also complement the glass-ceiling phenomenon. Women are generally the home maker and primarily family caregivers for children and of the elderly. It is invariably assumed that women won't be available to a job when family matters will intervene. It is considered that women in general give priority to family. This becomes the greatest hindrance to their success. Apart from that, all the corporations and big companies feel that women going on long leave during pre- and post-maternity would hamper the progress of the company. This biological factor also goes against the favor of women managers.

Finally, opportunities for promotion often favor men. By socialization men have more developmental opportunities. These are all male activities networks often tend to exclude women. This contributes to gender barriers in the workplace.

Adverse Effect Of Globalization On Women Force

The global economy has become detrimental for millions of working women around the world. The rules of the global economy make it possible for companies to chase the lowest wages and highest profits, regardless of the consequences for people and communities. Most of the Multi-National Companies are turning to women and children to cut their labor costs and increase their profits. Most women throughout the world are relegated to low-skilled, low-wage jobs. Their work often is dangerous and is likely to face additional threats on the job such as discrimination, sexual harassment, physical abuse and pregnancy exams as a condition of work.

Eighty percent of the nearly 50 million workers in export processing zones (EPZs) are women, most of them between the ages of 16 and 25. [xv] EPZs are tax-free industrial areas for foreign companies in which labor laws often are suspended and workers are unprotected.

In Mexico, women who work in the factories in the EPZs are subjected to numerous forms of violence, including murder. Even in developed countries, such as the

United States, women are working longer hours and making less than men. It is expected that in coming years more women would be in a professional line. A new demand for time restrictions and work rules may improve working conditions and dislocate jobs simultaneously.

Whether working in a factory in Thailand sewing athletic shoes for less than $4 a day or in a Mexican factory making parts for U.S. cars at $10 a day, women are among the hardest hit by the global economy. It is a fact that mostly women all over the world, work and are not paid according to their caliber. In most of the cases they are treated as a lesser human being and are preferred in low skill jobs despite having potential. The need of money for family and children compel them sometimes to go for hazardous work and many women risk their lives. The Free Trade Area of the Americas trade pact, now being debated by Big Business interests behind closed doors, would spread the massive joblessness created by NAFTA throughout the Western Hemisphere and have a detrimental impact on women workers. Women who pursued demanding careers encountered subtle but widespread societal prejudices. As women are expected, culturally and at times legislatively, to assume household responsibilities, they are subject to a double-shift burden.

Barriers faced by women in global business are innumerable. The most common amongst them are the absence of business literacy, inadequate networking and stereotyped thinking. Challenges common to all enterprises include securing funding, developing marketing and management skills, and devising suitable business strategies to thrive in globalize social and economic environments.[xvi] Other impediments for women are double-shift syndrome and sexual harassment along with corruption.[xvii]

Action Plan For Women To Break The Glass Ceiling

In order to have an equal participation in the global economy, women must overcome sexual stereotyping of occupations. This can be overcome by governmental policies and societal attitudes. In general women's occupational choices are profoundly influenced by men's authority so that they should be prudent enough to choose careers on their own instead of being emotionally dependent on anyone else. Women managers in a global economy should accept the challenging nature of the world business and its impact.

The Public Policy Forum conducted a census of women in corporate leadership in the 50 largest revenue-generating Wisconsin-based public companies (the Wisconsin 50). The various women directors were interviewed and gave the following advice to the CEO or chairperson of a company:

1. The overwhelming consensus was that networks need to be broadened.
It was discussed that CEO's and chairpersons need to relook things from the women's perspective and communicate to them about corporation's requirements. They should incorporate young women in the committees. They should look to new venues in which leadership skills may be showcased.[xviii] They emphasized that they should get more creative in tapping into the talent pool.
2. Another point suggested by the interviewees was to broaden the definition of leadership. The recruitment of highly qualified women should be evident. Another director suggested that women entrepreneurs who operate successful businesses should also be considered for the post of board member.
3. In addition, it was that felt that CEO's need to encourage and train more women leaders within their own companies. The skill and expertise needed for being on the board can be

developed among the existing women leaders within the companies through mentoring programs, in-house networking groups, training and development programs.

4. The directors also suggested an improvement of the criteria for nominating committees. One recommendation put forward by a director was that the nominating committee should have an open and transparent process and should be willing to accept names from many areas.

Thus, the study report indicated there were many ways in which CEO's and Board Chairs can be catalysts for the inclusion of women on higher managerial posts. The best result will be when no company can afford to waste valuable brainpower on gender discrimination, simply because it's wearing a skirt. [xix]

Conclusion

Recently, a participant from the Russian Far East, who had attended a US Department of Commerce business planning seminar, remarked that she really appreciated the changing global vision towards women entrepreneurs. She avers that her skills became a driving force to help a company to reach what it wanted to achieve.

Without directly tracking, observing, surveying, and interviewing individual women enterprise owners it is difficult to understand with clarity the current entrepreneurial movement or women's economic opportunities. Even the data collected over the past 10 years are insufficient and hardly correlate with the growing number of women entrepreneurs. Women must assess their own financial contributions to the global economy. Individually, business ownership provides women with the independence they need and with economic and social success they desire. Business ownership has great importance for future economic prosperity. [xx] Globally, women are enhancing, directing, and changing the face of business. Now they have carved a niche in the global economy and have their own position in a male dominated economic area.

Endnotes

i Women Entrepreneurs in the Global Economy, Susanne E. Jalbert, Ph.D., March 17, 2000.
ii quoted in Roy, K.C., Tisdell, C.A., & Blomqvist, H.C. Economic development and women in the world community. Praeger. 1996.
iii World Bank (1999). Private sector development: Small and medium-scale enterprise development. http://www.worldbank.org/html/fpd/private sector/sme.htm.
iv IMF,World Growth Grinds to Virtual Halt,IMF Urges Decisive Global Policy Response, at http//www.imf.org/external/plus/ft/survey/so/2009/reso128o9a.htm
v Carter& Cannon,Estes,1999;NFWBO,1998,Women in Business-Lesotho,Jalbert,1999
vi http:www.scribed.com/doc/49987561/Issues-and-challenges-for-woman-enterpreneurs-in-Global-Scene.
vii http:www.scribed.com/doc/49987561/Issues-and-challenges-for-woman-enterpreneurs-in-Global-Scene.
viii http:www.scribed.com/doc/49987561/Issues-and-challenges-for-woman-enterpreneurs-in-Global-Scene.
ixhttp:www.scribed.com/doc/49987561/Issues-and-challenges-for-woman-enterpreneurs-in-Global-Scene.
x http:www.scribed.com/doc/49987561/Issues-and-challenges-for-woman-enterpreneurs-in-Global-Scene.
xi http:www.scribed.com/doc/49987561/Issues-and-challenges-for-woman-enterpreneurs-in-

Global-Scene.
xii http:www.scribed.com/doc/49987561/Issues-and-challenges-for-woman-enterpreneurs-in-Global-Scene.
xiii http://www.smu.ca/events/icsb/proceedings/creao1f.html
xiv Sharmila Rudrappa, In destined for equality: The inevitable rise of women status, Harvard press,1998.
xv International Monetary Fund, World Economic Outlook Update: Global Economic Slump Challenges Policies, 26 January 2009/update/01//index.htm
xvi H.S.Astin and C.Leland,1991,Women of influence, Women of vision, San Francisco, P.13.
xvii R. S Greenberger,. 1999 ,Women Entrepreneurs in the Global Economy, Washington, D.C, PP.67-78.
xviii T.L.Friedman,2005,The World is Flat, New York,P.23

References

Accion International. (1997). http://www.accion.org

Allen, S. & Truman, C. (1993). Women and men entrepreneurs: Life strategies, business strategies. In S. Allen & C. Truman (Eds.), Women in business: Perspectives on women entrepreneurs (pp. 1-13). London: Routledge.

Association of Women in International Trade (WIIT). (1998). Second annual survey of public opinion on international trade. Washington, DC: 4. Babaeva L. & Chirikova, A. (1997). Women in business. Russian social science review, 38(3), 81-91.

Bales, K. (1999). Disposable people. Berkeley: University of California Press.

Bennis, W. & Nanus, B. (1985). Leaders: The strategies for taking charge.
New York: Harper & Row.

Bhatt, E. (1991). Women and self-employment case study of SEWA.

Kalbagh (Ed.), Women and development: women in enterprise and profession, Vol. 1, pp. 145-155. New Delhi: Discovery.

Bodrova, V. (1993). Glasnost and the 'the woman question' in the mirror of public opinion: Attitudes towards women, work, and the family. In V.Moghadam (Ed.), Democratic reform and the position of women in transitional economies (pp. 181-196). Oxford: Clarendon Press.

Brush, C. (1998). A resource perspective on women's entrepreneurship: Research, relevance and recognition. OECD's Women entrepreneurs in small and medium enterprises, pp. 155-168. Paris: OECD.

Brush, C. (1992). Research on women business owners: Past trends, a new perspective and future directions. Entrepreneurship theory and practice,16(4), 5-30.

Buttner, E. H. & Moore, D. P. (1997). Women's organizational exodus to entrepreneurship: Self-reported motivations and correlates with success. Journal of small business management, 35nl, 34-36.

Caminiti, S. (1999, September). Straight talk. Working woman, 66-69.

Carter, S. & Cannon, T. (1992). Women as entrepreneurs. London: Academic Press Limited.

Center for International Private Enterprise. (1997) Conference: Organizing for success: Strengthening women's business organizations. Washington, DC: Author

Chun, J. (1995, August). Equal access: women business owners find their place in the world. Entrepreneur 23, 84-87.

Clark, P. & Kays, A. (1995). Enabling entrepreneurship: Microenterprise development in the United States. Washington, DC: The Aspen Institute. Women Entrepreneurs in the Global Economy

Clements, B., Engel, A., & Worobec, C. (1991). Russia's women. Berkeley: University of California Press.

Counts, A. (1996). Give us credit. New York: Times Books.

Creevey, L. (1996). Changing women's lives and work. London: IT Publications.

Davis, S. & Meyer, C. (1998). Blur. Reading, MA: Addison-Wesley .de Melo, M. and Ofer, G. (1994). Private service firms in a transitional economy: findings of a survey in St. Petersburg. The World Bank: Washington, D.C.

Dignard, L. & Havet, J. (1995). Women in micro- and small-scale enterprise development. Boulder, CO: Westview Press.

Ducheneaut, B. (1997). Women entrepreneurs in SMEs. Report prepared for the OECD Conference on "Women entrepreneurs in small and medium enterprises: A major force for innovation and job creation". Paris: OECD

Eavis, P. (1995). Calling Russia to account. Emerging Markets Investor, 2 (3), 21-22. London: Risk.

Engel, B. A. (1991). Transformation versus tradition. In B. Clements, B. Engel, & C. Worobec (Eds.), Russia's women (pp. 135-147). Berkeley: University of California Press.

Epping, R. C. (1992). A beginner's guide to the world economy. New York : Vintage Books.

Estes, V. (1999, November 18). Women & business development: promoting economic growth and job creation. USAID/Europe & Eurasia Bureau: author.

Fabowale, L., Orser, B., & Riding, A. (1995). Gender, structural factors, and credit terms between Canadian small businesses and financial institutions. Entrepreneurship theory and practice, 19 (4), 41-65.

Fong, M. (1993). The role of women in rebuilding the Russian economy, Studies of economies in transformation, paper number 10. Washington, DC: The World Bank.

Friman, H. R. (1999). Obstructing markets: Organized crime networks and drug control in Japan. In H. R. Friman & P. Andreas (Eds.), The illicit global economy and state power (pp. 173-198). New York: Rowman & Littlefield Publishers, Inc.

Gessen, M. (1997). Dead again: The Russian intelligentsia after communism.
London: Verso.

Getecha C. & Chipika, J. (1995). Zimbabwe women's voices. Harare, Zimbabwe: Zimbabwe Women's Resource Centre and Network.

Gilligan, C. (1993). In a different voice (2nd ed.). Cambridge, MA: Harvard University Press. Women Entrepreneurs in the Global Economy 62

Goodwin, R. & Emelyanova, T. (1995). The perestroika of the family? Gender and occupational differences in family values in modern day Russia. Sex roles: A journal of research, 32(5/6), 337-351.

Green, R., David, J., Dent, M. & Tyshkovsky, A. (1996). The Russia entrepreneur: A study of psychological characteristics. International journal of entrepreneurial behavior & research, v 2, 1, pp. 49-53.

Greenberger, R. S. (1999, July). Working for a fair trade. Hemispheres, 40.

Grossman, G. (1989). Informal personal incomes and outlays of the soviet urban population. In A. Portes, M. Castells, & L. Benton (Eds.), The informal economy (pp. 151-170). Baltimore: The Johns Hopkins University Press.

Haas, H. (1992). The leader within: An empowering path of self-discovery. New York: Harper Business.

Handy, C. (1996). Beyond certainty. Boston, MA: Harvard Business School.

Harder, S. (1981). Advocacy networks. Graduate woman, 19-22.

Helgesen, S. (1990). The female advantage: Women's ways of leadership. New York: Doubleday.

.Helgesen, S. (1995). The web of inclusion: a new architecture for building great organizations. New York: Doubleday.

Hesselbein, F., Goldsmith, M., Beckhard, R. (1997). The organization of the future. San Francisco: Jossey-Bass.

Heyzer, N. (1995). A commitment to the world's women. New York: UNIFEM. Hill, C. W. L. (1998). International business: Competing in the global marketplace. Boston, MA: Irwin McGraw-Hill.

Hisrich, R. & Brush, C. (1987). Women entrepreneurs: A longitudinal study. Proceedings of the Seventh Annual Babson College Entrepreneurship Research Conference. Frontiers of entrepreneurship research. 187-199.

Hunt, S. (1997, July/August). Women's vital voices: the costs of exclusion in Eastern Europe. Foreign affairs, 2-7.

Jalbert, S. E. (1999a). Contemporary Russian women: Entrepreneuring for survival. Doctoral dissertation, Colorado State University, Fort Collins.

Jalbert, S. E. (1999b). Economic empowerment for women: An evaluation of the advocacy activities of the National Association of Business Women (NABW). Washington, DC: Center for International Private Enterprise.

Jalbert, S. E. (1999c). Report on the Zimbabwe and Malawi focus group outcomes. Washington, DC: Center for International Private Enterprise. Women Entrepreneurs in the Global Economy

Jalbert, S. E. (1999d). Forming a women's business association in Nepal. Economic reform today, pp. 28-29. Washington, DC: Center for International Private Enterprise.

Kaufmann, P., Welsh, D. & Bushmarin, N. (1995). Locus of Control and Entrepreneurship in the Russian Republic. Entrepreneurship theory and practice, 20(1), 43-56

Kauppinen-Toropainen, K. (1993). Comparative study of women's work satisfaction and work commitment: Research findings from Estonia, Moscow, and Scandinavia. In V. Moghadam (Ed.), Democratic reform and the position of women in transitional economies (pp. 198-412). Oxford: Clarendon Press.

Kay, Rebecca (1995). Surviving the market in the first two years of transition: Women in Russia rise to a new challenge. In S. Bridger (Ed.), Women in post-communist Russia (pp. 3-21). Bradford, West Yorkshire: Department of Modern Languages, University of Bradford.

Khotkina, Z. (1994). Women in the labour market: Yesterday, today and tomorrow, p. 86-108. Women in Russia, a new era in Russian feminism. London: Verso.

Kiplinger, K. (1999). World boom ahead. Washington, DC: Kiplinger Books Kouzes, J. M. & Posner, B. Z. (1997). The leadership challenge. San Francisco: Jossey-Bass Publishers.

P., Jatusripitak, S., & Maesincee, S. (1997). The marketing of nations. New York: The Free Press.

Kvint, V. (1996). Development of international joint ventures in Russia: Risks and opportunities. In A. Woodside & R. Pitts (Eds.), Creating and managing international joint ventures (pp. 159-174). Westport, CN: Quorum Books.

G. (1993). Gender and restructuring: The impact of perestroika and its aftermath on soviet women. In V. Moghadam (Ed.), Democratic reform and the position of women in transitional economies (pp. 138-161). Oxford: Clarendon Press.

Layard, R. & Parker, J. (1996). The coming Russian boom. New York: The Free Press.

Lazreg, M. (1998). Gender and agricultural privatization in ECA. Washington, DC: The World Bank

Lee, B. (1996, March). Women's groups still don't understand power. San Diego business journal,

Lehmann, S. G. (1995). Costs and opportunities of marketization: An analysis of Russian employment and unemployment. Research in the sociology of work, 5, 205-233.

Lessing, D. (1992). African laughter. New York: HarperCollins. Lever, A. (1997). Women's business organizations: the hidden strengths and potential. Economic reform today. n 2, 4-9.

Littlejohn, V. (1997, September). A global action agenda for women entrepreneurs. Center for Private Enterprise (CIPE) Conference: Strengthening Women's Organizations. Washington, D.C.

Lukianenko, T. (1994). New women's opportunities in the process of economic reforms in Russia. In Women of Russia-Yesterday, today, tomorrow (pp. 186-191). Moscow: Association of Women in Slavic Studies.

Mamonova, T. (1984). The feminist movement in the Soviet Union. In T. Mamonova (Ed.), Women and Russia (pp. xiii-xix). Boston: Beacon Press.

McCarthy, D., Puffer, S. , & Naumov A. (1994). Cast study--Olga Kirova: A Russian entrepreneur's quality leadership. International journal of organizational analysis, 5(3), 267-290.

Millman, A. (1998). The role of networks. OECD's Women entrepreneurs in small and medium enterprises, pp. 121-128. Paris: OECD.

Milner, L. S. (1997). Business associations for the 21st century, a blueprint for the future, p.11. Washington, DC: Center for International Private Enterprise.

Mockler, R., Chao, C., & Dologite, D. (1996). A comparative study of business education programs in China and Russia. Journal of teaching in international business, 8(2), 19-39.

Moghadam, V. (1990). Wider working paper: Gender and restructuring: Perestroika, the 1989 revolutions, and women. Helsinki: World Institute for Development Economics Research of the United Nations University.

Moon, G. (1995, August). Free trade: What's in it for women? Trade and women in developing countries. Background Report No. 6. Community Aid Abroad

Moore, D. P. & Buttner, E. H. (1997). Women entrepreneurs: Moving beyond the glass ceiling. Thousand Oaks, CA: Sage.

Moss-Kanter, R. (1995). World class. New York: Simon & Schuster.

National Foundation for Women Business Owners (1999). Women business owners of Canada: Entering the new millennium. Washington, DC.: Author.

National Foundation for Women Business Owners (1999). Women business owners in Sao Paulo, Brazil: A summary of key issues. Washington, DC.: Author.

National Foundation for Women Business Owners (1998). Women business owners in Mexico: An emerging economic force. Washington, DC.: Author.Women Entrepreneurs in the Global Economy

National Foundation for Women Business Owners (1998). Business women of Ireland: Concerns and expectations. Washington, DC.: Author.

National Foundation for Women Business Owners (1997). Women entrepreneurs are a growing international trend. Women's Connection Online, Inc., http://www.womenconnect.com/channels/business/ mar8b-19977htm, 1-2.

National Foundation of Women Business Owners (NFWBO). Women-Owned Businesses: Breaking the Boundaries. (1994). Washington, DC.:

Neff, T. J. & Citrin, J. M. (1999). Lessons from the top. New York: Doubleday. Noonan, N. (1988). Women & politics (8 (1) ed.). London: Haworth Press, Inc.

Noonan, N. (1996). Crossroads in Russian history: A brighter road ahead for women? In W. Rule & N. Noonan (Eds.), Russian women in politics and society (pp. 167-171). Westport, CN: Greenwood Press.

Organization for Economic Co-Operation and Development (OECD). (1998a).Fostering entrepreneurship, pp. 28-30. Paris: OECD

Organization for Economic Co-Operation and Development (OECD). (1998b).Women entrepreneurs in small and medium enterprises. Paris:ECD.

Pilkington, H. (1995). Can Russia's women save the nation? Survival politics and gender discourse in post-soviet Russia. In S. Bridger (Ed.), Women in post-communist Russia (pp. 160-181). Bradford, West Yorkshire: Department of Modern Languages, University of Bradford.

Posadskaya, A. (1993). Changes in gender discourses and policies in the former soviet union. In V. Moghadam (Ed.), Democratic reform and the position of women in transitional economies (pp. 163-179). Oxford:Clarendon Press.

Prugl, E. (1999). The global construction of gender: Home-based work in the political economy of the 20th century. New York: Columbia University Press.

Remington, T. (1994). Partisan Competition and Democratic Stability. In T.Remington (Ed.), Parliaments in transition (pp. 217-222). Boulder, CO: Westview Press.

Remnick, D. (1997). Resurrection: The struggle for a new Russia. New York: Random House.

Research Dimension, Inc. (1999). Women's enterprise development conference: Tbilisi, Zugdidi & Kataisi, Georgia - October-December, 1997,Counterpart International. Washington, DC: Author

Rimm, S. (1999). See Jane win. New York: Crown Publishers. Women Entrepreneurs in the Global Economy,P.66.

Roy, K. C. & Tisdell, C. A. (1999). Women in South Asia with particular reference to India. In K. C. Roy, C. A. Tisdell, & H. C. Blomqvist (Eds.) Economic development and women in the world community. (pp. 98-124.Westport, CT: Praeger Roy, K. C.,

Tisdell, C.A. & Blomqvist, H. C. (1999). Economic development and women in the world community. Westport, CT: Praeger

Sadat, J. (1997, September). Opening Keynote Address: Women: Preparing for the future. Paper presented at the conference of Center fo rInternational Private Enterprise Conference: Organizing for success: strengthening women's business organizations, Washington, D.C.

Scanlon, T. M. (1999). What we owe to each other. Cambridge, MA: The Belknap Press of Harvard University Press.

Scherer, C. (2000). The internationalists. Wilsonville, OR: Book Partners

Schwenninger, S. R. (2000, February/March). NGOing Global: Can civil society on an international scale compensate for the anarchy of world affair? Civilization, pp. 40-41.

Senge, P. M. (1990). The leader's new work: Building leaning organizations. Sloan management review, 7.

Severens, C.A. & Kays, A. (1997). 1996 Directory of US microenterprise programs. Washington, DC: Self-Employment Learning Project and The Aspen Institute.

Shawa, M. (1999). A forum and study on "Policy options for promoting the economic empowerment of women: The case of Malawi." Lilongwe, Malawi: United Nations

Economic Commission for Africa and Malawi's Ministry of Women, Youth, and Community Services

Shelley, L. (1999). Transnational organized crime: The new authoritarianism. In H. R. Friman & P. Andreas (Eds.), The illicit global economy and state power (pp. 25-51). New York: Rowman & Littlefield Publishers, Inc.

Sher, B. (1979). Wishcraft: How to get what you really want. New York: Ballantine.

Siegel, B. (1990). Business creation and local economic development: Why entrepreneurship should be encouraged. In Organization for Economic Cooperation and Development (Ed.), Enterprising women (pp. 11-20). Paris: Organization for Economic Co-operation and Development.

Slusky, L. Yampolsky, V., Partow, P. Dubina, G. & Goldfarb, V. (1997). Pilot project in international electronic distance education in Russia. T.H.E.journal, 24(6), 61-66.

Stevenson, L. (1990). Some methodological problems associated with researching women entrepreneurs. Journal of business ethics, 9(4,5), 439-446.

Thach, L. (1996). Training in Russia. Training and Development, 50(7), 34-37.

Tinker, I. (1995). The human economy of micro entrepreneurs. In Dignard L. & Havet, J. (Eds.), Women in micro- and small-scale development (pp. 25-39). Boulder, CO: Westview Press.

Turk, M. (1993). Interview: Strength is in the individual. Slovenian business United Nations (1990). The world's women 1970-1990: Trends and statistics. New York: author.

United Nations (1995). Women in a changing global economy: 1994 Worldsurvey on the role of women in development. New York:

Van Der Wees, C. & Romijn, H. (1995). Entrepreneurship and small- and microenterprise development for women: A problematique in search for answers, a policy in search of programs. In Dignard L. & Havet, J. (Eds.),Women in micro- and small-scale development (pp. 25-39). Boulder, CO:Westview Press.

Webster, R., Gray, T. & Johnson, R. (1999) Partnerships for sustainable enterprise growth. Washington, DC: USAID.

Wedel, J. R. (1998). Collision and collusion. New York: St. Martin's Press Weeks, J. (1995). Style of Success: Research on gender differences in management styles. Small business forum, 52-62.

World Bank (1999). Private sector development: Small and medium-scale enterprise development. http://www.worldbank.org/html/fpd/private sector/sme.htm

World Bank (1994). Enhancing women's participation in economic development.

Washington DC: Author.Yergin, D. & Stanislaw, J. (1998). The commanding heights: The battle between government and the marketplace that is remaking the modern world. New York: Simon & Schuster.

[1]H.S.Astin and C.Leland,1991,Women of influence, Women of vision, San Francisco, P.13.

[2]Albedia Randy,1997,Economics and Feminism, New York,Twayne,P.12.

[3] Nancy J. Adler and Dafna N. Izraeli, Women managers in a Global economy,P.3

[4] T.L.Friedman,2005,The World is Flat, New York,P.23.

Chapter Twelve
Technological Communications
in a Global Economy
-Rajesh Chedda

Global Economy Requires Global Communication

Advances in information and communications technologies have revolutionized the business environment of the 21st century, making it possible for people in different cities, states - even nations - to work together on one team. If businesses are to succeed in this global culture of collaboration, experts say they must understand how people in various parts of the world prefer to communicate with one another.

Today's business environment is totally different than the one that existed just a decade ago. We really do have a global economy, and an economy which no longer just consists of Japan, the United States and Germany. We have one technological revolution that's pretty far along - information technology, the web being the latest and most radical example.

Success today requires a new way of doing business, "competing like crazy with another company" on one hand, and "doing joint ventures with them" on the other. There is an awful lot more flexibility. So you see seven companies in six countries from three continents get together to create an answer to a software issue or an aircraft issue.

And that's what is called collaboration. Today, our work requires us to collaborate with someone that's somewhere else in the world. "So when we're global, collaboration is working together without physically being in the same location, we've got to connect through some technology like e-mail, web conferencing and other kinds of technology."

Because people who collaborate using those communication tools often have different cultural backgrounds, it's inevitable that culture interacts with technology, and that often leads to miscommunication.

The Americans are rugged individualists. They love to work on teams, but they love working alone as well. So they are very comfortable leaving voice mail, sending e-mails and even when they are in real-time meetings, going off on their own and doing multitasking.

European business culture is very different. People in Europe love real-time communication. So if they are at their desks and the phone rings, they are going to answer it. That's not true in the United States. When the phone rings, Americans may very likely let it ring into the voice mail so they don't get interrupted. Those were some of the findings of an international study of nearly 1,000 business leaders from the United States, Europe and Asia.

Business professionals in the Asia-Pacific region are also the most frequent telecommuters. There are a lot of people that are doing telecommuting and using technologies to get a hold of one another.

The Meetings Around the World study - sponsored by Verizon Business and Microsoft - also found that people in the Asia Pacific region feel that meetings conducted via audio or videoconference technologies can be more productive than meeting face to face and less costly. As more international virtual teams are set up, management consultant Jaclyn Kostner says companies around the world are not only pushing their corporate performance to new heights, they are bringing people a bit closer, in spite of geographic and cultural distances.

Systems Theory As A Tool For Understanding The Relationships Among Human Evolution And Civilization, Technology

In a society based on consumerism and a reductionist scientific paradigm, technology is used to further the goals of military, industry, transportation, and resource management. The capitalist government and economy of the United States are intimately entwined into an elitist, hierarchical power structure. The ruling hierarchy is a corporate bureaucracy that utilizes the media through informational propaganda and advertising to influence its populace.

Human endeavors implement technology to create, sustain, and improve global communication networks. The internet allows geographically remote groups of people to interact effectively as one community. An example in the emerging global economy is the multinational corporation. Yet, the internet is a global media network that is available to any community that can muster the financial and technological wherewithal to get connected. In fact, the system of communities arising and flourishing on the internet, what Marshal Macluhan describes as the "Global Village," may be the emergence of a new order of self-organization, life, and consciousness on this planet. Perhaps this is the teleological culmination of a process of increased complexity and eco-diversity in the co-evolution of the human species and technology.

The Communication-Driven Economy

I recently read an extremely interesting special section in The Economist, concerned in particular with how mobile communications and "mobile finance" was positively affecting emerging economies. One figure that stuck with me was that adding ten cell phones into a population of 100 people had the net effect of raising the country's GDP by 0.8%; that's a simply staggering figure relative to the investment involved. Particularly in countries that have been historically lacking in infrastructure, mobile communications can be paradigm-changing: it allows instant communication with places and people that might have been days off or otherwise inaccessible. By providing a flow of information of all kinds, where none existed before, especially over long distances, mobile communications make new markets and new products possible in ways that would have been out of reach otherwise.

Today, more people access the Internet, globally, from cell phones than from traditional computers. Many people have never accessed the Internet any other way. This is a continuation of the major "paradigm shift" which began in 1995 when "the Worldwide

Web" moved from being a province belonging solely to the technically adept, to something which was accessible and usable by anyone at all—with the right equipment, anyway. The "right equipment" was, of course, hideously expensive in global terms: a computer cost at least a couple of thousand dollars. Today, we see cell phones that are, in terms of power and performance, the full equivalent of "desktops" or "laptops" of only a few years ago and at a fraction of the cost. And the cost only keeps getting pushed down. A phone that is capable of accessing the Internet, and hence the world, is within the reach of more and more people in the world. And, as The Economist points out, having that phone enriches and improves people's lives in tangible and quantifiable ways.

But cell phones and mobile devices don't only drive economic change, they can drive political change as well. Five years ago, cell phones and text messaging played a crucial role in Moldova's "Orange Revolution"; today, it's at least as likely to be Twitter that is used for mass communications. Communications of this sort cannot be censored, and we can expect to be seeing such facilities playing an increasing role in all kinds of political discourse.

The device-manufacturing members of the LiMo Foundation ship on the order of a quarter of a billion phones worldwide annually. The economics of the electronics industry keep driving the cost of a device with a given feature set ever-downward; efforts both in the open source world and in organizations like LiMo do the same with software. Virtually every phone on the market comes with a web browser of some sort—ACCESS alone ships scores of millions of new installations of our browser product a year on phones at all price points.

Change on a global scale is rarely sudden. It's a series of small changes - incremental ones. In the past twenty years, cell phones have gone from being a luxury available only to the wealthy to something that's within the reach of the majority of people on the planet. At the same time, the power and functionality of the devices themselves has only increased. With that increased availability and functionality has come better flow of information and news, improved economic prospects, better education, and the ability to stay in contact with those who are physically distant, and for people around the world. We're only beginning to see the changes that will come out of a transition like this.

The "One Laptop Per Child" effort set out to produce a general-purpose, portable computer suitable for children's education at a cost of $100. It didn't quite achieve all of its goals, but it led to a number of interesting and useful experiments and results. It may be that the modern and increasingly functional cell phone turns out to be, to a large extent, the real "hundred dollar laptop" and not just for children.

Digital Economy

In order to understand the digital economy, it is important to explore the business pressures and understand the reasons why businesses are turning from traditional economy into digital economy. Most of the business pressures can be categorized as market, technological, or societal.

Market Pressures
Much of the market pressure organizations endure are caused by the global economy, the changing characteristics of the workforce, and the power of consumers.

Global Economy and Strong Competition

Over the past decades, the foundation for international trade has been developing. The use of information technology, especially the internet, has been a great factor for the expansion of globalization. Furthermore, international treaties and the unification of the European market under a single currency, the euro, have greatly increased international trade.

Aside from the influence of political forces, the cost of labor has played a large part in globalization and the use of information technology. While the wage of labor in some countries is higher than others countries, many companies are moving their factories to foreign land to hire cheap labor. Such business plans require extensive communication and collaboration, which can be supported by the use of IT.

Need for Real-Time Operations

The business world is becoming increasingly fast, and decisions need to be made quickly. With information technology, executives and managers are able to make quick decisions with instantaneous information.

Changing Nature of the Workforce

The demographics of the workforce in developed countries are rapidly changing. The workforce is becoming more diversified with increasing number of women, single parents, minorities, and disabled persons. Also, the education level of the workforce is steadily increasing with more knowledgeable workers available. The use of information technology is easing into the transition from the traditional economy into the digital economy.

Consumer Power

With the development of the internet, consumer expectation has been on the rise as they have more knowledge about availability and quality of products and services. As the internet makes the job of researching easier for consumers, consumers are able to compare products, services, and prices. At the same time, consumers are demanding more customized products with low cost. Such examples include Dell's customization over the internet and Nike's design-your-own sneaker online. Since customization require fast delivery of information to satisfy customers, companies are pressured to use information technology to retain customers.

Technology Pressures

Aside from market pressures, businesses also face technological pressures. The two main pressures in technology consist of technological innovation and information overload.

Technological Innovation and Obsolescence

Technology plays a large role in many organization's manufacturing and services. While technology is very helpful in an organization, it is important to understand that new and improved technology is constantly released in the market. The continuous improvement in technology forces organizations to keep up with new technology or suffer the consequence of obsolescence and become out-competed.

There is no doubt that information is abundant in the world. With the use of the internet and other telecommunication networks, more information can be accessible to organizations and individuals. With information growing exponentially each year, it is important to employ information technology such as search engines and intelligent databases to improve decision-making.

Thinking About A New Economy - The Effects Of Technology On An Economy And Society

The Industrial Revolution that began about 200 years ago lives in the collective memory as a cavalcade of inventors and machines: James Watt and the steam engine, Eli Whitney and the cotton gin, Cyrus McCormick and the reaper, Charles Goodyear and vulcanized rubber, and many more. But the Industrial Revolution brought a remarkable change in the human condition that went beyond any particular invention. It instilled a belief that the standard of living did not have to be forever stagnant.

Looking back from today's privileged vantage point, after two centuries of economic growth, it may be impossible to feel in our bones what it meant to live in a world without economic progress. Consider, for example, the note of genuine wonder in the voice of Karl Marx, writing of the new realities in the Communist Manifesto in 1848:

The bourgeoisie during its rule of scarce one hundred years has created more massive and more colossal productive forces than have all preceding generations together. Subjection of nature's forces to man, machinery, application of chemistry to industry and agriculture, steam-navigation, railways, electric telegraphs, clearing of whole continents for cultivation, canalization of rivers, whole populations conjured out of the ground-what earlier century had even a presentiment that such productive forces slumbered in the lap of social labor?

Modern economists, with their highly developed talent for reducing the drama of human production and consumption to dry statistics, describe the Industrial Revolution more simply: It was the era when economic growth in countries like the United States rose from essentially nothing to 2 percent per year. This 2 percent growth rate should not be understood as a physical constant like the boiling point of water, but rather as a rough guideline to the average experience of the most highly developed economies over the last two centuries.

Before trying to unravel how information technology may change the economy in measured, unmeasured, and even immeasurable ways, it is useful to begin by exploring what the productivity statistics say.

Productivity growth in the 1990s:

U.S. productivity growth in the last 50 years is typically divided into three periods. In the first period, running from 1950 to 1973, productivity (as measured by growth of output per labor hour in the business sector) rose at 3.0 percent per year. This period of relatively rapid growth has been attributed to many factors: the application of new technologies (especially those that had been developed during World War II), a burst of pent-up economic energy after the dark economic times of the 1930s, and growth of global trade.

Then productivity slowed down. From 1973 to 1995, productivity growth averaged just 1.4 percent per year. The years from 1973 to 1982 were worst of all. Over that time, productivity grew at only 0.9 percent per year. From 1982 to 1995, productivity grew a bit more briskly at 1.7 percent per year. Various events of the 1970s might explain the slower productivity: higher oil prices, higher inflation, a slowdown in government research and development spending after the Apollo moon landing, the growth of environmental legislation, and so on. But no single factor, nor any combination of factors, has proven sufficient to explain the depth and length of the productivity slowdown.

The default explanation for the slowdown was that the 1950s and 1960s had been an extraordinary time, following in the aftermath of world wars and depression, and that perhaps more modest growth rates were all a highly developed economy like the United States could expect. But then productivity bounced back, growing at an annual rate of 2.9 percent per year from 1995 to mid 2000. A lusty academic dispute in recent years has sought to explain the reasons for the turnaround. The standard methodology for these "growth-accounting" studies is to try to explain the overall rise in productivity by tracing it to gains in different sectors of the economy. Interestingly, studies done by both believers in, and skeptics of, the Information Revolution reach many of the same conclusions.

For example, they agree that business investment in computers and related equipment, which quadrupled from 1995 to 1999, is one main reason for the recent surge in productivity. The average worker is now working with more powerful technology than a few years ago. This involves more than faster personal computers; it also means better computer-aided design and manufacturing and better information systems for tying together inventories, purchasing, and accounting.

Moreover, it is broadly agreed that faster productivity growth in the production of computers themselves, especially in the underlying semiconductor chips, explains part of the productivity increase. The price of computing power had been falling about 15 percent per year in the late 1980s and first half of the 1990s, but beginning in the mid 1990s, it started to fall by 30 percent per year.

Yet another area of broad agreement is that commerce over the Internet, whether of the business-to-consumer or business-to-business variety, has nothing to do with the surge in productivity since 1995. By the end of 2000, only about half of Americans had a home connection to the Internet, and most of those connections were over painfully slow telephone modems. Business-to-consumer e-commerce was about $30 billion in 2000, or 1 percent of retail sales. In mid 2000, only about one-third of American manufacturing firms had even started using the Internet for buying inputs or for sales. Business-to-business e-commerce was about $140 billion in 2000, about 1 percent of business-to-business sales. One can sketch plausible scenarios in which e-commerce offers dramatic productivity gains in the next few years. But it hasn't been large enough over the last five years to have been driving economy-wide productivity trends.

Probably the main area of disagreement in these growth-accounting studies is whether the majority of the productivity increase in the past five years should be viewed as an increase in the long-term trend or as a short-term blip. At a conceptual level, productivity is economic output divided by inputs. When GDP growth is red-hot, as it was during much of the late 1990s, it boosts the productivity statistics by driving up the ratio of outputs to inputs. For example, real GDP, projected at an annual rate, grew at a rate of 5.7 percent in the third quarter of 1999 and a whopping 8.3 percent in the fourth quarter. But when the pace of economic growth settles somewhat, not necessarily because of a recession but simply because of a more moderate pace of growth, then productivity growth will also be slower.

Those economists who are most sanguine about the Information Revolution give it the lion's share of credit for boosting productivity by about 1 percent per year. The pessimists, who fear that a substantial share of the productivity resurgence is partly due to unsustainably fast short-term growth, give information technology credit for only about 0.6 percent of the annual increase in productivity growth.

In short, the additional GDP from the Information Revolution could within two decades be a direct cause of $3 trillion per year in output, which at that point would represent about one-seventh of the entire economy. The power of increasing growth rates by even small percentages, if sustained over decades, is phenomenal.

The wonders of e-commerce

Technology enthusiasts often assert that the New Economy is already upon us. But, for the sake of clarity, it is important to keep one's verb tenses straight. Although the U.S. economy has experienced a strong surge of investment in ever-faster computers over the last five years, the bow wave of the e-commerce revolution is just beginning to rock the economy. This is good news, because it opens up the exciting possibility that the Information Revolution will have staying power. The future prospects of e-commerce are especially important because the underlying sources of increased productivity growth over the last five years won't last forever.

For some years now, semiconductor-industry insiders have been pointing out that the process of etching ever-smaller computer chips will, at some point, run into physical limits. Current chip technology involves working at a scale of nanometers--billionths of a meter. At this scale, electrons sometimes hop unpredictably across very small distances. The tendency of certain molecules to clump together, which doesn't matter at a larger scale, poses a production problem. To overcome these sorts of problems, even a continuation of the brilliant engineering advances of the last few decades won't be enough. It seems plausible that the rate of increase in chip technology could slow substantially.
The surge in information-technology investment in the last five years will be increasingly difficult to duplicate in the future as well. Certainly, investment in computers will continue rising, but it will be difficult to repeat the quadrupling of such investment that occurred over the last five years in the next five years--and it would be even harder to quadruple yet again in the five years after that. It's always easier to quadruple from a smaller base than from a larger one.

Thus if the Information Revolution is to last for the medium run, it cannot rely only on improvements in computer chips and increases in technology investment. The underlying drivers of productivity growth will have to shift. In the medium term, it is e-commerce that can potentially maintain the Information Revolution and productivity growth.

In addition, because of tighter, faster links between suppliers and buyers, there is less need to have inventories sitting in warehouses. Since the U.S. economy holds about $1.1 trillion in inventories, gains in this area will mean a few hundred billion dollars worth of stuff not sitting around gathering dust. Thus, although the first stage of the Information Revolution over the last five years has been characterized by high investment in more powerful computers, the second stage, over the next decade, seems likely to be characterized by a dramatic change in how transactions are carried out and processed.
Welcome to "web world"

The economic gains from reducing transaction costs and holding down inventories are potentially enormous - but again, they are also self-limiting. While the costs of transactions and the levels of inventories can be cut, in the nature of things those costs will never fall below zero. Market forces will encourage firms to seek out the juiciest cost-cutting targets first, but once the low-hanging apples are picked, it will become harder and harder to squeeze out further cost savings. If the Information Revolution is to last beyond the next decade, and if it is to rival society-transforming inventions like the internal combustion engine, it will have to do more than reduce paperwork and empty out some inventory warehouses. It will need to change how people live in fundamental ways.

When thinking about the possibilities of this stage of the Information Revolution, one leaves behind hard data and enters the realm of plausible speculation. It's useful to begin by visualizing the technology as it someday may be. The Internet, as we presently know it, is a technological marvel but also clunky, buggy, and slow. Now imagine web pages that appear as quickly as a television set changes channels, with television-style clarity, movement, and sound. Think about calling up these web pages with voice commands, or some form of channel clicker or mouse, not with laboriously typed web addresses. The great increase in speed will make these web pages interactive: Ask a question, get an immediate answer. Now combine all this with hand-held, wireless access to the Internet, with communications anywhere in the world at costs lower than today's long-distance telephone rates. Just for fun, or perhaps for terror, mix in the capability of the Global Positioning System to know exactly where you are in relation to everything else and databases that have complete records of your past purchases and viewing habits. In a decade or two, I suspect that we will look back on the current state of the Internet the way we reminisce about black-and-white photographs or old radio programs.

Questions

1. Explain how communication technology has brought people and nations together?
2. What are the latest modes of communication?
3. Site some examples of collaborations.
4. How are 'mobile communications' and 'mobile finance' positively affecting emerging economies?
5. How much credit **do** you give to Information Technology for the boost in world economy?

References

homepages.tig.com.au

http://www.berr.gov.uk

http://www.docstoc.com

http://www.oecd.org

Rice, MF ,Information and Communication Technologies and the Global Digital Divide Technology Transfer, Development, and Least Developing Countries', Comparative Technology Transfer and Society.(2003)

Walsham, G,Reserch paper on 'Globalization and ICTs: Working Across Cultures'.(2001)

"Global Information and Communication Technologies". The World Bank.(2009)

Managing Information Technology in a Global Economy", by Mehdi Khosrowpour.(2001)

Chapter Thirteen
Intentional Leadership
-Kevin N. McGuire

Introduction

Leadership matters. Titans of business, legends of sport, and outsized political officials on the world's stage reinforce this precept, as distilled through self-promotion and nonstop media coverage.   Yet as much as leadership has been lionized, recent world events have also resulted in the overwhelming vilification of high-level leaders. The sentiment seems legitimate and appropriate. We have lost respect for executives in positions of influence because they have not demonstrated the basic qualities that leaders must project and the intensity of feeling in this matter is now acute. When corporate executives – the most promoted and vaunted workers of our time – require taxpayers to rescue them (and their institutions), attitudes regarding leadership are bound to change. Wall Street excesses, the tragedy and failures to follow-up in New Orleans after Hurricane Katrina, banks and insurance companies jeopardizing the value of homes and industries across the globe– to mention a few image breakers –have angered and disappointed the populace.

The public probably thought that corporate leaders focused on the future, making steady progress toward greater accomplishments, and marshaling human capital, technological advances and financial resources to facilitate that progress. Of course, citizens expect that progress would occur within an environment marked by integrity and ethics as part of the everyday fabric of decision-making. Unless leaders commit to higher values than short-term goals, personal gain, or enrichment of stockholders and special interest constituents, we will have few reasons to applaud leaders.

Beyond the expected cynicism, the acute public disappointments resulting from broad-based leadership failures have resulted in heightened awareness about the nature and potential of leadership. Specifically, leadership success does not come in a simple package that one opens and wears the new garment. Further, an emerging awareness in the public assumes that there is no single leadership personality, style or explicit set of traits for success (Hesselbein 1996).

As the public has come to realize, leadership is properly concerned with facilitating the work of others to achieve common goals, which include day-to-day results, personal and institutional accomplishment, and long-term progress; it is not about "what I want," but rather "what needs to be done" (Matshusta 1994).

One of the amazing dimensions of leadership is its complexity, as it is replete with paradoxes that present challenges to all who choose to assume a leadership mantle. That's because from a career perspective, leadership is dangerous and difficult work. It frequently means identifying uncomfortable issues, asking people to live up to their words, or facing up to frustrating realities.

Teaching and Learning School Leadership

Effective practices of districts and schools

The attempt to improve student achievement has generated focus-group discussions related to how both school districts and schools individually improve teaching and learning. Two key questions arise in these discussions: first, what personal characteristics or behaviors are associated with improved student achievement; and second, what behaviors support the teachers and keep them in their positions more than 5 years after being hired?

School districts and their schools have been a focus point for analyses by the U.S. Department of Education and the NYS Department of Education during the past three years. The effort has been coordinated to identify key challenges in leading a public education enterprise. The common challenges that emerged included:
unsatisfactory academic achievement, political conflict, inexperienced teaching staff;,low expectations and a lack of demanding curriculum, lack of instructional coherence, high student mobility, and unsatisfactory business operations (Manpower Demonstration Research Corporation 2004).

Some districts in the study represented "faster improving" districts. Their history indicated a past characterized by political and organizational stability and an agreement that educational reform plans and practices adjusted to meaningful change in student learning. To the study initiators, it appeared that these conditions might be preconditions for rapid improvement.

A consensus for change began with the acceptance of a new role for the superintendent and the school board. As a collective body, they would focus on policy-level discussions that supported improved student achievement. They would remove themselves from the day-to-day operations of the district and schools. Second, these districts accepted the superintendent's key role as developing a shared vision with the board that would delineate goals and strategies for reform.

Guidelines for reform would become the framework for a collaborative school-level goal/effort, and would allow the central office to revamp district operations to serve and support the school-based efforts for reform. Two additional factors emerged from the discussions: first, the identification and use of crucial stakeholders; and second, the ability of the school to articulate its plans for school improvement to the central office.

District-Level Practices

An analysis of the project revealed five success strategies consistent with faster improvement.

> 1. Primary attention directed toward student achievement, characterized by specific achievement targets for individual students and grade levels or departments plus a deliberate effort to align curricula to state standards, and *conversations* about connecting standards to classroom practice.
> 2. A school-wide agreement among all stakeholders to use available data to adjust classroom instructional practice. This required support from the central administration in the form of training for teachers, and support from

154

the school administration in the use of data-driven decision-making.

3. Reforms, although understood (conceptually) as district-wide, began at the elementary level.

4. Reading and mathematics instruction had to strengthen at the middle schools and high schools, even at the expense of other subjects.

5. The lowest performing schools in the district became the focus for additional support in the form of direct funding and teacher-quality initiatives.

School-Level Practices

At the school level, principals identified common practices they implemented that contributed to improved student achievement. The principals communicated the importance of school-wide change and encouraged and advocated for substantial reform. They motivated and assisted the staff to accept new school practices. Each of the principals described his/her leadership as primarily influenced by personal knowledge of teaching and learning. As a group, principals taught a class regularly, observed instruction in numerous classes each day (to stay informed), or modeled instruction for their teachers in classrooms. While there were many overlapping practices highlighted by the group, the practices that correlated with observations reported by New York State's Center for School Leadership included:

1. *Expectations* set at higher levels than previously accepted and indicators would include data review sessions. Students and teachers were aware of the higher levels of expectations and staff agendas referenced disaggregated achievement, longitudinal histories and projections about students.

2. *Curriculum standards and assessments* were a topic for regular discussion, with the goal being alignment across the grades and throughout departments, as well as the use of alternative evaluation models.

3. Principals expressed respect for *exceptional teaching,* and the teaching profession in general. They clearly believed that teacher attitudes influenced student achievement, and they believed that they should allow their teachers to take risks, while providing support for those who did experiment with new classroom practices.

4. *Personalization* of instruction was a frequent topic for sharing initiatives. The desire for increased personalization of instruction and support for students at the middle and high schools was a goal shared by the group. While advisor-advisee programs were in place, no one was willing to evaluate their success at the time of the interviews because they were too early in their implementation.

5. *Experimentation* was taking place with professional development in each of the schools. All experiments, professional development activities, and training events connected to school improvement initiatives were supported by the central administration.

6. *Community involvement* was one of the key points highlighted, with a variety of strategies, to encourage parental contact with the school and spur changes in teaching and learning. Technology and technological training became assets that supported changes in teaching and learning. All stakeholders regarded community involvement as an expectation, not an option.

The Demands on School Leaders

Demands have changed and priorities have shifted in recent years, as is typical with the school district enterprise. Instructional leadership has become the number one indicator of effective leadership in public schools, but this is not a broadly shared characteristic in the nation's schools, as various studies have indicated that current assistant principals and principals do not consider themselves skilled in fundamental concepts of instructional leadership.

In interviews with superintendents and principals, they described instructional leadership as "improving the quality of teaching and learning." Not surprisingly, different school districts view the practice of instructional leadership differently. In some districts, there is an emphasis on principals visiting every classroom frequently; in others, principals serve as instructional facilitators, designating teacher-leaders who spend time with every teacher.

No matter the school or district design for improving student achievement, foundational imperatives are necessary to achieve success. While district wide strategies are critical, some basic understandings at the school level are equally important. Instructional leadership does not mean usurping the job of the teacher. It does mean providing teachers with feedback, support and appropriate professional development. In providing this level of support, leaders have to demonstrate key abilities (Murphy 2008), including the ability to communicate and collaborate relative to the organization's purpose and direction.

In addition, several other abilities are essential, such as using a leader's influence and time to encourage the development or expansion of a school environment and organizational culture that celebrates academic, emotional and physical achievement. Joseph Murphy (2008) and the licensure consortium have detailed and refined six standards of performance for school leaders:

1. A school administrator is an educational leader who promotes the success of all students by facilitating the development, articulation, implementation, and stewardship of a vision of learning that is shared and supported by the school community.

2. A school administrator is an educational leader who promotes the success of all students by advocating, nurturing, and sustaining a school culture and instructional program conducive to student learning and staff professional growth.

3. A school administrator is an educational leader who promotes the success of all students by ensuring management of the organization, operations, and resources for a safe, efficient, and effective learning environment.

4. A school administrator is an educational leader who promotes the success of all students by collaborating with families and community members, responding to diverse community interests and needs, and mobilizing community resources.

5. A school administrator is an educational leader who promotes the success of all students by acting with integrity, fairness, and in an ethical manner.

6. A school administrator is an educational leader who promotes the success of all students by understanding, responding to, and influencing the larger political, social, economic, legal, and cultural context.

These standards formulate a foundation for a Cohesive Leadership System that integrates leadership development within New York State.

The Leadership Paradox

Individuals in leadership positions can inadvertently hinder the accomplishment of their organization's goals by not accepting the changes in leadership required in the early 21st century. In a striking departure from 20th century leadership models, *authority*, one of the assumed and obvious inherent tenets of management and leadership, must be *earned* these days. For education leaders, difficulties ensue because community leadership demands a paradoxical combination of abilities (Handy 1996).

The first paradox that every individual leader learns is that self-esteem and courage are critical dispositions – not arrogance, but a confidence that allows the individual to see into the future, step into the unknown, or uncover what is needed. Add the courage to confront the brutal facts and persuade community members to change direction and commit to higher levels of achievement for their students than they had thought possible.

Self-esteem and courage balanced with humility (Collins 2001) and a reasonable doubt keeps the leader open to the ideas of others. Many of those who would follow want to provide insight or help shape the path towards goal attainment. Successful leaders recognize the strength and value of incorporating the best thinking from within the group.

The second paradox surfaces as contrasting forces that frequently refer to the work ethic and personal responsibility leaders must assume. Charles Handy (1996) calls it a "passion for the job" that needs to be balanced by activities and interests that are not directly job related. Great leaders have interests and spend time with people outside of their professions, engage in cultural (arts), recreational (athletics), and other endeavors. They find the inspiration that strengthens job performance sometimes comes from the least-expected places and sharing these experiences with co-workers expands the day-to-day relationships that revolve mostly around specific work goals.

A third paradoxical facet of leadership has to do with relating to employees, genuinely recognizing them and caring for and appreciating them for their ideas, contributions and their anticipated contributions in their future. This caring attribute, however, mirrors the leader's capacity for aloneness (Handy 1996). All effective leaders must learn to "walk alone," as well as engage with others. When a decision is required, leaders are keenly aware that without their personal action, further progress will not happen. It is then, after the speeches, the focus groups and the feedback loops, that leaders have to commit, and commitment is an individual process.

While there is no agreed-upon inclusive or uniform set of leadership characteristics, these and other paradoxes do exist and leaders must hold them in balance in order to advance the organization's mission and goals.

Another dimension of the walk alone concept was presented by the ancient Greek, Herophilus (300 B.C.), who wrote, "When health is absent; wisdom cannot become manifest, strength cannot be exerted, wealth becomes useless, and reason is powerless." Leaders not only have to walk alone; they must care for themselves, or their vision, talents and commitments never will be realized.

Organizational Development and Leading Others

Leadership should focus on facilitating the achievement of others toward a common goal. To this end, an understanding of the people that follow leaders (I will refer to them as 'followers') has proven to be imperative. This point cannot be overemphasized. It is just as important for leaders to understand their followers, as it is for followers to understand their leader(s). If one leader can move 100 followers to a shared goal by understanding the thinking, motivations, and practices of the followers – and put systems and practices into place that realize the goal – then the leader has exercised successful leadership. If 100 followers understand a leader's articulated vision (only part of the process), and are not moved to act upon that vision because the leader has failed to prepare the followers for action, then the leader has failed.

Leaders think of followers as, literally, following them. This is an incomplete, perhaps even mistaken notion. Yes, followers choose to be led, sometimes because they admire or even love the leader. Other times they choose to be led because they agree on a shared goal. Either way, leaders and followers join forces on a shared quest, not simply a set of resources assigned to specific tasks.

These three elements combine for effective leadership: follower, leader, and shared goal. They need to connect in a profound way to support leadership for organizational advancement, and in the leader's mind, there should be no visible hierarchy between follower and leader to prevent advancement.

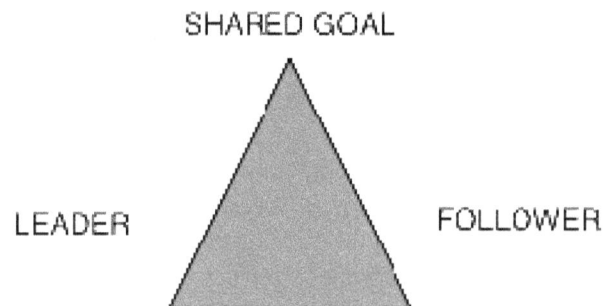

SHARED GOAL

LEADER   FOLLOWER

The Culture of the Workforce

Interpersonal relationships in the workforce comprise much of the culture within a company or an educational enterprise and they embody agency expectations. Joseph Murphy (2008) identified, in the ISLLC Leadership Standards, a culture of collaboration, trust, learning and high expectations that is critical to organizational success. This dimension of leadership that influences corporate culture has a powerful connection with integrity and ethics because no one can build trust and true collaboration in an environment that lacks open, dependable, and honest communication.

Effective leaders never resort to deceit or misleading messages. Constructive relationships build upon knowing and caring for one another. Von Krogh (2000), in addressing culture, emphasizes that caring is vital to successful performance. Indeed several corporate leaders, including KPMG, the U.S. Army, British Petroleum as well as many others, consider "quality relationships vital to their success."

Honest communication is an outgrowth of caring for employees and trusting them to work effectively toward the achievement of the organization's mission and goals. There is no secret to developing this type of culture. An effective leader proceeds with deliberate pace, communicates clear goals, and insists on order and honesty to win the trust of others. The organization is strongest when both truth and trust are pervasive.

In a trustful environment, communication is open and employees feel free to think and share creative ideas that influence the future. Von Krogh (2000) is explicit in reinforcing the difference between information and knowledge, indicating that knowledge attaches to human emotions, hopes, and intention. There is a connection between personal internal commitments and actions align with the vision and mission of the agency. Knowledge expands when the human side of the organization is diverse and nurtured.

Wisdom and Personal Growth

Schools have been recognized as a primary source for the development of competence and also, a public place where character should be developed directly or indirectly. In addition, while students accumulate information in school, leaders must hope that they will grow in wisdom. Wisdom acquisition occurs when leaders plan to develop wisdom among their followers or students by insisting that experiential learning and community service be part of every curriculum.

Wisdom will not be the outcome if the focus is exclusively on information accumulation. While a wealth of knowledge is important, the application of knowledge is the path to wisdom. This development should parallel the medical model that begins with theoretical knowledge and then advances to a clinical experience to apply new learning. Wisdom only occurs when a person has appropriate experiences to practice the application of clinical knowledge with a broad-based group of patients or peers.

Collective Wisdom

The most important factor in successful business ventures of any type is the caliber of the work force (Collins 2001). Yet, some executives behave as though they do not understand this basic truth. Konosuke Matsushita (1994) has proposed that "the proprietor" is responsible for injecting a human quality into the organization. In a school, the principal must humanize the enterprise.

While every organization must be concerned with the growth of the collective intelligence among staff; within schools, collective intelligence must increase at a steady and continuous rate among administrators, teachers, students and their parents. Teachers, administrators and students must continuously develop skills and abilities for their knowledge and wisdom to grow. School leaders must lead by example, demonstrating an uncommon focus, perseverance and determination to achieve academic growth and personal growth in the civic virtues of honesty, integrity, compassion, empathy and personal responsibility.

The "tail trails the head" (Matsushita1994). If the head continues to learn and apply research, the tail will follow. If the head is distant and detached from the basic mission or moves slowly to respond to opportunities, the tail will follow. In addition, top management must always listen to the workers. The leader must move between the big picture and the action on the front line. Gathering knowledge and insight from the front line will enhance organizational progress and will reinforce the understanding that everyone in the enterprise is important to the mission.

Survival Strategies

The demands on school and district leadership have changed dramatically due to the increased attention to standards testing and accountability. In the USA, the new public is interested in results because it is afraid that international academic development is outpacing graduates of high schools in the United States. The pressure in this environment is palpable and the work of educational leaders has become more difficult and professionally hazardous.

School leadership in these conditions means coordinating schools, boards of education, teacher unions, and families, in addition to teachers and administrators.

Leadership often involves asking people to face up to frustrating realities, and at times challenging people to follow through on their own words, to close the space between spoken values and behavior.

According to Richard Elmore, managing school districts to improve student achievement is one of the hardest jobs in America (Harvard Business Review 2007). Ronald Heifetz and Marty Lansky (2000) believe that many school leaders fail to recognize the dangers inherent in changing systems that operate within a district. People are set in their ways and resist change even though they, in theory, support innovations. Changing systems means changing beliefs and relationships within organizations and such changes create the professional minefields for leaders.

After working with hundreds of school superintendents, principals and teacher leaders, it is apparent to me that even the most successful leaders minimize the dangers in charting a new course for a school or district. I have learned that there are certain success strategies to manage change that serve as survival techniques for leaders who must move the organization forward.

First, the leader must accumulate followers prior to taking on significant alterations to the status quo. It is important to locate well-regarded partners who share the same goals. Having a convincing voice from multiple educators and others demonstrates the universal benefit of recommended changes. 'Going it alone' can appear arrogant, egocentric or foolhardy, and more importantly, risks the acceptance of important ideas.

This strategy highlights the importance of trusting relationships within the organization and with influential people outside of the school or district. Heifetz indicates that the quality of human relationships is more important than almost any other factor in determining results (2000)

Second, leaders must learn from the opposition. Understanding opposing viewpoints expands the leader's awareness of various perspectives on a topic, program, or recommendation. Often, by courting the opposition, the intensity of disagreement subsides to the point where all parties can see elements of agreement. If one is open to ideas from "across the aisle," progress can be crafted based upon a greater appreciation of subtle differences not identified by allies or the uncommitted.

It is also crucial not to overlook the quiet, yet uncommitted. They will frequently make the difference in the leader's success, like swing voters in an election. Although not outwardly clear in their lack of support, they may just be fearful of change due to an uncertain future.

Leaders who have experienced success in any field know the importance of personal relationships. Tending to the ideas of allies, the uncommitted and opponents will not only expand the knowledge base for all participants, such attention to details and stakeholders assists leaders to avoid misdiagnosing a problem or misunderstanding a solution. Leadership can be dangerous, and the risks associated with failure should diminish as they are tempered by those holding different viewpoints. Seek to understand and you have achieved the potential that others will understand you.

Discussion Questions

From your personal experience and/or current events in your community, please identify a successful leader who meets the criteria set by Joseph Murphy's Six Standards of Performance.

Please explain how the leader meets the Six Standards.

Is there an important leadership ability that you think is overlooked or underappreciated in your field or profession? Please explain why it is important and how you will develop that ability.

References

Bennis, W. (1989) *On Becoming a Leader.* Addison-Wesley Publishing Company, Inc.

Collins, J. (2001) *Good to Great: Why Some Companies Make the Leap and Other Don't.* Harper-Collins Publishers Inc.

Gardner, H.(1995) *Leading Minds: Anatomy of Leadership*Basic Books, A Division of Harper Collins Publishers, Inc

Handy, C.,& Hesselbein, F. (1996). *The Leader of The Future*The Drucker Foundation, Jossey-Bass.

Heifetz,R.,& Linsky,M. (2004). *When Leadership Spells Danger* Educational Leadership, Vol. 61, Number 7, pp. 33-37

Kouzes,J.M., & Posner,B.Z., (1998). *Encouraging the Heart: A leaders guide to rewarding and recognizing others.* San Francisco; Jossey-Bass.

Manpower Demonstration Research Corporation (MDRC), (2004). *Foundations for Success: Case Studies of How Urban School Systems Improve Student Achievement.* The Council of the Great City Schools

Matsushita,K. (1994). *Not For Bread Alone.* The PHP Institute,Inc. Dai Nippon Printing Co. Ltd.

Murphy,J.(2008) *Educational Leadership Policy Standards: ISLLC 2008.* The Council of Chief State School Officers

Von Krogh,G., & Ichijo,K., & Nonaka,I. (2000). *Enabling Knowledge Creation* Oxford: Oxford University Press

Wills, G. (1994). *Certain Trumpets: The Nature of Leadership* Simon & Schuster, New York

Chapter Fourteen
Deans, Authentic and Moral Leadership, Decision Making, and Higher Education
-Richard Bernato

Every Dean in higher education faces multiple decisions daily that require actions, implementation efforts, cajoling of faculty and staff, sanctions, reprimands, rewards and praise. Each action the dean selects reflects a pathway that is a decision-choice.

A "decision – choice" may be depicted graphically in the manner that the National Council for the Social Studies offered in 1984.

Figure 1 Decision making pathways

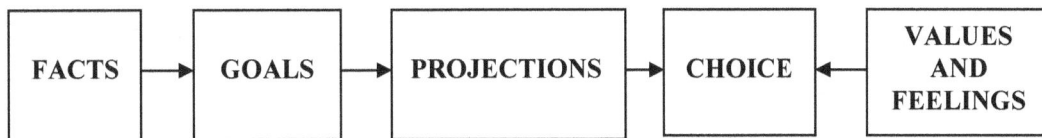

| FACTS | → | GOALS | → | PROJECTIONS | → | CHOICE | ← | VALUES AND FEELINGS |

In this model, a decision begins with a "decision – occasion" that generates a goal and a set of alternatives. Projections of these alternatives will suggest a series of possible, probable, and preferable futures. While any outcome may be possible, some outcomes are more probable than other outcomes. Thus, the decision choices narrow to what is preferable. What is preferable, the right side of the model dictates with its expressions of values and feelings. That is, when alternative possibilities are "computed" the choice for which we opt is a product of our values and feelings modified by our experiences and skills.

For example, the United States was shocked and angered by the Japanese attack on Pearl Harbor. Our desire for revenge and our determination to reverse Japanese military expansion is what drove our actions during the Second World War. When the United States secretly developed the atomic bomb, President Truman faced three distinct choices. One was to use an atomic weapon on Japanese major cities. A second was not use it. A third was to demonstrate the weapon's enormous power on a deserted Pacific island to threaten the Japanese and motivate them to surrender. While the potential outcomes of these choices were under debate, according to historical accounts, the president never deviated from his choice, to use it on Japan. Truman had a strong conviction that using the atomic bomb would shorten the war and save American lives. Thus, his values, i.e. saving American lives, drove the decision.

Hypothetically, a college president may face a decision where college finances contingent on tuition, are declining in an economic downturn. She may feel pressure to lower admission standards in order to garner more enrollees. Doing so will bring in more tuition and help assure the institution's financial health. However, another consequence would be to dilute the quality of the students who customarily attend and graduate from the school. What values are at stake for the president? What choices does she feel? What individual dimensions of the president's moral structure are at play? What principles of authentic moral leadership apply?

While the act(s) of deciding, especially the if-then computation of possible, probable, and preferable futures is subject to much analysis by a variety of theorists, what is common to all is the right side of the model offered in Figure 1, values, principles, and moral beliefs. That is, the strength and quality of the decision maker's values affect the moral quality of the choice made. Taken further, if the choice's actual outcome does not satisfy the decision maker's values, it is likely that the leader will opt for a new choice if the option is available.

The moral dimension for higher education administrators may be at the intersection of several similar mindsets that drive current views of leadership. These are charismatic, transformational, servant, and authentic models where proponents of each observe the existence of ethical and moral precepts often based upon shared values.

Avolio and Gardner (2005) differentiated among these models to describe their advocacy for an authentic leadership paradigm. Authentic leadership's central premise is "that through increased self-awareness, self-regulation, positive modeling foster the development of authenticity in followers" (p.317). Further, they cite Michie and Gooty (2005, p.318) who find that authentic leaders practice "transcendent values (e.g. universal values such as social justice, equality and broadmindedness; benevolent values, such as honesty, loyalty and responsibility) and positive other –directed emotions …. (318). Taken from a converse viewpoint, they note that Seeman (1960, p.320) examined inauthenticity in order to more fully explain how it differed from authenticity.

Seeman stated that inauthenticity was "extreme plasticity on the part of the leader seeking to comply with perceived demands arising from public roles" (320). Finally, Avolio and Gardner define authentic leaders as "those who are deeply aware of how they think and behave and are perceived by others as being aware of their own and others' values/moral perspectives, knowledge, and strengths; aware of the context in which they operate ; and who are confident, hopeful, optimistic, resilient, and of high moral character" (p. 321).

Avolio compared charismatic, transformational, servant and authentic models against several components of leadership practices and found elements of positive moral perspective, leader self-awareness and values in each of them.

Charismatic Leadership involves creating a self-image so powerful that people draw close to the leader naturally (http://changingminds.org/disciplines/leadership/styles/charismatic_leadership.htm)

Gardner and Avolio note in a prior article where they asserted, "while charismatic leaders employ rhetoric to persuade, influence and mobilize followers, an authentic leader energizes followers by creating meaning and positively socially constructing reality for themselves and their followers (p. 330)."

Transformational Leadership occurs where the leader takes a visionary position and inspires people to follow him (http://changingminds.org/disciplines/leadership/theories/bass_transformational.htm).

Gardner and Avolio differentiate between transformational leadership theory and authentic leadership theory by noting the key "distinction … authentic leaders are anchored by their own deep sense of self; they know where they stand on important issues, values and beliefs" (p.329).

The *Servant leadership*'s style of leadership puts the leader as responsible to one's followers (http://changingminds.org/disciplines/leadership/styles/servant_leadership.htm).

The authors acknowledge similarities in the morals / values perspective to authentic leadership, but also find that theoretical advocates such as Greenleaf and Blanchard have not offered verifying empirical evidence to validate their advocacy for a servant leadership style (330).

Bearing in mind that morals / values / ethics appear to be valid predictors of leadership, there is research that argues for authentic leadership in the practices of educators both in Kindergarten through Twelfth grade and higher education. Doscher and Normore (2008) use Starrat's (2005) five domains of moral responsibility as a framework for discussion. These domains begin with humble citizen, public servant, educator, educational administrator, and educational leader (p.3). They describe the role of the educational leader as one in which the leader has a duty to "transform the educational institution." Transformation extends beyond the typical low-level expectations of managing a school system and embraces the practices of proactive leadership where through planning and model behavior leaders embed particular values and morality into the culture of the school. They also support Strike's assertion (2008) that leaders "must be competent, caring, and collegial….morality is all about creating the reality" (p.4).

In particular, the educational leader infuses a value-laden layer over all acts and decisions. Finally, they incorporate Fullan's postulation that a moral leader obliges moral purpose and a special set of principles and practices in a systematic process that transform an enterprise. Fullan argues that systemic reform would reduce the so-called charismatic – hero model of leadership- to one where the leader facilitates others' leadership within a mission-based context.

Meacham (2007) used the Avolio and Gardner authentic leadership model to study higher education administrators who were self-aware of their values, beliefs, ethical philosophies and character strengths. Since higher education is often characterized by shared governance practices, administrators may be challenged by conflicting viewpoints and agendas that might be unethical or illegal. Higher education leaders hold the ethical line in their support of authentic change or they lead the pathway to immoral behavior.

This premise may also be similar to the power and leadership variables of the High Involvement model as described by Bernato (2001) where the school leader must define power boundaries and seek to distribute leadership responsibilities as appropriate. Meacham's qualitative study revealed that authentic administrators in higher education noted that they had to use considerable moral courage to take principled-based action against unethical behaviors or illegal policies.

Upperman (2007) examined how exceptional moral and ethical character shaped leaders of higher education institutions. The study recognized the complexity of character development in leaders and posited that those higher education leaders' views of their own leadership, their own moral values and ethical principles, the institution's own values, combined to shape the leader's development.

Markwardt (2001) examined servant leadership characteristics in higher education (2001) and substantiated the need for a foundation of moral absolutes to guide college leaders. Similarly, Plinske studied the critical characteristics, competencies and professional experiences of the next generation of community college presidents. A Delphi study of forty-one college trustees reduced sixty-eight potential attributes and competencies to nine critically important ones. Second among these was good moral character – honest, and trustworthy. Wilson's article about the resurgence of Drake University (2008) cites President Maxwell's basic principles that guided all of his regeneration work: honesty, inclusiveness and accountability (1).

Dikeman (2007) observed that the community colleges' mission obligates their college leaders to nurture a close relationship with the communities they serve and that this necessitates a focus on ethical leadership. She surveyed fifty-eight North Carolina community college presidents about their leadership practices and their ethical perspectives. She found a predominant tendency towards ethical absolutism in which "The respondents…scored highest in enabling others and modeling the way." Each of these practices is associated with authentic leadership. Similarly, studies about business leadership affirm aspects of authentic leadership and argue for their incorporation into higher education curriculum and practices (Marsh, 2008, Caldwell, 2007).

Wepner's, Donofrio's, and Wilhite's study of the leadership exhibited by educational deans is of particular value (2008). They presented vignettes to fourteen deans of education that embodied a four dimensional framework of leadership: intellectual, emotional, social, and moral. They grounded their research in the self-concept theory that "We come to know our professional identities because of intersubjective exchanges that occur as we test the meaning of our exchanges with others in the workplace" (p.154).

Thus, they suggest that a leader's construction of self evolves with inter and intra personal relationships and experiences. The key element for them is the quality of the leader's reflection about and distillation of events, exchanges and relationships.

They developed vignettes to represent aspects of intellectual, emotional, social and moral dimensions to which the deans described how they would react and why. They used a coding method to delineate and characterize the deans' responses to the various vignettes. Where the researchers initially expected the moral dimension to be the leading decision making determinant, they were surprised to find that the intellectual dimension was the dominant behavior set that informed decisions of these college deans.

They found little consistency among responses within the moral dimension with the exception that arguments pertaining to a sense of "duty" were commonly expressed by the deans as part of their decision making process. The authors suggest that the community college deans were not very self-reflective. They note: "However, education deans functioning in the context of U.S. higher education appear to rely on the intellectual dimension as the basis for employing the other three dimensions (p.165)." They lament that education deans may not have been prepared to examine their core values. They conclude that deans need to engage in continuous self-reflection and institutions should develop cultural support systems to see that this happens..

It may not be surprising that education deans in this study tended to use their intellectual dimension at the expense of the other three dimensions. Deans, after all, are esteemed and recognized individuals who likely achieve their posts because of their intellectual prowess. The deans in this study appeared to use their moral dimension to a lesser extent than the intellectual dimension. They may reflect the decision model where they define a decision opportunity, generate probable alternatives for analysis and project likely outcomes of each including which ones hold a personal advantage. Their decisions may be faulty unless they ground their choices in a clear sense of purpose and mission clarified by a strong sense of their ethics and values.

The formula $D = (S)(E) / M$; i.e. Decisions are a result of the products of Skills and Experiences, whose denominator is Mission, may capture the essence of ideal authentic leadership practices. The skills mastered, whether leadership, scholarship and research, experiences and opportunities develop during an individual's lifetime.

If however, the mission is inauthentic, unclear, or ungrounded, if the values shift as situations shift or if values relate to expedient opinions, the mission's moral validity is questionable. A mission weakened by ethical incertitude may taint the relationship of the skills and experiences the leader brings to the decision – opportunity. These reciprocal relationships must be authentic, clear, and grounded for valid moral leadership in Higher Education and any other leadership role.

Thus, even as institutions of higher learning sway with the winds of unprecedented economic pressures, and uncertain futures, college leaders must engage, develop, implement, and sustain authentic leadership.

Such leaders should make every effort:

- To seek and to reflect on experiences, accomplishments, and decisions in order to distill them for continuous development of oneself and one's enterprise,
- To practice and master "futuring" skills that help to predict likely outcomes of actions and non-actions,
- To create and lead a dialogue about identifying, and implementing adherence to a "vision" for the institution that is founded on unshakeable ethical codes and commensurate value-practices,
- To embed the formula: Decision = (Skills) x (Experiences) / Mission in their leadership and vision practices.

Seeking and Engaging Opportunities

Socrates' admonition that "an unexamined life is not worth living" may be worthy advice for leaders in higher education. As Wepner, et al. advised, it would be wise to employ systemic practices that Senge (1990) advocated such as Team Learning and Personal Mastery as college administrators take on the mantle of ethical and moral behavior.

Institutions of higher education might require their administrators to demonstrate that they practice reflective thinking with facilitators and participate in retreats devoted to matters of ethical behavior. As Senge suggests, dialogue and inquiry sustain ethics and moral behavior.

Practicing and Mastering "Futuring" skills

Futuring skills are formal if-then, predictive, and forecasting techniques that enable strategic planners, futurists, and thinkers to anticipate and extrapolate from trends. Through this simple technique, they recognize ripple effects, narrow probable consequences of decisions, acts, and plans and select the best course of action. Futuring skills that disburse throughout an organization begin at the top. Mastery of these skills enable the ethical and authentic leader to choose actions that align with and support consequences that are acceptable to the espoused values of the institution.

Creating a Dialogue

Avolio and Gardner use the word followers to denote those constituents, stakeholders, faculty, and staff who recognize, embrace and aspire to authenticity in their own practices. Followers and leaders share a collective vision with common principled values and ethics. The shared vision is more likely to sustain an authentic higher education organization in difficult times than the influence of any one leader. An authentic leader creates a dialogue about identifying and implementing adherence to a "vision" with an unshakeable ethical code and commensurate value-practices. The vision emanates from the dialogue that the participants create as they work their way through many discussions of "if we want this...then, we must do."

Decisions

Decisions are a function of one's skills and experiences insofar as they represent one's mission and values. This "formula" seeks to represent the dependence between both sides of the equation and implies the extent to which the facets of authentic leadership described by Avolio, Gardner and others apply to a decision – maker. Leaders construct decisions in the dynamic tension among skills, dispositions and experiences of the participants modified by their values, understanding and commitment to their shared mission.

The research appears to indicate that practices of modeling and reflection are characteristics of authentic leadership. When a leader reflects upon how the skills one has developed and one's life experiences contribute to one's self concept, one may see how one's actions are driven qualitatively by the ethical and moral convictions one holds about one's mission.

Algebraically, if one of these variables, the decision, the skills, the experiences, values or the mission harms others in unnecessary and negative ways, and reflects unethical or immoral behavior, the whole equation no longer represents of authentic leadership. The equation is now a representation of coercive leadership, manipulation and tyranny. Conscious recognition and awareness of the ingredients contributing to this formula may help leaders adhere to their aspirations to be authentic and create forums for higher education that are based upon service and opportunities for others to grow and develop skills and valuable experiences. Deans serve in the first line of academic integrity and must reflect mission and leadership practices consistent with the vision of the enterprise if their schools are to flourish.

Discussion Questions

1. The model of decision-making offered in Figure 1 represents a Classical Theory of decision-making. In practice, the model for leaders in institutions of higher education should represent a more fluid, multifaceted approach to decision making. How would you suggest we modify, add to, delete from, or create a more likely model of what comprises ethical, authentic decision making? 2. The formula, $D = (S)(E) / \text{Mission}$ seeks to "algebraically" demonstrate the interrelationship of the act of deciding and its dependence on the emergence of one's skills and experiences insofar as the authenticity of one's mission. Does the "formula" hold? How would you rearrange or rewrite it to reflect specific applicability to authentic leadership practices not only in higher education but in other venues?

References

Avolio, Bruce J., Gardner, William J. "Authentic Leadership development: Getting to the root of positive forms of leadership." The Leadership Quarterly 16 (2005) 315 – 338.

Bernato, Richard. "High Involvement Behaviors of Elementary Blue Ribbon and Non-Blue Ribbon Schools in Long Island. Dissertation. Dowling College. 2001.

Caldwell, Cam, Lily, Jeane. "Ethical Leadership and Building Trust – Raising the Bar For Business". Journal of Academic Ethics 5 (2007) 1-4.

Dikeman, Randi. Leadership practices and leadership ethics of North Carolina community college presidents. Dissertation. East Carolina University.2007.

Doscher, Stephanie Paul, Normore, Anthony H. "The Moral Agency of the Education Leader in Times of National Crisis and Conflict." Journal of School Leadership 18 no.1 (January 2008) p.8

Markwardt, Richard Arthur. Servant Leadership: Moral Foundations and academic manifestations. Dissertation. Kent State University. 2001

Marsh, Catherine. Business executives' of ethical leadership and its development: Implications for higher education and human resource development. Dissertation. Northern Illinois University 2008.

Meacham, Margaret Anne. Life stories of authentic leaders in higher education administration. Dissertation. The University of Texas at Austin. 2007.

Plinske,Kathleen. The next generation of community college presidents: Critical characteristics, competencies, and professional experiences. Dissertation. Pepperdine Univesity. 2008.

Ploussiou, Leah Joanna. Establishing legitimacy: An analysis of a college president's first year at the helm. Dissertation. University of Pennsylvania. 2005.

Upperman, Phillippe J. Shaping exceptional moral and ethical character among leaders of higher education institutions. Dissertation. Seattle University. 2007.

Wepner, Shelley B., D ' Onofiro, White, Stephen C. "The Leadership Dimensions of Education Deans." Journal of Teacher Education 59; (2008) 153

Wilson, Robin. "At Drake, Leadership by Example is Effective." The Chronicle of Higher Education 54 no. 45 1 July 18 2008.

http://www.changingminds.org/
http://changingminds.org/disciplines/leadership/styles/charismatic_leadership.htm
http://changingminds.org/disciplines/leadership/theories/bass_transformational.htm
http://changingminds.org/disciplines/leadership/styles/servant_leadership.htm

Chapter Fifteen
Financial Crisis, Global Imbalance, and Globalization: A Cry for Cooperative Action
-Anand Shetty

Introduction

Economic and financial globalization and the accompanying increased cross-border investment and trade, spread of technology, educated workforce, emphasis on market economy and sound macroeconomic policies have made substantial contribution to economic growth and prosperity around the world. The value of trade as a percentage of the world GDP increased from 42.1 in 1980 to 62.1 in 2007. Foreign direct investment increased from 6.5 percent of world GDP in 1980 to 31.8 percent in 2006. The stock of international claims (primarily bank loans) as a percentage of the world GDP increased roughly 10 percent in 1980 to 48 percent in 2006.

The number of minutes spent on cross-border telephone calls on a per-capita basis increased from 7.3 in 1991 to 28.8 in 2006. The number of foreign workers has increased from 78 million people (2.4 percent of the world population) in 1965 to 191 million people (3.0 percent of the world population) in 2005. The percent of the developing world living in extreme poverty has been reduced in half.

Greater openness and increased competition in a globalized market place means increased access to capital and modern technology, innovation and greater efficiency. Joseph Stiglitz, a Nobel Laureate, has observed that globalization "has reduced the sense of isolation felt in much of the developing world and has given many people in the developing world access to knowledge well beyond the reach of even the wealthiest in any county a century ago" (IMF, Globalization: Brief Overview, Issues Brief, Feb. 2008).

The road to growth and prosperity through globalization has not been without setbacks. Financial and currency crises that the world witnessed in recent years pushed back the progress made by globalization. What is significant about these crises is that they do not stay localized thanks to the increasing interdependency that has followed the globalization process.

In 1994, the Mexican Peso crisis, which engulfed the Latin American countries, had unsettling effect on the cross-border capital flows that fueled the process of economic growth and development. Soon after the world economy dealt with the Peso crisis, the Asian currency crisis erupted in 1997. Starting in Thailand, it quickly spread to most of the Asian countries. It took almost two years to recover from the impact of this disaster and the damage done to economic growth in these countries.

The Asian currency crisis followed by the collapse of the Russian bond market in 1998, the collapse of the stock market bubble in 2000 and the terrorist attack in New York in 2001, shook global markets. Although the global economy was resilient enough to bounce back each time, it did not happen without major setbacks to growth and prosperity that globalization helped to bring about.

2008-09 Financial Market Crises

The 2008-09 collapse of global financial markets threw the world into a recession unmatched by any since the great depression. It literally placed globalization on hold by decreasing trade flows, reversing cross-border capital flow and increasing trade restrictions and protectionism. The World Trade 0rganization (WTO) predicted that the trade flows would fall 9% in 2009, the largest in 80 years.

A part of this decline was attributed to shortage of trade finance. Multinational banks, which greased the wheels of world trade with necessary financing, pulled inward to address their problems at home created by the credit crunch. The WTO estimates that there is a credit shortfall between $100bn and $300bn a year. Cross-border capital flows also saw similar decline. Americans alone repatriated $759 bn. in the three quarters following the rescue of Bear Sterns in March 2008 (Financial Times (FT), 4/30/09).

According to the Institute of International Finance, the net private capital flow to emerging markets in 2009 is shaping to be the worst on record. The figures released by the BIS in April 09 showed that the cross-border lending shrank by $4,800bn to $31,000bn in nine months as of December 2009, the sharpest fall on record.

The OECD projected its member countries' total output to fall by 4.3% and the unemployment rate to reach 10% in 2009. When the world is in recession, trade becomes the major victim as international and domestic interests collide to restrict trade.

In spite of their commitment to avoid trade restrictions at the November 08 meeting of the G20 countries in Washington, 17 out of the 20 countries have been reported to initiate 47 policies that have trade restricting effects in some form by the time they met again in April 2009 in London (FT, April 2, 2009).

The protectionist trend seen since the crisis was made worse by the falling US dollar and consequent undervaluation of Chinese renminbi relative to all other currencies that float with the US dollar.

It is an historical fact that when a currency seeks to gain or maintain trade advantage by manipulating its currency, other countries respond with devaluation of their currencies or other trade restricting measures such as tariff and quotas to protect their exports. Vietnam's decision to devalue its currency by 5% in November 2009 to protect itself from renminbi undervaluation and the discomfort expressed by other Asian countries to renminbi's undervaluation, were clear evidence of such response. The ultimate victim of the protectionist policies is global trade and development.

Analysis

Prevention of financial crises is one of the major issues facing the world community today, and the future of globalization depends on it. Understanding the causes of such financial crises is the first step towards finding a resolution. A crisis may be triggered by a set of forces that is unique to the country or the market where it originates.

The increasing dependencies and interconnectedness brought about by financial and economic globalization plays a key role in globalizing such a crisis. Each participant in the global economy has certain responsibilities towards maintaining the free flow of trade through appropriate macro-economic and balance of payment policies. Any policy failure can give rise to undesirable consequences, including the financial crises that the world has experienced over the years.

U.S. Role

The financial crisis of 2007-08 has been attributed to the growing global imbalance and the U.S. failure to reign in the surging liquidity (a development caused by global imbalance) in the late 1990s and early 2000s. The global imbalance is reflected in the trade surpluses and deficits that countries experience. Since the sum of all deficits must be equal to the sum of all surpluses, when some counties enjoy surpluses, it has to be at the cost of deficits in other countries.

Table 1 highlights the extent of this imbalance from the perspective of the US, the country that has experienced the largest trade deficit and also where the 2008-09 financial market crisis originated.

The US Trade Deficits and Per Cent Share of Major Trading Partners:

Year	US	China	Canada	Mexico	Germany	Japan	OPEC	Total
1985	121880	0.00	17.85	4.51	9.18	37.87	8.47	77.88
1986	138538	1.20	16.54	3.54	10.51	39.72	6.43	77.95
1987	151684	1.84	7.43	3.75	10.10	37.13	8.50	68.76
1988	114566	3.05	8.53	2.30	10.49	45.21	7.83	77.40
1989	93142	6.69	9.82	2.34	8.56	52.67	18.70	98.78
1990	80864	12.90	9.53	2.32	11.63	50.83	30.11	117.32
1991	31136	40.76	18.99	-6.90	15.53	139.34	43.65	251.37
1992	39212	46.69	20.49	-13.72	19.31	126.49	28.67	227.93
1993	70311	32.39	15.32	-2.37	13.70	84.42	17.41	160.87
1994	98493	29.96	14.18	-1.37	12.71	66.67	14.03	136.17
1995	96384	35.06	17.79	16.40	14.99	61.36	16.68	162.27
1996	104065	37.98	20.84	16.82	14.85	45.72	21.15	157.35
1997	108273	45.90	14.29	13.44	17.24	51.83	17.09	159.77
1998	166140	34.26	10.02	9.54	13.95	38.53	5.28	111.60
1999	265090	25.91	12.11	8.61	10.72	27.69	8.23	93.27
2000	379835	22.07	13.66	6.47	7.65	21.47	12.64	83.97
2001	365126	22.76	14.47	8.23	7.96	18.90	10.87	83.20
2002	423725	24.32	11.37	8.77	8.47	16.52	8.13	77.57
2003	496915	24.97	10.40	8.18	7.90	13.29	10.28	75.02
2004	607730	26.70	10.94	7.43	7.54	12.54	11.49	76.65
2005	711567	28.43	11.03	7.01	7.11	11.71	13.43	78.71
2006	753283	31.08	9.53	8.57	6.36	11.91	14.88	82.33
2007	700258	36.92	9.73	10.68	6.39	12.04	16.73	92.49
2008	681130	39.35	11.50	9.50	6.31	10.88	26.09	103.64

Source: US Department of Commerce

The US trade deficit increased almost six fold between 1985 and 2008. One country that stands out prominently as having the largest share in this deficit is China. It's share rose from less than one percent in 1985 to almost 40 percent in 2008. The second major contributor to the US deficit is OPEC, with its share rising from 8.47 per cent in 1985 to 26 per cent in 2008. The shares of Canada, Mexico and Germany have more or less stayed the same. Japan's share has fallen from 37.87 per cent to 10.88 percent during the same period, a trend that is opposite to that of China.

Many leading economists, including the Federal Reserve Bank Chairman, Ben Bernanke, argued that the global imbalance is the root cause of the current crisis. Savings glut in China and other developing countries flooded the financial markets of the deficit countries like the U.S. and created an environment for low interest rate, asset price inflation and the bubble. Chinese exchange rate policy, by holding the renminbi value against the U.S. dollar and prices of Chinese manufacture goods low, played a major role in creating trade imbalance between China and the U.S. Martin Wolf of Financial Times observed, "China's decision to accumulate roughly 2000bn in foreign currency reserve was a blunder" (FT, 6/10/09).

The situation was made worse by the lack of proper supervision of the financial markets that were busy innovating and introducing complex financial instruments in managing the credit flows. The U.S. regulators are also responsible for letting the cheap money policy create consumption boom that sucked a record volume of cheap imports and expanded household debt with excessive borrowing.

There is a third dimension to the financial crisis and the imbalance problem. Often, it is asked why is the U.S. so prone to excessive spending, running current account deficits, and financing it with foreign debt? The answer lies in the reserve currency status of the U.S. dollar.

As the issuer of the world's major reserve currency, the U.S. can use its own currency to finance its trade deficit and as the supplier of the reserve currency, it has no choice but to run persistent deficits to meet the growing demand for this reserve currency. The reserve currency status of the U.S. dollar places the U.S. in a dilemma.

As the global economy expands, the demand for dollar denominated assets for reserve will expand forcing the U.S. to run larger and larger current account deficit. If it stops issuing dollar denominated assets, it will create a shortage of liquidity and risk pulling the world economy into a spiraling contraction.

The problem with this paradoxical situation is that as the quantity of outstanding dollar assets increases, it would eventually undermine the value of the dollar. Yale economist Robert Triffin, famously known as Triffin's Dilemma, pointed this out nearly 50 years ago.

Foreigners holding these assets will start questioning the U.S.'s ability to maintain the dollar's value. In fact, such questioning has already started. China, Russia and other BRIC countries have been making demands for the dollar's replacement as the reserve currency. On the eve of G20 meeting in April 09, the head of the People's Bank of China published a paper proposing replacement of the dollar as the reserve currency.

Towards a Solution

What does the world do to prevent future financial crisis after witnessing the most severe downturn since the 1930s depression and place the world on a sustainable growth path? No single country can prevent a global financial/economic crisis on its own in an interdependent world. It calls for coordinated efforts by major players in the world economy. The world must address several things on a priority basis. First, nations must reduce their trade imbalance caused by savings glut through concerted efforts to increase domestic spending in surplus countries as an important first step.

Why do imbalances matter? They matter because they are a factor as was the case with the 2008-09 financial crisis and they make recovery from the crisis difficult. When the imbalances persist, the countries with big external deficits will be under pressure to continue with fiscal deficits to maintain demand. This will place pressure on interest rates and ultimately crowd out private investment and lower potential growth. If on the other hand, the deficit countries reduce their deficits sharply without offsetting changes in surplus countries, it will result in sharp decline in global demand.

The imbalance also has implications for the financial markets, as it was evident in the 2008-09 financial crisis. They had a share in the market meltdown. They created a huge demand for liquid and safe assets as the surplus countries placed their reserves in the market. The financial market responded to this by fabricating financial assets in a hurry without regard to their safety and soundness. The result was the financial market crisis that we witnessed in 2009.

The surplus countries can stimulate domestic demand through appropriate macroeconomic policy measures and the deficit countries, like the U.S., should do their part by curtailing excessive consumption. These measures by themselves are not enough.

Exchange rates must also adjust to aid the elimination of the imbalance and the prevention of future imbalances. Currencies of the deficit countries must decline relative to those of surplus countries so that their products become more attractive to foreign buyers and the domestic consumers are encouraged to find domestic substitutes for imports.

The decline in the value of the U.S. dollar following the financial crisis is part of this natural process of adjustment. What must also happen, but has not happened, is the decline in the dollar's value against the renminbi, the currency of the country with a very large trade surplus, along with other currencies.

Renminbi, has been kept pegged to dollar at 6.82 renminbi. This has made the situation worse for other countries whose currencies have appreciated against the dollar by making exports from these countries to China expensive and Chinese imports attractive. This is reflected in the surge of China's exports from $276 bn. in the second quarter of 2009 to $325 bn. in the third quarter (Martin Feldstein, FT 10/30/09).

The introduction of a new reserve currency, preferably a super-sovereign currency as is suggested by some leaders, to avoid the burden on a single currency such as the US dollar, may have some merits as a solution to global financial crisis. It can help to relieve the U.S. from its sole responsibility as a supplier of reserve currency and restore confidence in the U.S. dollar. The U.S. can focus more on dealing with its mounting current account deficit and foreign debt problem instead of taking on the burden of providing liquidity to the global financial markets.

China has repeatedly called for replacing the dollar as the reserve asset by a composite currency similar to Special Drawing Rights (SDR). Beijing has also shown interest in extending the composition of SDR to include major emerging market currencies including its own currency. Even if such an idea is good, having renminbi in the composite without making it freely tradable and without having open access to Chinese capital markets may not make such a composite currency easily acceptable to major central banks.

It is not clear how replacing the dollar by a composite currency, however constituted, will be an answer to the global imbalance problem and to the issues facing the global financial markets. Even the idea of a reserve currency may be irrelevant in a highly integrated global economy where fewer and fewer countries are adhering to fixed-exchange rate regimes.

In a recent article in the Financial Time (12/10/09), Martin Feldstein observes that countries no longer hold dollars or other currencies as traditional reserve assets to bridge gaps between imports and exports. Instead, these assets are being used as long-term investment funds. Countries engage in sophisticated portfolio strategies in the management of these funds. The currencies can suffer ups and downs as the portfolios are rebalanced. Current decline in the dollar value against major currencies can be attributed to such portfolio rebalancing activities.

One interesting outcome of this new role of reserve currencies is that when the dollar declines relative to other currencies because of rebalancing, it will shrink the U.S. trade deficit and create a shortage of dollars in the currency market. This shrinkage, in the course of time, will stop the decline in the value of the dollar and may reverse the process.

Since the failure of financial markets that process the financial flows is equally responsible for the current crisis, there is an urgent need for stricter regulation and prudent supervision of these markets to prevent asset price bubbles and their eventually collapse. In an interdependent world, financial regulations also need to be coordinated and leveled to prevent participants in the financial market from taking advantage of policy differences known as regime arbitrage.

One policy leveling issue that is discussed is the bank levy to pay for the bank rescue carried out by various governments during the financial crisis. It is important that if one government does it, other governments who represent the centers of major financial markets must also do it.

The coordination of macroeconomic and financial policies is best done through a greater cooperation among the G20 countries that represent 85 percent of world output. When G20 countries met in London in April 2009, they addressed the issue of international cooperation to deal with the global recession. The following statements in the preamble to its September 09 meeting in Pittsburgh are evidence to the commitment of G20 countries:

> "Today we agreed to launch a framework that lays out the policies and the way we act together to generate strong, sustainable and balanced global growth. We need a durable recovery that creates the good jobs our people need.
>
> We need to shift from public to private sources of demand, establish a pattern of growth across countries that is more sustainable and balanced, and reduce development imbalances. We pledge to avoid destabilizing booms and busts in asset and credit prices and adopt macroeconomic policies, consistent with price stability, that promote adequate and balanced global demand. We will also make decisive progress on structural reforms that foster private demand and strengthen long-run growth potential.
>
> Our framework for strong, sustainable and balanced growth is a compact that commits us to work together to assess how our policies fit together, to evaluate whether they are collectively consistent with more

sustainable and balanced growth, and to act as necessary to meet our common objectives.

We commit to make sure our regulatory system for banks and other financial firms rein in the excesses that led to the crisis. Where reckless behavior and a lack of responsibility led to crisis, we will not allow a return to banking as usual, and to act together to raise capital standards, to implement strong international compensation standards aimed at ending practices that lead to excessive risk-taking, to improve the over-the-counter derivatives market and to create more powerful tools to hold large global firms to account for the risks they take. Standards for large global financial firms should be commensurate with the cost of their failure. For all these reforms, we have set for ourselves strict and precise timetables"

The Pittsburgh meeting is also important for declaring G20 as the premier forum for international economic cooperation and establishing the Financial Stability Board (FSB) that will include major emerging countries with responsibilities for coordinating and monitoring progress in strengthening financial regulation.

It is not, however, clear from the debate how the group is going to resolve the policy differences and convince the members of the importance of shared responsibilities. The Pittsburgh summit gave finance ministers a task of bringing about an agreement on shared policy objectives. By the time the ministers met in Scotland in November, 2009, agreement had not been achieved. They claimed that progress has been made on the timetable for assessing whether countries have adopted policies that are in the collective interest rather than the narrow self-interest of countries.

At this meeting, the G20 agreed to set out national policy frameworks by the end of January 2010, conduct the first cooperative mutual assessment process by April 2010 and develop a set of policy options for the next summit in June and develop more specific policy recommendations for leader at their summit in November 2010.

There are, however, a number of difficult and sensitive issues, such as the Chinese exchange rate and coordination of financial market regulation in each country, that they did not address. And, on other areas, such as climate change, or the flow of funds from rich to poor countries to help reduce carbon emissions, was also limited.

Five prominent members of the group, including the Canadian and South Korean leaders, who will chair the group's two summits this year, sent a letter recently to the rest of the G20 countries indicating frustration at slow progress this year. They warned them that "without cooperative action to make the necessary adjustments to achieve (strong and sustainable growth), the risk of future crises and low growth remain". They emphasized the need to design cooperative strategies and work together to ensure that our fiscal, monetary, foreign exchange, trade and structural policies are collectively consistent with strong, sustainable and balanced growth (FT 11/09/09).

One thing is clear, that the role the U.S. played as an engine of global growth for so long is not sustainable anymore. It's ability to act as the consumer of the last resort along with a few other small economies that kept the world in balance is impaired.

The U.S. households are burdened with enormous debt and there is an urgent need to clean up their balance sheets. In an article in Financial Time on 12/21/09, Kemal Dervis of Brookings Institute called upon developing countries to step in to cure the global imbalance and help the U.S. clean up its balance sheet.

The rest of the world must generate more imports in relation to exports, and the major burden of this must fall on surplus countries like China, Germany and Japan. China with the fastest growing economy and with a savings rate of 49 percent of the GDP and 28 percent of the global savings in 2009 can make a big difference. China's export share of GNP has risen from 20 percent to 36 percent between 2001 and 2007. Its current account surplus in 2008 is $426 bn. The IMF expects the surplus to rise again after a temporary decline, to $595 bn. in 2012. It is estimated that if China's current account surplus rises to 10 percent of its GDP, its surplus could be as high as $800bn by 2018.

Stimulus measures introduced by China were helpful in preventing its economy from slipping into recession, but they were not by themselves of much help in reducing the imbalance. China's efforts must be accompanied by appropriate adjustments to its exchange rate to make a difference. With a large foreign exchange reserve valued at $2,273 bn. in September 2009, "China has kept its exchange rate down to a degree unmatched in world economic history." Its real exchange rate has remained more or less at the same level since 1998 and depreciated by 12 percent over the last seven months (Martin Wolf, 12/09.09). Moreover, China's policy of keeping the exchange rate down is the same as providing an export subsidy that is protectionism.

Germany, another major surplus country, also faces criticism for not being helpful in solving the trade imbalance problem. Forecasts suggest that Germany will have a surplus of $187b this year, second only to China with a forecast of $291b. Just like China, Germany believes that their customers should continue to buy from them and not borrow which is inconsistent with the fact that their surpluses mean the customers' deficits. How can a country continue to borrow and run a deficit to support the exports of surplus country without running into financial disaster, including eventual default? This is definitely not in the best interest of the surplus countries.

Many members of the 16-country eurozone economy have been facing serious imbalance problems. Germany has been called upon to take a lead in boosting growth across the region. Berlin has refused to give up its competitive advantage earned by being a low cost producer or to share the advantages of being a surplus country. Berlin could boost demand and help other countries in the zone.

When the world is trying to struggle out of a deep recession, demand matters, and as the world's fourth largest economy, Germany has a role to play in rebalancing global demand. It is difficult to understand why the surplus countries refuse to accept that their reliance on export surpluses (lending to customers to buy their goods) must eventually harm them if their customers go bankrupt. A disruption of eurozone will be bad for Germany and so will any protectionism move by the US towards China (FT, Matin Wolf, 3/17/10).

Discussion Questions

What is global imbalance? What factors are behind the global imbalance? Why is it a problem for the continued and sustainable growth of the world economy?
Explore the leadership role played by G20 group. What are the potential problems they face in dealing with global issues?

Chapter Sixteen
Leading Social Agencies in a Democratic Society
-Richard J. Hawkins

Let us face facts. The title of "leader" and the accompanying responsibilities the role entails is becoming less and less attractive to many who possess the talent but not the will to lead. While private sector leaders seem motivated by huge and irrationally large compensation packages, social agencies can rarely compensate their leaders in a way that remotely reflects their passion, commitment, hard work, and responsibilities. Fortunately for social agencies, like schools and other governmental and non-profit organizations that exist to improve the human condition, the work itself and the ability to lead organizations with a higher moral purpose is still somewhat attractive to some very talented people.

Yet, fewer and fewer people seem willing to fulfill leadership roles where compensation does not adequately address the risk factors of assuming responsibility. Whether selecting a CEO or seeking candidates for non-profit boards, the pool of qualified and willing candidates to fill these roles seems to be diminishing. More and more social agencies struggle to find qualified leaders. We seem to be on the precipice of a leadership void of epic proportions in the realm of social services.

As Thomas Friedman (2005) noted, globalization has begun to level the playing field and other nations challenge the United States of America's dominance on the world stage in virtually every domain. While still a dominant player on the world stage, the USA is clearly finding itself in the midst of major social, political and economic shifts.

A vast difference between the "haves" and the "have-nots" is growing exponentially and the resultant social unrest is far too tangible both in the US as well as internationally. The level of mistrust between citizens and their leaders at virtually every level has never been higher. Perceived arrogance and an unwillingness to listen to constituents in the face of this unrest have inflamed citizens worldwide.

The internet and the availability of news on an almost instantaneous basis, 24 hours a day, has led to the average world citizen becoming far more aware of every leader's indiscretion and governmental misstep. The advent of on-line social networking sites and blogs create a level of individual and organizational transparency never before seen. The sheer volume of the data available to anyone on the internet on any subject is overwhelming.

Add the self-serving "spin" of the "data" to the mix and often two individuals looking at the exact same information can easily arrive at two diametrically opposing interpretations of the same data set. Whom do you believe? Almost any individual citizen can find a way to engage in a very public expression of thoughts on virtually any leader, topic, person, or organization, whether they have command of the facts or not. Opinion has begun to supplant knowledge as the standard for "action."

The worldwide recession has added fuel to the fire of discontent that leaders face among their constituents and enemies. In the USA, the crisis in our financial markets has taken a financial toll on virtually all social agencies regardless of whether funded privately or publically. The loss of sustainable revenue and the reliance on "one-shot" financial quick fixes hamper our ability to redesign and align social agencies with Twenty-first century needs, particularly the issues associated with our shifting and increasingly diverse demographics and globalization.

Our leadership void in government has become so ubiquitous that citizens have simply begun to accept poor leadership as typical and normal. The scary truth is that the failure of leadership in our social agencies is starting to resemble, in the worst possible ways, the leadership of our elected officials. The emphasis on short-term gains more often serve the interests and needs of the leaders and their boards than the interests and needs of constituents and the core purpose of the organizations. Frankly, if left unchecked this emphasis on short term gains and the concentration of wealth into the hands of fewer and fewer members of society, can put the future of our democratic society and perhaps democracy itself in jeopardy.

Our social agencies, particularly schools, lie at the core of our democracy. The founders of our democratic society understood the importance of developing an informed citizenry who had the will and capacity to participate in the democratic process. The stakes are simply too high for our social agencies to fail.

Despite the daunting circumstances we face, we must develop leaders with the skills and dispositions to navigate successfully the roiling waters of our changing world. Twenty-first century leaders of social agencies must see opportunity in crisis and be willing to lead and serve their organizations with moral purpose. We must develop collaborative educational leaders who can make our schools and other social agencies immune to political statehouses dedicated to their own self-interests. With enlightened leadership in our social agencies, we can design and build social agencies that focus on their core missions and provide many clients the services that they need.

Twenty-first Century Leadership

Twenty-first century leaders know the difference between leading "organizations" and leading "people." Effective leaders lead people, not concepts or slogans. As pointed out repeatedly by Gary Wills (1994) in his book, *Certain Trumpets*, leaders require followers. Without followers, who can lead? Followers require inspiration and clarity from leaders.

Leaders of social agencies know that people *are* the organization, thus building relationships and treating everyone with dignity and respect is paramount. Adults can exercise choice. They can choose to work for your organization or not. They can choose to believe in and support an organization's purpose or not. The more effective the leader, the more those they lead will make choices that benefit the organization as a whole enterprise.

In social sectors, where the intrinsic commitment and dedication of the faculty, staff, or employees is essential for organizational quality, leaders must focus on the skill, capacity, and beliefs of the people. If people believe in the organization, understand and believe in its core purpose and its vision, the leader's main job to create common understanding and commitment is easy to accomplish.

A leader's orientation toward collaboration and the creation of collaborative teams seems essential to democratic institutions. One person cannot manage, comprehend, or synthesize all the facets or factors affecting their organization. As Peter Senge states, "It is no longer sufficient to have one person learning for the organization... It's just not possible any longer to 'figure it out' from the top, and have everyone else following the orders of a 'grand strategist.' The organizations that will truly excel in the future will be the organizations that discover how to tap people's commitment and capacity to learn at *all* levels in the organization" (2007, p. 4).

An individual who dispenses solutions to every problem with 100% accuracy and believes that he or she avoids unintended consequences does not lead successful organizations. While some leaders like to perpetuate the myth of their infallibility, their careers are often short. Unfortunately, their negative effects on the organizations they "lead" are felt for decades later. The world is simply too complex and the speed at which change occurs blurs every individual's vision. No individual sees all and knows all.

Leading With Vision

Twenty-first century leaders lead with vision. Simply put, they design, teach, and steward every aspect of their organization in alignment with the organization's shared vision of success (Senge, 1999). In organizations led by effective leaders, vision is a living, breathing, inspirational picture of one's desired future. A vision encompasses everything from performance goals to the way everyone expects to behave as a community. Everything revolves around the vision: decision-making, strategic goals, hiring, firing, supervision, programs, budget, professional development, and community engagement. In successful organizations, vision enables proactive behavior by many employees and is palpable throughout every aspect and dimension of the organization. It provides focus and purpose.

A friend of mine, Dr. Ray Jorgensen, tells a story of management consultants who were brought in to work with NASA in mid-1960. They observed and interviewed many, many individuals representing various job classifications throughout the agency. One evening, they came upon an elderly man cleaning a sterile "white room." While having low expectations of a man who, for all practical purposes, they considered a janitor, they asked him what his job was. The gentleman, without missing a beat said, "My job is to put a man on the moon." His response is the epitome of a common understanding and shared vision.

In poorly run organizations, vision is relegated to a paragraph posted on the wall of the employee lunchroom. Few know what it says and fewer still know what it means.

Many organizations, particularly in the social sectors, have missions but no vision as to what success looks like or how the organization would look and behave if the mission were achieved. Vision and mission complement each other. Vision informs the mission. If the vision is a detailed, 3D, Technicolor picture of what success looks like then, the mission is the written expression detailing the means to achieve it.

Senge wrote: "Great leaders develop the capacity to hold a shared picture of the future we seek to create" (1990). I would add that they also possess a laser-like focus on aligning every sub-system within the organization toward the shared vision. Frequently, leaders and employees get lost in their bureaucracies and lose sight of their purpose.

Obviously, schools should not be designed for the benefit and convenience of the teachers; hospitals should not be designed for the benefit and convenience of the doctors. The core purpose in each enterprise should be quality education for children and quality care for patients. This is not to say that the employees are not considered; the needs of all internal and external stakeholders must be aligned to the vision and core purpose of the organization.

In many of my leadership classes, I have groups of students put together complicated jigsaw puzzles that have no clearly defined borders. I do not give them the picture of the completed project at the outset of the exercise. After only a few minutes their frustration is palpable and they beg to see the picture – a wish I will not grant. They struggle through the task. The stronger groups start to organize their work differently. They collaborate. Immediately, they sense the "complexity" of the task, and how without a picture (vision), the task takes vast amounts of time, unnecessary experimentation and frustration. They quickly make the connections to working in organizations without a commonly held vision.

The leader of an organization without a specific vision of success – how it looks, feels, smells, and behaves – is tantamount to a captain sailing his boat with no specific destination in mind, yet he continually adjusts the sails in reaction to every shift in the wind and then acts surprised when the boat ends up on the rocks.

Effective organizations have a destination in mind. Their destination is attuned finely to their internal organization's culture, capacities of the organization's resources and the needs of their external clients. They adjust the sails only when the adjustment takes them to their desired destination (vision). The vision, if well designed, never changes; however, they often adjust strategies to reach their vision.

In the social sectors, leading with vision and a sense of moral purpose is critically important, especially now, in the midst of a global fiscal crisis. The organizations we lead are usually dependent on other agencies for fiscal well-being. For example, schools, hospitals, and other social agencies face massive cuts in government aid during recessions.

In the USA, taxpayers are screaming that their taxes are too high and, given the hefty reductions in government aid, leaders must reduce expenses to remain solvent and they must invent new ways to guide their agencies to fulfill their core purpose. With a clear vision and mission, the painful process of cutting and redesigning programs becomes less emotional, more logical, and less arbitrary. Having all stakeholders involved and invested in the process creates common understanding of the problems the organization faces.

Through reinforcement and alignment to the vision and mission, decisions regarding reduction of services focus on and preserve the essence of the organizational vision and mission. Those programs and personnel essential to the vision and mission are preserved. Granted, no matter what, this process is painful. Yet, the leader's role and goal should be to preserve the vision and mission and to insure that students, clients, patients, and residents still receive essential services. They adjust strategy, not the vision or mission. The task may take longer and be more difficult to accomplish, but the destination remains the same.

Communication Leads to Collaboration

A very wise colleague of mine once told me that within every organization, stories *would* be told. In the absence of effective communication from leaders, the members of an organization will fill the communication void and tell their own stories. More often than not, their accuracy and veracity will be suspect. Nonetheless, the power of perception is not to be underestimated. Left to their own devices, these stories become the fabric of organizational culture. Effective leaders understand the power and necessity of truthful and consistent communications with their internal and external stakeholders.

Effective leaders create and communicate context for their organization and its place in the world. They insure that their stakeholders know about organizational progress and successes as well as the challenges their organizations face. Over time, clear, consistent, and truthful communication builds trust among leaders and their followers. Trust enables organizations to accept risk and value creativity. Trust is the fuel that allows organizations to "see the glass as half full" and to face all challenges as another opportunity to excel.

In the case of the fiscal crisis facing most social organizations, effective leaders keep their stakeholders well informed about the issues they face. Constituents have the information necessary to understand the true matter at hand, and can therefore contribute to the collective wisdom necessary to deal with any challenge.

When leaders create dialogic space for *all* stakeholders to process and understand the potential ramifications of any large issue affecting the organization, there are no surprises; no one is unaware. More importantly, rumors and other "defensive routines" that opponents of change introduce into the culture and their negative effects on the organizational culture are minimized (Argyris and Schoen, 1978).

Effective leaders, especially in the face of adversity, continually reflect on their organization's vision and mission and ensure their stakeholders that all strategic modifications align with the organization's core purpose. They encourage their followers to participate in the development of solutions for the short and long-term that will enable the agency to achieve its vision and mission.

Leading With Inquiry

If we accept the premise that no one person should be the chief learner for an organization and that collaboration is critical to both short and long-term organizational prosperity, then leaders must engage the workforce in deep introspection. Collins (2001) indicates that confronting the organization's "brutal truth" is essential to creating a desired future. Leaders address the gap between the current reality and the desired future reality. Confronting the brutal truth can be very dangerous for all concerned, especially if they resort to the "blame game." It is downright treacherous if leaders lack inquiry skills and fail to incorporate "leading with inquiry" into the process of confronting the current reality that their agency faces.

Inquiry, in its simplest form, is a discipline that requires constant practice and refinement. It requires genuine inquisitiveness and sincere, respectful, and purposeful questioning techniques. It involves the ability to listen deeply to the answers, no matter how much they hurt or conflict with one's mental models. Inquiry is not the exclusive province of the leader. In fact, inquiry is a discipline that must be taught, practiced and assessed as a learning tool that everyone within the organization uses.

Inquiry is a skill that, when used ethically and carefully, builds relationships with the all those engaged in the exchange especially those who serve and are served. Inquiry allows the leader to take the pulse of the entire organization. Inquiry provides some of the most valuable data available to a leader: the practices, performance, attitudes, beliefs, biases, and assumptions that members of the organization hold.

Armed with this knowledge, the leader has the ability to see the gap between the values the organization espouses and the actual values held by the people who comprise the organization. Leaders must insure that common understanding is actually common and one cannot know the common understandings unless one asks questions and listens deeply to the answers.

One cannot become aware of an issue critical to the vitality of an organization without tackling the "elephant in the room." The "elephant" surfaces through leader-generated inquiry. Accusation or advocacy must be downplayed when inquiry into organizational health and prosperity are under evaluation. Leaders who have successfully developed the capacity to lead with vision and inquiry are less fearful of raising these critical inquiry issues about the status of the agency. They have already set context and direction for their organization, and have developed strong professional relationships. They build organizational trust and have faith in those with whom they work, so they can elicit honest evaluations of the agencies status.

Effective leaders, in every sector, must possess the courage, desire, and skill to ensure that their organization prospers through good times and bad. Common understanding of the critical issues affecting the vitality of one's organization cannot be unearthed without providing forums for inquiry and analysis of current realities contrasted with desired future visions of the agency. Inquiry is the discipline that builds trust, creates common understanding of the shared vision, provides safe space for the discussion of difficult issues, and keeps the organization focused on its desired future.

Multi-culturalism

It is probably best to address the multi-national and multi-cultural shifts that affect all organizations in today's world – particularly those in the social sectors, from the perspective of productivity. Organizations in a global economy, whether schools, hospitals, or other social service agencies, clearly serve a diverse clientele both internally with employees and externally with clients and other recipients of our services. Effective leaders understand that "stakeholders" are not simply those who look, think, believe, or act exactly as the leader. They know that diversity offers keys to designing more creative, effective, and dynamic organizations. In a collaborative setting on a world stage, diversity is power and a necessary ingredient for productivity (S.E. Page, 2008).

All organizations are social systems. Effective leaders are always mindful of their organization's culture and the context in which it operates. Hoy and Miskel (2001) observed "As a social system, schools are characterized by an interdependence of parts, a clearly defined population, differentiation from its environment, a complex network of social relationships, and its own unique culture . . . the school as a social system calls attention to both the planned and unplanned—the formal and informal—aspects of organizational life" (p. 22). It is easy to see that one can substitute the word "school" for any other socially oriented organization.

No matter the service provided, organizations are complicated and, as Senge reminds us, leaders who understand complexity and the dynamic nature of all systems are more likely to encounter success with their organizations (2000). Effective leaders, particularly those who value and practice inquiry and collaboration, understand that multi-cultural perspectives are one of the most powerful tools at their disposal to promote creativity, enhance change, and position their organizations for greatness.

Effective Leaders Design, Teach, and Steward

With all of this talk about vision, mission, core purpose, and collaboration, one may wonder how leaders bring about changes that ensure their organizational success on a practical level. First, leadership is not a linear process. It is anything *but* linear, therefore there is no handbook containing "if this/do that" advice on how to handle a situation.

Peter Senge, in one of his brilliant books, The Dance of Change (1999), boiled down the role of leadership into three core concepts: Design, Teach, and Steward. For my purpose, I will focus primarily on the "design" aspect of the equation, however designing, teaching, and stewarding an organization to their vision of success are clearly inseparable. Within the context of the whole organization and its culture, leaders primarily work within these three domains, using inquiry as one of the key leadership behaviors unifying all domains. The illustration below (Illustration 1.0) is my attempt to display my thinking visually.

Illustration 1.0

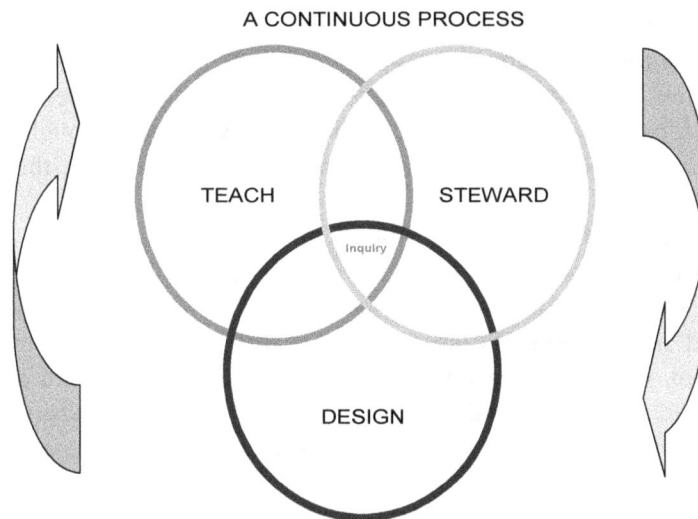

A CONTINUOUS PROCESS

TEACH STEWARD

Inquiry

DESIGN

The question before you at this point may be, "Yes, but what is it that we are designing, teaching, and stewarding?" The answer, of course, is the organization's desired future or shared vision. Without vision, any design is random, often contradicts organizational purpose, and worse, steers the organization in a direction opposite the one intended.

Design

The performance of any organization is a direct reflection of its design. Things you do well and things you struggle with reflect your current design. In the absence of a shared vision, every behavior and performance, output is what you designed for – good or bad. Poor performance, is less a people issue than a design issue. Deming (1986) actually suggested that 80% of systems' issues are design problems and only 20% relate to the employees.

Ineffective leaders are notoriously quick to design solutions to the problem "du jour." Some leaders believe that *their* job is to solve everybody's problems, right? They often react impulsively, with an absence of pertinent data and no vision of organizational success. Without a vision guiding the decision-making process, each "fix" becomes more and more reactive and random. It is a reaction to a set of circumstances, which can change very quickly.

Worse yet, some leaders design solutions that are ineffective and blame everyone but themselves for bad results. Over time, the people of the organization become angry and confused. Given the "chaos" perpetuated on them from the "suits" above, they create equilibrium for themselves at the expense of the "whole" organization by protecting their own turf. This behavior allows sub-organizations to become isolated, set their own goals and disconnect from the organization on a daily basis. The aforementioned scenario describes a bureaucracy that exists for the preservation of itself, not for the benefit of the entire organizations and its mission. This suboptimal design is all too familiar to workers in social agencies and the constituencies they serve.

If your organization does not have a shared vision of its desired future, begin designing and developing one. This is an organizational imperative. While slow going at the start, it allows leaders and their organizations to adjust strategically to any new data or situation they face. From a systems thinking perspective, design processes illustrate how organizations go slow to go fast. Vision is the organizational equivalent of a building's foundation; all designs draw forth from the foundation. Without a thoughtfully designed and sound foundation, a clear vision and mission for the organization, the structure will disintegrate eventually.

If there is a clear, explicit vision in place, current reality and every major decision facing the organization undergoes an examination through the lens of the vision. When there is a clear vision for the agency, leaders can engage stakeholders to think collaboratively and deeply about the issues before them. When inquiry reveals the "root cause" of a problem, brainstorming solutions and analyzing the intended and unintended consequence of each decision and its potential affect on the vision commences. Ultimately, the leader or leadership team decides the best pathway based upon the data collected.

Since the stakeholders have been involved since the beginning, common understanding of the issue already exists and the vast majority of the stakeholders affected by the decision support the leadership team. More importantly, the vision remains intact and how the new strategy and related decisions align with the vision is transparent.

Collaborative processes provide an even more important role. Not only do they help to communicate and reinforce how decisions align with organizational vision, they also provide the data necessary for the leader to evaluate how ready the organization is to accept and implement the change under consideration. Readiness for change affects the timetable of any initiative for change.

Change initiatives require the organization to rethink their current strategies and often the organization is unprepared conceptually or practically to effectively implement them. The effective leader constantly participates in the interplay between current reality and desired future. The gap between an organization's current reality and its desired future is where effective leaders focus their initial design work. The best ideas often fall to the wayside because the employees do not understand their purpose nor do they believe they have the training or the capacity to implement them well. The interplay between culture and initiative is modified from Senge's original "Framework for Strategic Leadership (2000).

Illustration 1. 1

The Interplay Between Current Reality and Vision

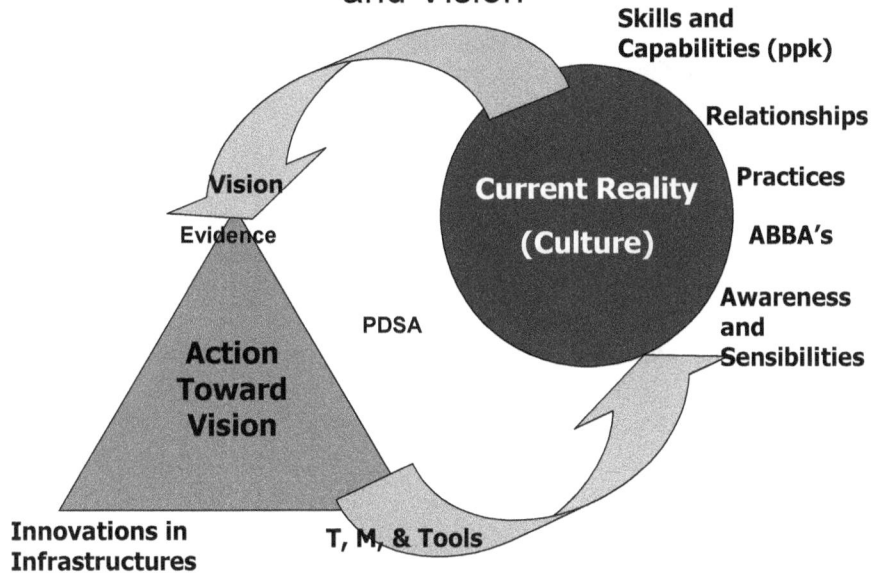

An examination of the design process depicted in Illustration 1.1 above, PDSA references Deming's notion of a continuous improvement process (Plan, Do, Study, and Act). When planning for change, the effective leader considers the readiness of the culture to understand and enact the desired change that, in turn, influences the design (triangle). This illustration applies at the macro or the micro level of organizations that seek to design a vision, processes and programs that support the institutional mission and achievements.

Failed Federal Legislation in the USA

For example in the USA, the federal vision imposed on all schools is that "no child shall be left behind no matter their race, gender, income levels or disability." Federal Legislators have defined the evidence of success as Proficient Performance on standardized tests and each of the 50 states had to develop benchmarks to measure progress towards standards of "excellence" that in turn, became Race to the Top standards of testing that states had to use to measure teacher and principal effectiveness in 2012.

In the USA, states have the constitutional authority and responsibility to regulate education for their citizens. The "Innovations" the states put in place are few and largely ineffective. The Theories, Methods, and Tools (TMT's) that the schools need to comply with the federal vision of all students graduating at proficient levels have to be developed by each individual school or district. The entire design, which was flawed to start, failed to consider school culture and the readiness of educators to produce the required changes by the year 2013. Had the federal legislation provided incentives for continuous improvements in student achievement in each school, a simpler and less costly model of change might have been achieved in American schools.

One can interpret the USA federal *No Child Left Behind Act (2000)* and *Race to the Top (2010)* as imposed visions with specified evidence of progress required for each school annually. There was no guidance in the form of innovations to achieve the vision, and little or no suggestion as to what a school needed to know and be able to do to make annually yearly progress. Worst of all, the legislators never considered the current reality (culture) and its' capacity to implement NCLB or RTT effectively.

The Federal legislators expected educators to shift a 100-year-old paradigm about student performance that fits nicely on a bell curve into a new paradigm designed to eliminate the bell curve and have every child achieve proficiency within approximately 14 years of the initial legislation. Schools that did not make average yearly progress were subject to sanctions and closure. Predictably, schools that did achieve a minimum of 90 percent of their students scoring at or above proficiency have consistently represented communities of middle to high wealth constituents. The whole purpose of education is to raise the quality of life for each citizen, not torture the children of the poor with excessive testing and sanctions.

Obviously, legislators with a true sense of history, empathy for the poor and some sense of human motivation would design with both the culture and vision in mind. They would provide for organizational "stretch" that was attainable in time, and account for new goals when the organization achieved initial objectives. Such legislators would reward progress towards programmatic structures and policies that produce the desired vision. Innovations are required to produce a different result than the organization is presently producing.

By systemically rewarding schools for effective growth in student achievement, school personnel would be encouraged to examine current reality through multiple lenses and make effective changes. Most social agencies produce outcomes that their systems call for. It can be no other way. Systems follow their designs and produce what the designs require.

New designs require extensive collaboration, inquiry, confrontations with brutal facts, courage, leadership and teamwork. To produce a new result that aligns to a new vision and desired future, one needs to innovate. To expect a different result from an old system is to recreate Einstein's notion of insanity.

Discussion Questions

1.   Based on an honest reflection of your organization's current reality through multiple lenses (productivity data, relationships, personnel, policies, practices), what has your organization actually been designed to produce? Where are the gaps between the espoused vision for your agency and its reality?
2.   How engaged are internal and external stakeholders in designing your organization's desired future? What might be the effect of their participation on your organization?

References

Argyris, C. (1994). *On Organizational Change* (2nd ed.). Malden, MA: Blackwell.

Bohm, D. (1996). *On Dialogue*. London: Routledge.

Bolman, L. G., & Deal, T. E. (2008). *Reframing Organizations: Artistry, Choice, and Leadership* (4th ed.). San Francisco: Jossey Bass.

Collins, J. (2001). *Good to Great*. New York: Harper Collins.

Deming, W. Edwards. (1982, 1986). *Out of Crisis.* Cambridge, MA: Massachusetts Institute of Technology, Center for Advanced Engineering.

Deming, W. Edwards. (1994). *The new economics.* Cambridge, MA: Massachusetts Institute of Technology, Center for Advanced Engineering.

Friedman, T. L. (2005). *The World Is Flat: A Brief History of the Twenty-First Century.* NewYork Farrar, Straus and Giroux.

Issacs, W. (1999). *Dialogue and the art of thinking together: a pioneering approach to communicating in business and in life*. New York, New York: Currency.

Kotter, J. P. (1996). *Leading Change*. Boston, MA: Harvard Business School Press. Jossey-Bass (Ed.). (2007). *The Jossey-Bass Reader on Educational Administration* (2nd

Manley, R. J., & Hawkins, R. J. (2010). *Designing School Systems for All Students: A Toolbox To Fix America's Schools.* Lanham, MD. Rowman and Littlefield.

Page, S.E. (2008). The power of diversity. *The School Administrator* 65 (9). Scharmer, C. O. (2005). Presence in Action [DVD]. Waltham, MA: Pegasus Communications.

Schon, D. A. (1983). *The Reflective Practitioner. How professionals think in action.* London: Temple Smith.

Senge, P., Roberts, C., Kleiner, A., Ross, R., & Smith, B. (1999). *The Dance of Change.* New York, New York: Currency Doubleday.

Senge, P., Cambron-McCabe, N., Lucas, T., Smith, B., Dutton, J., & Kleiner, A. (2000). *Schools That Learn - A Fifth Discipline Fieldbook for Educators, Parents, and Everyone Who Cares About Education.* New York, NY: Doubleday.

Schein, E. (2008). *Organizational Culture and Leadership* (4th ed.). San Francisco: Jossey-Bass.

Sergiovanni, T. J. (1994). *Building Community in Schools* (1999 ed.). San Francisco: Jossey-Bass.

Walton, M. (1986). *The Deming Management Method.* New York, NY: Putnam.

Wills, G. (1994). *Certain trumpets : the call of leaders.* New York: Simon & Schuster.

Chapter Seventeen
How to Ensure Equity for Students in an International Online Learning Community
-Thomas Franza

While the concept of making an international online seminar series equitable for all participants may initially appear extremely challenging, it is a valuable task. The benefits derived from the varying degree of perspectives, interpretations, approaches, and solutions generated by a multi-national gathering far outweigh whatever inconveniences and obstacles the development of such a seminar presents.

The first step is to identify and acknowledge the four major hurdles that the presenter and participants will face:

- Technological resources
- Time zone discrepancies
- Cultural biases/perceptions
- Language commonality

This chapter's sole purpose is to address these four main concerns and their potential solutions so that other enterprising institutions with limited technological resources may replicate this experience for their students or employees. In this chapter, we explore the preparatory work for an international seminar or conference, the layout of its content, the priorities arising during its development, and the assessments required after its presentation. The process in this seminar series focuses on asynchronous methods of communication, the development of a sense of community, and multiple methods of content delivery; all of which are designed to maximize the participants' (and presenter's) level of satisfaction with the overall online experience.

In order to have a successful online international seminar, or course, there needs to be a significant amount of work done prior to its onset. Online events need to be more highly organized because of heightened prior development needed to foster interactions (Bowman, 2001). The Internet Exchange event often requires extensive preplanning before an institutional proposal is generated. In the case of the seminar, used as an example herein, the planning phase began one year before an official proposal was created. This preplanning phase helped to shape the proposal and was instrumental in obtaining institutional approval since all costs in personnel time and equipment usage had been determined.

No matter the topic(s) to be covered, there are certain universal steps that must be undertaken.

- The format for the documents must be well- designed with basic headings and sub-headings. A sample or template of what the presentation material should look like should be distributed to all of the presenters. The model provides cohesion and consistency in the overall experience for participants. Individual presenters must be free to expand and alter the model as they see fit.

- The presenters must have deadlines and hold to them. At least one month prior to the onset of the event, emails must be sent to presenters requesting the submission of their final materials. All content must be created and uploaded to the delivery system before the event starts. At this point, authors of the lectures should be focusing on their approaches to anticipated discussions and not the organization of the materials. The lecturers must adjust constantly to the student reactions in an effort to improve communication and the sense of community. The sense of participating in a learning community and personal growth that participants experience determines the overall satisfaction with the event. In traditional courses, professors may be able to react spontaneously in a lecture hall. In the virtual classroom with asynchronous international commentaries, discussions must be managed during a 48 hour cycle and professors are the key guides who point out interesting pathways to pursue. Based on their knowledge of the material, and the goals of the lecture, the lecturer has to permit students to take multiple leader and teacher roles in the exchange of ideas. The unpredictability and the diversity of participants' exchanges produce the greatest productive learning in these events. The moral imperative for the lecturer is to be a steward of learning, guide to students, and in the closing hours of the week, the one who asks what each student has learned and the final arbiter and presenter of what the lecturer has learned. The didactic element opens and closes the lecture and in many cases, may be quite divergent.

- Written documents need to be proof read. Spelling and grammar mistakes are much less forgivable as they send a negative subliminal message to the reader/participant. It is also important for international seminars because translation dictionaries may not recognize misspelled words. Homophones will also detract from the participant's ability to comprehend and interpret the presenter's true meaning.

When hosting an online event, one cannot assume the type of technology each participant possesses will be similar. International events can be particularly difficult. In the case of the seminar referred to earlier, the technologist reached out to people at the participating institutions to understand what technologies they had available and what level of familiarity students would have with the technology. In many instances, specific resources were scarce or non-existent and shared Internet access would be limited.

While an obvious prerequisite for an online seminar would be that all participants have access to a computer with Internet access, these resources may be present in the form of public access computers such as those found in a school or library. It cannot nor should it be assumed that all participants have personal computers or high-speed internet access in their homes. Acknowledging limited access to online time and equipment will dictate the methodology used to present the material. In short, it is important to use a method of communication that is accessible to all. In fact, simple principles of social justice require that the design of the exchange facilitates learning with limited access time to the Internet.

Take for example, the problem with bandwidth. If internet bandwidth is limited, the use of pure videos and real time interactions should be minimal. In such situations plain text, office suite applications such as Microsoft Word documents and PowerPoint presentations, and Adobe Acrobat files should be the dominate method of delivery for seminar information.

- Plain text documents, while devoid of graphics and lacking in luster, are viewable by all participants regardless of the computer they are using. They are also small, making them quick to download, and easily saved to other devices.
- Since these do not possess fancy formatting or graphics, a presenter does not have to worry about how they will look on the various participants' computer screens.
- Plain text files also have the added benefit of working very well with translation programs.

Participants can take the text and either copy and paste it into a language translation program or open it within the program. This allows the participants to read the information in their native language. Although not all participants may have initial access to this type of software, there are more than adequate free versions available on the internet including one offered by Google.

Two caveats are: (1) these programs provide a translation that is an approximation and readers must recognize when a translation does not make sense. Often, the translation is sufficiently accurate to help clarify the main idea; (2) lecturers should avoid idiomatic language as an absolute necessity. Idiomatic or colloquial language, while part of our everyday language to English speakers, to a non-English speaker these may prove to be a major obstacle both in comprehension and in translation. Think of how the Americanism "a cool idea" could be interpreted by a native of India, Denmark and Nigeria ... or what they would do with the phrase "stumbling block" instead of "obstacle."

External Obstacles to Overcome

Even though MS Word and PowerPoint require presenters to own the software necessary to create the content, there are free web browser add-ons available so that participants can view documents and presentations. These web browser add-ons lack the ability to edit the documents, but that is acceptable from a participant's perspective.

In a traditional seminar, participants need to be able to see the presenter's presentation. They do not need to be able to edit it. Additionally, documents created in this manner possess a greater degree of appeal because they have a cleaner look, can support multiple fonts, and incorporate graphics. The sole disadvantage is that the person creating the documents has little to no control of what they will look like on the computer of the person who is viewing them, as factors such as not having the correct fonts loaded or a default printer can change how documents and presentations will appear on a viewer's screen. They may be larger in size because of the graphics, formatting, and fonts.

Adobe Acrobat files (PDF) are also very useful. While they are larger than plain text files, they are often smaller than their office suite originals. Several office suite applications have the ability to create PDF files without purchasing additional software. PDF documents also keep their formatting regardless of the system on which they are viewed. Additionally, because they are not editable by the participants, there is no danger of data being accidentally manipulated or deleted. Finally, because Adobe's Acrobat

Reader is a free download, it does not incur a further expense for the participants of the online seminar.

Occasionally, presenters who submit their documents and materials may have trouble creating PDF documents. In these cases, early intervention by the people that are handling the technology for the seminar can lead to a simple solution where by the local technology center copies the document into the PDF format.

Because international seminars will have participants and presenters from different parts of the world and, therefore, different time zones, in order for it to be equitable to everyone the delivery mechanism needs to focus on time-independent information delivery tools. Synchronous communications take place in real time or same-time (Lever-Duffy, McDonald, 2011). Consider a person presenting at a traditional conference. The presenter talks while the audience listens. If one is not in the room at the time the presentation is given, one cannot participate. Synchronous communication content delivery tools are live streaming video and video conference type technologies.

Asynchronous communications are time-shifted meaning that the people can be separated by both space and time, and still be part of the event (Lever-Duffy & McDonald, 2011). Email, texting, and discussion boards are examples of asynchronous communication tools. The people involved in the event do not all have to be at their computers at a particular time or in a specific place in order to participate in the event.

Even though email is most likely the most popular asynchronous communication tool, it should be used sparingly in online seminars. In the case of the seminar series described in this chapter, email was used for the original outreach to the presenters and participants so that they could have the directions necessary to connect to the virtual learning environment. After that original email, they were encouraged to keep all communications within the site. By keeping information within the learning management system, it was easier to maintain complete records (Elbaum, McIntyre & Smith, 2002). In addition, the process was more equitable because emails tend to be between specific individuals and not the group as a whole. Emails as a method of communication has the potential to discourage the active flow of ideas. By using Discussion Board for all communications or a Chat Center in Dowling College's Blackboard software, this leadership lecture series ensured that all students even those without a personal email account had access to all discussions. No one was excluded.

Structure Learning for Equitable Participation

While asynchronous communication is better suited for events that span multiple time zones, it does not imply that there should not be a time structure behind it. In the seminar referenced here, the International Leadership Seminar, there was a time outline displayed in the "Course Information" section of the site. Each lecture was one week in length. The material was available to the students in the "Course Documents" section of the site at a designated time each week. A question based on the material was released at a specified time three days later in the "Discussion Board" section. After that, the students would have two days to respond. That discussion thread would be closed, another question would be released, and the students had two days in which to respond. This cycle continued for the sixteen weeks of the seminar.

The structure created a pacing for the seminar series that allowed both the presenters and participants to know what to expect and when to expect it. Providing individuals with windows of opportunity to respond and interact, allows the seminar to deal with the time zone discrepancies and still maintain a structure that keeps it organized and creates a sense of progression.

Discussion boards allow for multiple forums and each forum may have multiple threads. These threads are convenient tools because they help the reader to follow the flow of the posted information. Discussion boards are often referred to as message boards (Shelly, Gunter & Gunter, 2010), electronic discussions or electronic forums (Lever-Duffy & McDonald, 2011).

Some of these programs allow the users to post anonymously. While technology system administrators can still determine the originator of every post, to the rest of the participants in the conference, the author of the information is unknown. This has incredible potential for eliminating cultural or gender biases, making it more equitable for everyone. It can even be used by the presenters to respond to an individual without foreknowledge of who that person is.

Because discussion boards are asynchronous, it also allows the person posting the information to craft a response offline. An individual participant can utilize a variety of tools such as translation programs, word processing programs, spelling and grammar checkers or even a peer to review material before making it available to others partaking in the seminar or conference. In addition, because all participants have the ability to reply to the questions posted, people who would tend to be normally shy or soft-spoken can have their ideas heard. In a true seminar series, where an international learning community is a desirable outcome, participants should be comfortable revealing their thoughts in identifiable statements. Personal references to culture, values and beliefs may illuminate discussions and exchanges and enrich the experience for all participants.

Building a Learning Community

The Discussion Board section noted here also had two forums not directly related to the lectures themselves. One forum, labeled "Tech Spot" and the other, labeled "The Water Cooler" were sites where students and professors gathered to discuss concerns or interests beyond the content of the lectures (Elbaum, McIntyre & Smith, 2002). The purpose behind these two areas was to provide a space for the participants and presenters to interact with each other in ways that were not in direct relationship to the presentations.

The Tech Spot was designed for people to post any technical or computer related problems that they might be encountering. The Water Cooler was created as a place where people could post any information or questions that were not related to the lectures. In a traditional office, people tend to congregate around the water coolers. They go there to get a drink of water and usually stay for a while until they finish their drink. While they are there, they encounter other people and usually have conversations. During the course of the International Leadership Seminar Series people posted questions about the weather, projects they were working on, and even the rigors of taking the seminar. Information posted in this section is designed to replace the conversations that would normally take place in the time periods between the sessions of a traditional seminar. The Water Cooler Chat Center allowed people to get to know each other and their interests outside of the presentations.

The Master Communication System

Depending upon the organization, the delivery mechanism for the lecture series has to be the host software. If the initiating organization has only one learning management system, it is the only choice. It cannot, however, be assumed that all of the participants know how to use the delivery mechanism. The host institution has to keep communication in the forefront. The technology team should assume that the groups involved have never used the system before. An initial email to the presenters should explain to them that participants will receive an email shortly, helping them to learn how to connect to the system. This will help the presenters to feel like they are part of the process. It will go on to explain why certain aspects of the program are time released and therefore not presently visible. The email should inform the presenters how they and the participants can find learning management system tutorials at the institutional site and within what specific sections of the virtual learning site.

Directions should include a document explaining how presenters can post their content to the site, use forums and manage discussions. The seminar's information technologist should send emails that deal with technical issues, while those that deal with policy and schedules, the seminar's host faculty member should send to presenters and participants. This differentiation of roles helps to make it clear who is responsible for each part of the lecture series and speeds up problem resolution.

In order to begin the seminar series, each of the participants received a separate email at their college or home. This email consisted of a welcome and a basic explanation of how to authenticate one's participation within the online site with a name and password. For an international seminar, the email should consist of simple, plain text. This plain text permits the participants to copy and paste the document into a translation program. A PDF document with the same verbiage, but with additional screen capture graphics inserted, was attached to the email. Using screen captures of the actual site and keeping instructions as simple and straight forward as possible, allowed the students to follow any representative pictures. A cardinal rule to follow when dealing with multiple languages is to remember that pictures are the Rosetta Stone of the communication process. The visualization that they offer of segments within the software enables students to follow directions more easily.

Basic Steps Have to Be Followed

When creating "how to" documentation, there are basic steps to follow. First and primary is the "KISS" principle, "Keep it simple, Stupid!" (Wikipedia, 2012), and this must never be violated. To paraphrase … the KISS principle decrees that simplicity is best. When people are frustrated or confused, giving them complicated instructions will not help them. It actually has the opposite effect. It makes them feel even more overwhelmed and more likely to stop pursuing the activity. By creating simple and easy to follow instructions, one can help to build a student's overall sense of accomplishment.

Keep this in mind:
- Acronyms should be avoided unless their non-abbreviated forms were presented first.
- The person creating the instructions should select words that all students will find easy to translate.
- Instructions should only refer to one task at a time.
- Presenters and students need to find what they need without searching countless pages of a manual or website.

Setting Guiding Principles and Expectations

Another obstacle the college in this example had to overcome was that of expectations. An email sent through the learning management system and signed by the person designated as the leader/host of the International Leadership Seminar Series provided the rationale, vision and mission of the seminar series. One should never assume individuals know what they should do as a member or leader of a seminar.

In the seminar series, we used the "Course Information" section of the site, to display an overview of the seminar. A vision and a mission set the tone for the seminar. In a traditional course this might be a segment of a professor's first lecture, the part that helps make certain all participants know what they can expect from the seminar. The presenters' schedules were located in this section to show the timing of the lecture series. The schedule presented an overview of the entire program to help both presenters and participators to see the breadth of the program. This is the same as a scope and sequence for a typical college course.

In the seminar cited here, there was another section of the learning management system labeled, "Assignments." In this section, there were guidelines for both presenters and participants, so that everyone would know exactly what was required from them. Since there were different expectations for each group, there were two different sets of guidelines posted in such a way that all participants could read both guidelines. As stated earlier, the clearer expectations are, the easier it is for everyone to follow them. While this is true for both traditional and online environments, if one is more lax in a traditional environment, it is easier to correct because of the direct contact with the participants. Since the type of seminar under consideration is an asynchronous online event, it is more difficult to correct unwanted behaviors. Basic courteous rules stated: No ridicule of another person's ideas, culture or beliefs will be tolerated and every response must be worded with respect for the different beliefs and values the members bring to our learning community. Disagreements and requests for evidence to support a position or opinion are encouraged in all circumstances to further the exploration of knowledge and to expose members to new views and ways of interpreting our human communities.

The learning management system employed by the International Leadership Seminar Series had the advantage of a space where participants could create their own websites. These personal pages were visible to other members of the seminar series. The original email that participants received explained this feature and its purpose to act as an electronic equivalent of a "birds of a feather" pre-seminar meeting. This feature allowed the participants to create a personal presence of self and to help overcome a participants' disappointment by the lack of face-to-face interaction that might be available in video conferencing (Perreault, Waldman, Alexander & Zhao, 2002).

Since the learning management system did not allow the presenters to create personal web pages in the same way that it did for the participants, another learning management system was equipped with a "Staff Information" section and that location was used to post short biographies and pictures of the presenters, technologist, and hosts.

Feedback Loops

Once the online seminar concluded, presenters and participants received an email with a link to an online survey. This was similar to almost any survey one would expect at the end of a conference with questions both quantitative and qualitative in nature. It is preferable to make the responses anonymous, but allow the person to provide a name, phone, and email at the end should they wish to be contacted to give more feedback. Anonymous feedback allows a person to be honest without fear of personal harm. In an online seminar, presenters and students gain confidence from reading one another's commentaries and often, the honesty and tone of the presenter comments set the criteria for future quality exchanges.

The quantitative questions elicit an overall feel for the seminar series, its valuable aspects, its practical applications and its capacity to meet the needs and expectations of its participants. Asking people to rate items on a five point Likert scale provides information in a direct manner that ensures efficient interpretation and statistical analysis of how the seminar was perceived. There should be questions for both the seminar as a whole and ones for each presentation. The qualitative questions should be more probing, thereby allowing the generation of rich data. One will usually discover patterns and themes arise within the qualitative responses.

Chomsky in Language and Problems of Knowledge: The Managua Lectures (1988) states, "...teaching should not be compared to filling a bottle with water but rather to helping a flower to grow in its own way" (p. 135). International online seminar series, when implemented properly, have the ability to be equitable for all participants. The benefits derived from the varying perspectives, interpretations, approaches, and solutions generated by a multi-national gathering are both compelling and rewarding. At each international site, a lead presenter has to volunteer to monitor and to encourage participants to contribute to every presentation. The interaction and continuous exchange of ideas, emotions and social understandings that these students share allow the seminar to become a true learning community for all. Moral leaders in the global economy must be open to the development of every neighbor in the world community.

The International Leadership Seminar Series that Dowling College hosted with its partners at Shri M.D. Shah Mahila College of Arts and Commerce, Mumbai, India; Universidad Panamericana, Guadalajara, Mexico; Iona College, New Rochelle, New York, and Lecturers Jean Sussman and Edward Lyons, Chicago, Illinois affirmed for all participants that many people of diverse cultures respect a high quality of moral leadership. These participants hoped to emulate moral leaders, support moral leaders and lead fairly and equitably in all of their actions.

References

Alexander, A., Perreault, H., Waldman, L. & Zhao, J. (2002) *Distance Education Issues as Perceived by Faculty and Students.* 2002 OSRA Conference.

Bowman, J. (June 2001). *The Third Wave: Swimming Against the Tide.* Business Communication Quarterly v64 n2, p87-91.

Chomsky, N. (1988). Language and Problems of Knowledge: The Managua Lectures. Cambridge, Massachusetts: MIT Press.

Elbaum, B., McIntyre, C. & Smith, A. (2002). Essential Elements: Prepare, Design, and Teach Your Online Course. Madison, WI: Atwood Publishing.

Franza, T. (2006). Web based distance learning training and technology needs as perceived by faculty and students: A contrast between web based and traditional classrooms. (Doctoral dissertation) Dowling College, Oakdale, NY. (UMI No 3220844)

Lever-Duffy, J., McDonald, J. & Mizell, A. (2011). *Teaching and Learning with Technology: Fourth Edition.* New York: Pearson Education, Inc.

Perreault, H., Waldman, L. Alexander, M., & Zhao, J. (July 2002). *Overcoming Barriers to Successful Delivery of Distance-Learning Courses.* Journal of Education for Business v77, n6, p. 313-318.

Shelly, G., Gunter, G. & Gunter, R. (2020). *Teachers Discovering Computers Integrating Technology in the Classroom, Sixth Edition.* United States of America: Course Technology, Cengage Learning.

Wikipedia. (viewed March 2012). KISS principle. Wikipedia.org. [Online]. http://en.wikipedia.org/wiki/KISS_principle.

Wilson, C. (November 2001). *Faculty Attitudes about Distance Learning.* EDUCAUSE Quarterly. Available: http://www.educause.edu/ir/library/pdf/eqm0128.pdf.